Ben Gander

OCD & ME

GANDER PUBLICATIONS
Petersfield

ISBN: 978-0-9559926-0-5

"The mind can make a heaven out of hell or a hell out of heaven"

John Milton

This book is dedicated to my beautiful, loving, wonderful wife – I love you more than words can say (although that won't stop me trying!).

Introduction

If you've picked up this book with the intention of reading it, the chances are that you either suffer from Obsessive Compulsive Disorder (OCD) or are close to someone who is a sufferer. Alternatively, you may just have a curiosity about the subject. Whatever the reason, I have written this book primarily for people to know that, no matter how badly an individual may be suffering from OCD, it is possible to be free of it. It takes hard work, a lot of courage and a huge leap of faith, but I made that leap and am now reaping the rewards, leading a very happy, productive life.

Before we get into the nitty gritty, I thought it necessary to explain why I have chosen to write this book as semi-autobiographical. The reasons are simple: to protect the innocent; to excuse me for inaccuracies caused by having a bad memory; artistic freedom – I am, after all, a wanabee writer. However, the essence of my story is one hundred per cent the truth: the extent of my illness, the events that arose as a result, the symptoms, the obsessions, the compulsions, the tragedies – they all occurred as set out herein.

None of this would have been possible if it had not been for the help of one person in particular: I would like to thank my wife for being the most wonderful woman in the world and giving me the inspiration to cure myself of mental paralysis and debilitation. I could say that I am unworthy of her, but I don't think there is a man alive that is worthy. Without you I am nothing. You gave me so much, including such beautiful, funny, slightly crazy children. I love you forever, my little Pantalaimon.

I would also like to thank those that helped my wife and I through the worst of times: Simon and Carolyn (sorry for ruining your holiday!), the Donaldsons, Mike and Irene,

*Chris and Julie, Zara and Jon, Nick and your fellow
directors for ensuring I had a job, Mum for being so kind
and loving and Dad for being you (and please remember the
parents in this book are not accurate reflections!), my little
sister Jocelyn, Gerry and Dave for your continued support
and being the best baby-sitters ever!, Sue (the CBT Master!),
Jane and Chris ... this list goes on, but you know who you
are! If I show you half the support you showed me in your
hour of need, then I would consider myself the best of
friends.*

*I would also like to thank Lynne Barker and Ashley Fulwood
for your encouragement and help in getting this book to a
wider audience and making this process far more enjoyable!*

*Penultimately, I would like to apologise to handwashers for
picking on you a bit. I know it's not your fault and I am
perhaps a little jealous that you steal all of the limelight.
Your suffering is just as painful as mine and I wish you the
best of luck.*

*And finally, for all of those sufferers out there and their
friends and family, I hope you enjoy the book and that it
provides you with hope and the impetus to seek your
freedom.*

Yours truly,

Ben

CHAPTER ONE: THE GLASS ROOM

Maybe only those that have been to the very depths of sadness truly appreciate what it is to be happy. The night does nothing to ease mental suffering. Alone with my thoughts, reality obscured by the shadows of the night, it formed a perfect breeding ground for my illness. The compulsions were taking over; the obsessions of pain and suffering of loved ones, momentarily eased by the performance of a ritual, but to soon return with a vengeance. I stood alone in the middle of the living room, feeling so lonely and scared. My dear wife lay upstairs sleeping, blissfully unaware as to how far gone I was. I walked around the room, staring but not seeing, eventually arriving at the window and looking out through the gap in the curtains. Movement outside distracted me: a cat strolled by nonchalantly, a black cat. Like I could do with any more bad luck! But that was superstition. What I have is more than just superstition. It turned and gave me a look of disdain. I like cats, but sometimes they can be arrogant little bastards!

I was a sick man by then. Mentally ill.

Nobody really understands my disease unless they've experienced it too. And *really* experienced it. Not just had the occasional compulsion or the odd quirky habit. I mean total debilitation. Nearly every part of the day becoming filled with some ritual or other. With each day that past, I was picking up more non-productive behaviours. I was on the edge of becoming overwhelmed. No doctor could ever help me, I was sure of that. Some claimed to know what was going on, but I was never convinced: these experts went on about this part of the brain or that part of the brain, coming out with long Latin phrases, a lack of this chemical, and on and on. But they still never had a handy solution. No quick fixes for me; no little pill to take; no physiotherapy for the brain to get me up and running again. And deep down, even if they didn't say it, I knew what the doctor was really thinking when I sat there in front of her, my head in my hands, crying like a little baby, past the scientific curiosity and pity: 'Oh, just pull yourself together! There's nothing really the matter!' But the mind can make a hell of heaven.

My throat became sore from all the non-sensical coughing and throat clearing that I had forced myself to do. We're not all hand-washers, you know, despite all the media attention that lot seem to get! Countless were the nights that I woke in a state of anxiety, unable to get back to sleep, entering a fresh set of rituals. Picture the scene: a man in his mid-twenties, quite handsome, reasonable build, of Anglo-Saxon origin with jet black hair, friends, no immediate tragedy in his life, charismatic (well, in my opinion anyway), a well-paid job, a beautiful wife … So, why is he on his hands and knees, his eyes blood-shot from frustrated bouts of crying and too many sleepless nights? He lies there shaking with anxiety. He crawls over to the mirror and stares at himself, searching for an explanation, an answer for his misery that no one has been able to give. But the man looking back is just as frightened and confused and has no answers. He searches for signs of insanity – that would be an explanation at least! But no. Nothing decisive anyway. Only an expression of sheer panic; terror way out of proportion to what had just happened. Because all I'd done was cough. Ah, but how many times? And what went through my head when I coughed? And how loud had it been? So I had to cough again, but in another way, and then I had lost count. What if it had been a 'bad' number? The senseless counting and the checking… These were the symptoms of my illness. The problem went much deeper. I knew what it was, yet I didn't know. I knew that this was not doing me any good, yet I couldn't stop it. My throat was red raw with pain. But this poor, pathetic wretch could not control it. Not by himself. It's worth repeating: the mind can make a hell of heaven.

Having obsessive compulsive disorder, or 'OCD', is like living in a little glass room which is tinted on the outside. You're inside the room, seeing the world go by, observing and wanting to join in; but you're just too busy to leave the room through that very tiny door made of glass that's so difficult to find and, once found, so difficult to get through, requiring an octopus-like flexibility. Occasionally, you stray out of the room, but you're so often out of touch with how to behave normally that you have problems fitting in and, before too long, you're back inside that box – OCD has called you back in. The outsiders can't see your strange behaviour that you perform inside this glass room unless they lean up really closely to the glass and they know what they're looking for. Of course, other sufferers can spot you a mile off: they can see that little box and they know exactly what's going on inside. The story of my life is the story of my struggle to leave this box that had become so large over the years and, once out, to smash it down so that I never get trapped in there again. The rewards are endless. Living has intrinsic value.

But there were times that I came close to blowing the whole damned glass construction up and with me in it.

CHAPTER TWO: LAYING THE FOUNDATIONS

Anxiety had built up in her for forty weeks. Her brain released damaging chemicals into her body; they found their way to the placenta, mixing with the goodness therein; the baby was nourished with protein and a large dose of fear. She worried. She feared life itself. Everything she ever had to do, she was scared; there was not much joy in such an existence. No matter what the occasion, no matter what fun could be had, to her it was always far easier to see the potential difficulties. An attitude problem, that's all it was. If she were only to change her outlook, all of this fear could have been shown up for what it was: unfounded. But try telling that to her.

So a baby was born, inheriting a natural inclination to worry.

I would have weighed in at 7lbs 1oz if I hadn't pissed on the midwife. Instead, I weighed in at just under 7lbs. That's 2 ounces of piss! That's a lot of piss! My dear old Mum told me this. How she knew this, I've no idea. I'm sure that it's not a policy to weigh a new born baby before and after their first leak. And the perpetrator had drawn attention to itself, its existence a truth that was all too painful for the poor lady to bear: a penis! How could her beautiful bouncing baby possess such an imperfection for a girl? After all, she had desired so much for that little girl, a replacement for the one she had lost nearly two years ago, stillborn; she had bought all the clothes, sent 'girl' thoughts to her belly, even done the 'twirling the ring on a string over the belly' trick to confirm its sexual identity! So how the hell had this happened? A boy! Would she ever receive any good news in life? It was one tragedy after another.

And did she let me know about it? Boy, did she! Every time I misbehaved I was reminded of my selfishness in choosing to be a member of the less fairer sex. More than that, when she felt down – which was a regular occurrence –

she would break into tears and ask an imaginary listener, 'why her?' All she wanted was a little baby daughter. A prisoner of her own negative outlook, bless her. Still, I know how that story goes. But she was very gentle and kind too and I always knew she loved me more than anything else in the world.

My Dad buggered off pretty quickly. Not physically – he stayed with her till the end – but emotionally. He was not an emotional man. Didn't really understand women. His mother was a hard woman who didn't take any shit from anyone! (For example, on hearing that our dog had died, her carefully selected words of comfort were: "You realise you killed him by feeding him cat food. He'd still be here if it wasn't for you.") She was a lovely lady and always meant well, but she was very hard. Brought up in an emotionally tough environment, the constant crying and whinging and the, 'why me?!' soon pushed him away (my Dad, not the dog). It felt to me that he drifted into a world lacking in passion, love, care. Sometimes I would even go so far as to say he didn't just drift, he ran like a coward! Evenings were his opportunity to sit down and watch the TV without being disturbed; the weekends were for sport. Always for bloody sport.

We start out life as loners. We can't communicate, so we have to reason with ourselves. We can't express our emotions. It's a frustrating time. By the time we can communicate, we've already laid down some pretty strong foundations. What with Dad not being much more than a physical presence, much like a rock, and Mum caught up in her own little issues, I didn't have much of a chance to communicate anyway. Not having a brother or sister didn't help. But I reckon my Dad was so put off by then he had convinced his testicles to call it a day. And they weren't the most sociable of couples, so I rarely had other children to play with. A lonely childhood requires a strong imagination to get through; as time went on, that imagination was allowed to become stronger and stronger.

There was one other important development that arose as a result of this loneliness: an inability to step back into reality. I could quite easily step out of the world around me and live in a little room all by myself. I used to spend hours playing in my room by myself, acting out various adventures with my collection of Star Wars toys and Action Men (always felt sorry for Action Men – they had permanent pants stuck on; the frustration doesn't bear thinking about!).

I've always had a good memory for emotions, if not for facts. I can still remember how I felt, still picture the waves to this day, crashing against the side of the boat, the spray on my face, my sense of wonder and dread. One jump and I would be consumed by this other world, hidden by the blue fiery surface, a world full of undiscovered mystery. My Mother's voice crying out, rising above the cacophony of oceanic sound in a way that only its child could recognise. I knew that I'd done wrong from the moment I'd clambered over the side and peered over the edge. The poor lady had only looked away for a split second and her little angel was gone! Curiosity compelling him. Maybe this was the first time I had ever associated compulsion with anxiety, the tone of my Mother's voice releasing a chemical in me that would become so familiar in later years. It was just one of those silly things that every child does to frighten a parent. My Mother showed superhuman speed and agility when she flipped over the side, pulled me away, lifted me up and carried me to safety for a good squeeze and telling off, a finely-balanced mixture of love and punishment. That was during the period known as the 'troublesome twos'.

Memories become obscured by the subjective emotions of the moment and nostalgia for a time so missed but never really existed. Despite my parents' dysfunctional ways, my memories are of contentedness generally, with a slight frustration in my lack of control. I had a passion to do so many things, see places, discover new experiences; but I was impotent, completely under the control of a couple of dudes who had no intention of breaking out into the world of interesting things. My lack of control found its way into my behaviour as I tried to find ways to guide events. Mixed with magical Christmases and warm Summer holidays are attempts at avoiding cracks in the pavement and counting lampposts going by whilst trying to sleep in the back of the car.

I remember sitting there, staring at the digital clock on the washing machine, waiting to see how slowly a minute took to go by. It seemed like ages. It never seemed that long when watching Bugs Bunny cartoons. I began to appreciate the value of every minute. How I've wasted them since! But listen to me, the Drama Queen.

I was generally more compulsive as a child than I was obsessive. I can recall feeling a burning desire, as I sat there searching for chocolates on the Christmas tree, to grab a bauble and see if I could fit the whole thing in my mouth. Eventually, I succumbed! I felt a certain sense of peace once I'd done it, a sense of completion or satisfaction, like everything was now in order. That split second of bliss was worth the pain I felt as the smashed bauble pierced through my lower lip causing my Mum to nearly have a heart attack at the sight of her little boy with glass protruding from his face, rimmed with a spray of blood. From a purely boyish point of view, I'm still proud of the Indiana Jonesesque scar.

And my compulsive behaviour was not just restricted to hurting myself, as the boy who dared to partner the girl I fancied in country dancing lessons was to find out. In an ideal world, I should have asked her to dance myself. But they were both blondies, whilst I had very dark hair – I felt a certain sense of fate in their union. It was not revenge; there was no premeditation involved when, during hockey practice, I took a swipe at him, hitting him so hard that his arm snapped, forcing his radius to poke through the skin. It was pure compulsion. Just like when I tripped the boys skidding along the ice. Or when I felt the need to spell out the word 'fuck' whilst my Dad and I were watching TV together one day. As he would put it, I was up in that bedroom before my feet could touch the ground. (This was in the days when disciplining a child was legal.) But there was a certain sense of bliss for that split second between my literary achievement and the full force of a parent hurtling across the room. I had nurtured and formed this feeling of completeness upon acting out a compulsion.

I was seven or eight years old, sitting with my Mum and Dad watching a James Bond film. I can't remember which one, but Roger Moore was in it. Always difficult films to watch with your parents because there would always be a sexy scene when I would have to pretend not to be interested. I had a bit of a cough. My Dad could be very intimidating when he wanted to be. He told me to stop coughing. I carried on. I had a cough after all, for goodness sake! He told me that I was doing it on purpose. I wasn't. I remember trying not to cough from that point onwards. I lay there trying to hold it in; the anxiety built up in me; I knew that with each cough I would get a certain sense of relief, followed by fear as my Dad would tell me off in his harsh, mocking tone. I became more anxious the more he criticised and doubted my honest need to clear my throat. I wonder if that's how the connection started, if he sowed the seeds in my brain that evening.

My anxiety was kept to a minimum during those years as I feared nothing whilst still in the family 'womb'. My parents were excellent in making me feel secure: our way of life had structure; the unexpected very rarely happened; my Mum's constant worrying about me and my Dad's authoritarian, no-bullshit attitude made for a strongly fortified abode. So I did not need to worry about losing loved ones.

Having an obsessive nature involves being overly interested in a subject in a way in which its substance does not justify. The object of the obsession occupies your mind to the detriment of other thoughts and activities. It's not a huge problem when you're Jonny Wilkinson and obsessing about your goal-kicking; but when it's about something awful happening to a loved one then it's time to stop. My obsessions came when I was about eleven or twelve, just in time for puberty. It was around that time that I began to realise that there was a bad world out there and things were just waiting to happen. And I resented my continued lack of control. I didn't like the fact that bad things could happen and wanted to be able to prevent them. The frustrations of being a teenager and the irrationality that sets upon us during those turbulent years provides the perfect opportunity for obsessive compulsive disorder to recruit followers to its way of thinking.

I believe that there is a crucial moment in most potential OCD sufferers' lives when they come to a point where they can end up going one way or the other. Many of us will hit a phase when we suffer from anxiety over and above the norm, when we fear from a lack of control to make things right. It is during this time that OCD tests us over and over again. It is during this time that a person needs to be most vigilant if he or she is to repel it for good. Many people have told me that they started doing something weird around that time, such as, when they dropped a sweet on the floor they would need to drop another one to give it company, or they had to turn the light on and off a certain amount of times before going to sleep; but then one day they said to themselves, 'oh that's just stupid – I'm going to stop doing that!' And they did! They exposed the disorder for the little lying shit that it is and sent it packing, never to be able to fool them again. My phase of being tested was between 12 and 16. I would often beat it; but too many times, I failed. I was not all-consumed at this young age because I still didn't care enough to fear consequences and I was too arrogant to readily listen to any instructions to avoid danger. But there were still enough times when I gave in and lay the grooves in my brain for OCD to slide on down. Looking back, I remember making New Years' resolutions some years, promising myself that I would start acting normal, stop being such a freak. But my oddities crept up on me and by February I was back to abnormal. It didn't bother me, though, because it was such a small part of me.

OCD creeps up on you slowly, sucking you in with its false promises of an anxiety free existence, but before you know it you're completely under its wicked spell! A slave to its nonsensical whimsical commands! I think one in ten are potential victims, but only one in ten of those develops it and one in ten of those (one in a thousand, I think!) develops it in such a way that it becomes debilitating and requires help. But I could be wrong. If I could go back in time I would – I'd explain to me the wasted time, the emotional trauma and suffering, the unfulfilled potential and the not enjoying life to the full created by this most cunning of disorders! If 'ifs' and 'buts', blah, blah, blah!

So I hit 11 years old and a little while after went head first into puberty. It's the time when your penis suddenly comes to life, almost like a butterfly emerging from a cocoon, but without the aesthetic qualities (and it's a pretty safe bet that there are more butterflies that have been pressed and stuck in a frame than cocks). It was like he was saying to me, 'hey you, why don't you show me some more attention? We can have some great adventures together, you and I!' Every man is a wanker, it's just a question of degree! I remember the first few attempts at masturbation: I would get to this point where I thought I was going to piss myself and I would have to stop. But after a while I decided to carry it through – and, woah! what an amazing feeling! There is nothing quite like the first time you 'shoot your load'! After that, I couldn't wait to go to bed in the evening! And I cringe to think about the state my bedcovers were in. This is the only time I would agree with my Mum that she would have been better off with a girl. (I'm pretty sure that girls don't go through an equivalent experience – not by themselves, any way, but I may be wrong.)

There is not much of interest in Plato's *Republic*, but he does tell a fascinating anecdote: an old man, when asked by a young man, what was it like not being able to have sex anymore?, replies by saying, 'I'm glad to be freed from that master.' The lying git, was my first reaction – there's a feeling that Plato should have added a reply from the young man along the lines of, 'Bollocks! I bet you'd give your last breath for a shag!', but I don't remember any of the great philosophers ever being so uncouth. Anyway, the point is there: men are greatly influenced by their sexual desires. The teenage years are the hardest, and with the changes coming over the teenager there are two common side-effects: angst and arrogance, and I had both in bucket-loads!

The angst came in the form of doubting myself: sexually, physically, academically, intellectually, as a moral, ethical, decent human being. I asked the usual questions: does she like me?; is she sleeping with someone else?; do people think I'm gay?; is my knob too small?; will I get her pregnant?; what if I come too quickly?; what if I can't even get it up? The arrogance was more simple: 'who gives a shit?' was the pervasive philosophy. So the two played off against each other, sometimes one winning, sometimes the other, sometimes a stalemate. However, the arrogance held the OCD at bay and taught me vital lessons in coping with the disorder that I was to forget for several years.

I was fifteen and she was a year older. We had been intimate, seen each other's most prized possessions, enjoyed each other in the way that kids our age do. Then it came to losing the big 'V'! We discussed it. Or rather, she kept on about how she wasn't sure she was ready, whilst I pleaded with her to give me one. Then came the big day. I went out and bought some condoms that morning. I remember some bloke muttering to me something about how rubbish it is wearing one whilst I was putting money in the machine. I gave a, 'tut, yeah, you're telling me!' type of reply, even though I had no idea what he was talking about. My girlfriend and I got back to my house. It was the summer holidays and my parents were at work. We went up to my room and stripped to our underwear. I looked down: nothing happening downstairs! We hadn't actually 'got going', but I thought the mere taking off of clothes and wanting to have sex would be enough. Well I got that wrong! If anything it had shrunk! We tried to 'start things up', but it was too late: anxiety had set in. Then came the 'Is it me? Have you gone off me?' from my girlfriend. This didn't help. Then she avoided my phone calls and was always out whenever I went round. I found out later that she met some bloke down the pub soon after and they shagged in the bushes of the pub garden. Slag.

I did lose my virginity soon after that without any problems at all. I was at a party and fairly drunk and smooching with some girl in her early twenties; there was no mucking about, no time for thought, we found ourselves in a bedroom, on the bed, naked and shagging! Simple as that! And I've never had a problem since. What was the difference? That I had no time to think about what I was doing, to dwell on things, to worry, to get anxious. On my first attempt, I was full of angst and had too much time to think, to get the wrong juices flowing through my brain. The next attempt, I was a cocky little bastard who'd pulled a girl several years older and by far the prettiest at the party. I was alpha-male and didn't give a shit about anything but getting this beauty into bed!

I remember one day, whilst I was studying in the library, there was this strange looking figure slumped in the corner with a towel over his head and reading. Every now and then, he would pull something from under the table and rub himself with it. Watching him intensely, I noticed that he would do this every time I coughed. He was taking out a bar of soap and rubbing his clothes with it. Eventually, he stood and went to leave. Once he had past, I let out a loud cough – he stopped and seemed to shudder! The soap came out and he rubbed himself all over with it. I thought about coughing again. But I stopped myself, not wanting to be too cruel. Sad pathetic man, I thought to myself. I was so glad I wasn't like that.

This arrogant trait saw me through puberty and into early adulthood. University was a breeze. There were a few give-away signs of behaviour that I was not a normal human being: I used to check the cooker was off, looking at it four times for some reason, and I would thoroughly check the front door was locked too. When playing rugby, I would put my scrum-cap on four times and scratch the bottom of each foot four times just to make absolutely sure that I would not break my neck. But these little blips in my ability to think straight were just that. There was nothing overwhelming about them. They were not a pervasive part of my behaviour.

I loved the freedom of university, the control I had over my life. I had no one to care about except myself and I felt almost invincible; I had no fears. The world was my oyster. I had delusions of grandeur, completely unfounded; I would become the top dog in some big company, or possibly an

MP, maybe even Prime Minister! Then I would have so much control to do the things that needed to be done.

I left university feeling like I could do anything. Armed with my accountancy degree and bags of confidence, I left university at the age of just twenty-one. Then everything slowly went pear-shaped.

CHAPTER THREE: SUPPRESSION OF THE SELF

The banana was the first piece of fruit for the day. Three more to go. I got to the end of it and then chucked the skin in the bin. 'But had I eaten it all?' I began to wonder. Maybe there was still a bit of the tip left. I fished it out of the bin and scraped my teeth against where the tip had been, consuming what miniscule parts were left, taking up bits of skin as I did so. I threw it back in the bin, feeling a bit silly but less anxious for a minute or so. Then it dawned on me: I should have done that four times. So I repeated the above process three more times, making sure that the girl next to me did not catch me doing so. After the fourth time, the anxiety went away again, this time for a good few minutes. Then more thoughts entered my head: had I done it four times?; should I have gathered up increasingly more bits of banana with each scrape?; would I have to do this with each banana from now on? Stop!, I said in my head. This is ridiculous! I got out of my chair and went to the toilet.

Whilst peeing into the urinal, I noticed a paper towel on the floor. It wouldn't take much to pick that up and put it in the bin – that would give a sense of order. So, once finished, I picked it up and threw it in the bin. There were a couple more lying on the floor. I picked them up too and threw them away. Then I checked each cubicle, picked up any toilet tissue lying there and threw it in the loo, flushing it and put the lids down. I surveyed the whole room. It was tissue free.

"You should be a cleaner!" said a voice from behind. I looked around – it was one of my managers.

"Can't have this place looking like a pigsty, can we?" I joked, feeling incredibly stupid. I had the urge to wash my hands; no, I didn't want to turn into one of those bloody hand washers the media is so obsessed by. I had enough quirky habits already.

Walking out of the toilets, one of the other trainees pointed at me and laughed. Had he seen me with the banana? A feeling of shame came over me. I looked down to what he was pointing at. My flies were undone! In all my obsessing, I had forgotten to do them back up – that was all! I felt a strange sense of dignity that this was all I was being mocked for. I could handle ridicule of normal behaviour; as long as my weirdness wasn't being mocked, that was fine.

Sitting back down, I looked at my in-tray. It was full of work that needed to be done today and I was still stuck on something that should have only taken me an hour. Our work required that we recorded the time we spent on each job in order that we could charge clients the correct amount *and* to ensure that we were working efficiently. But little rituals would add to my day. It would only be silly little things, but I would end up losing my concentration and have to start again. This was happening to me far too often. I would have to stay late that night to get things done. Right, no more silliness, I remember thinking to myself, head down and get on with it. Easier said than done.

"You're late!" she said.

"Sorry," I replied. "I had to finish some work for Carlton before I left. I tried ringing you, but your phone was off."

"The battery's gone," she replied. "Well everyone's here anyway and the starters have been and gone – you've missed out, I'm afraid. I've ordered you ham and pineapple pizza, by the way."

"What about chillies?" I said. "You know I love chillies!"

"Well if you'd been here on time, you could have ordered," said Felicity. She knew how my body reacted to chillies, that's why she didn't order me any. "I'm going to the toilet. They're sitting over in the far corner."

"I'll wait," I said. I didn't really know them and didn't want to start introducing myself. My years at university had taught me a lot of things, but I still remained as unsociable and incapable of holding a normal conversation as ever before.

"No you won't," she replied. "Just go and sit down. You look stupid standing here waiting for me."

I sighed. Felicity gave me a look that said, 'just do it', so I made my way over to the table, feeling slightly anxious.

Introducing myself, I sat down opposite some bloke who I thought was called Tim. I didn't like him. He was too close to Felicity and she was *my* girlfriend. My boxer shorts had twisted and were causing havoc in the nether regions.

"Hi everyone," I said, trying to sound confident. A blend of 'hi's, 'hello's and 'how are you?'s followed.

"Hi Tim," I said to the idiot opposite. "How's things?" Bad I hope, I wanted to add.

"Good," he replied, unfortunately.

I stood up suddenly and quickly readjusted my boxers.

"Are you okay there?" asked Tim loud enough for everyone to hear. It was clear that he had been drinking. He was an obnoxious twat at the best of times, without drinking adding to it.

"Just readjusting, Tim" I replied, smiling. "Got to give the little fellow room to breath!" It felt good to make a joke of it, but in reality I was feeling anxious. I realised that I would need to stand three more times. I did it once more.

"If it's that little, surely it doesn't need that much room," said Tim, as I stood up. Everyone laughed. Amongst the laughing, I heard someone mutter, "why does he keep standing up?". So I did it again and bent at the lower back, holding it as if it was stiff.

"I think I've pulled a muscle, Tim," I said by way of explanation. I hoped that this would provide me with a cover. One more time and I was done.

"You should rub some oil on it," said the girl next to me.

"Baby oil should do the trick," said Tim. More laughter at my expense.

At that moment, Felicity returned from the toilets. I quickly took the opportunity to stand up. She looked at me and smiled curiously.

"Why are you standing?" said Felicity. "I feel quite regal!" At that point Tim stood up too.

"Just trying to be polite to my good lady," I replied, feeling a bit silly, but relieved that this little ritual was now over. I ignored Tim.

"Well, I'm just standing because I was feeling left out," said Tim, making his obnoxious presence felt. He turned to everyone else and motioned for them to stand too. A couple of them did so, laughing. I felt so stupid. I sat back down.

"You can all sit!" said Felicity. "As you can see, Tom still thinks he's funny. You've met him before, haven't you?"

Tom! The obnoxious bugger's name was Tom! Why didn't he say anything?

"I don't remember meeting him before," I lied, in a cheap attempt to make him feel insignificant.

"He seemed to think I was called Tim," Tom replied, blowing my cover and putting on a silly voice. "I didn't bother correcting him. I didn't want to make him feel silly."

So what have you been doing for the last five minutes, then? I hated this bloke with a passion and began to think of childish ways to get him back.

The pizza came and I ate it without the desire to stand up again. I didn't enjoy it much though: dickface Tom was chatting up Fliss and I was trying to cut him short, but kept receiving a load of drivel in my ear from the girl sitting to the left of me. She kept asking me about my work and where I had studied and where I intended to go. I had no interest in this conversation, but she was pleasant enough and I didn't have the heart to tell her to shut her face. Then I made the mistake of asking her about her plans and that was it – she never paused to take a breath! No idea what she said. Something about wanting to be a partner and Australia may have appeared there somewhere. And she kept on going off on tangents, as if she couldn't bear to leave anything out. Maybe she thought something bad would happen to her if she did – I could understand that. I drifted off from what she was saying, keeping a check on Tom's pathetic attempts at chatting up Fliss. I was beginning to wonder whether he fancied her or was just trying to annoy me. At the end of the evening as we all got up to leave, I put a piece of garlic bread in his hood. Childish, I know, but it made me feel better.

"I don't like him," I said to Felicity on the train on the way back.

"He's an acquired taste," she replied, which is always a polite way of saying that someone is a bit of a prat.

"Do you like him?" I asked.

"He's alright," she said.

"As in fancy him, I mean."

"That's a bit of an odd question," said Felicity. "He's alright, I suppose. He needs to sort his hair out, though."

Anxiety rushed through me. I felt an overwhelming desire to ask the question: "Have you ever snogged him?" I tried to sound nonchalant.

"What kind of question is that?"

"I'm just asking."

"Well don't!"

"Well have you?" I said. I didn't care about the answer. I just needed to hear one.

"No!" she said. "Look don't start doing this again! I can't stand it when you start asking all these questions!'

That was enough. "Sorry," I said. She looked the other way. We sat there quietly. I was relieved to get the question off my chest. But, I thought to myself, she may still do it in the future. How could I stop this from happening? The compulsion came over me to ask: "Would you shag him if you weren't going out with me?"

"What?!" she cried. "Just shut up, idiot!"

"I just need to know," I said quietly and in a calm tone, moving closer to her.

"Shut up! You're getting on my nerves now."

"Please, you have to tell me," I said, sounding slightly anxious.

"No!" she said.

I sat back, relieved with her answer. Then it hit me!

"What, no you won't tell me or no you wouldn't sleep with him?" I asked.

"Both!" she shouted. "You're really pissing me off now!"

That doesn't make sense, I thought. Still, I was satisfied.

"Sorry," I said, touching her hand.

"Get off me," she said, pulling her hand away. We didn't speak much for the rest of that night.

I met Felicity at work about eight months after joining. Two years had gone by since leaving university and it had taken half of that time to find a job. I had left there feeling optimistic and 'happy-go-lucky'! But optimism had soon turned to pessimism. The arrogance of youth had waned, whilst my anxiety waxed. The confident young man ready to take on the world was no more than a sprat in an ocean, lost and not knowing where to turn. As my anxiety increased, so did my strange behaviour. What I had brushed aside as quirks in my personality during my teenage years were fast becoming seriously damaging to my rationality. When I left university, anxiety began playing a big part of my life. I left the metaphorical door wide open for OCD to stroll in and cause havoc. I was soon sharing my life with the disorder. From then on, door handles stood no chance under the strain of a constant checker, key words in sentences found themselves cropping up in even numbers, socks would go on and come off again four times... But I remained on top of my illness and was rewarded with a job offer at a top accountancy firm.

The confidence boost of a well paid job reduced my symptoms in the short-term, but being surrounded by highly-motivated people who would stop at nothing to get to where they wanted to go soon took its toll and I lapsed after a few months. My illness then 'plateauxed' for a while. The rituals were tolerable and did not take up much of my day. Yes, I was a little slower than I should be, but it was an acceptable speed. I had nothing to worry about except myself and did not think enough of myself to let *me* bother me. Then I met a girl at a work party. She was in her mid-20s, an auditor, had high ambitions, was very clever and well-to-do. I was on the dance-floor doing the 'macarena' when I felt a hand across my stomach. I tried looking round, but she would not let me. I checked the hand and the smoothness, hairlessness, slender wrist, dainty rings and long polished nails – it was probably a girl, so I accepted my situation. I leaned back into her to ensure that she was of an adequate size and felt two firm lumps in my upper back, not one soft one in my lower back. All was good so far. She made me wait till the end of the song before I could turn round, which was only a minute away but felt like ages, especially with so many blokes around me giving cheeky grins of approval. Who was this? Turning round, as our Hispanic friends were replaced with yet another old song re-sung over a monotonous drum machine and keyboard, I finally got to see her! She was okay. Nothing special – just okay.

"I'm Felicity!" she bellowed in my ear, pulling me off the dance-floor and dragging me towards some chairs.

"Mark," I said. "I like your dress. If I was a girl I'd wear one like that. But I don't think I'd wear those shoes."

"What's wrong with my shoes?" she said, bemused.

"I'd look stupid in them," I replied.

"You'd look stupid in the dress!" she said, laughing. "I'd prefer for you to be out of it!"

And that was that! A clear invitation and I didn't need a second. We went back to hers that night and, brimming with confidence from excess alcohol, we shagged on the communal table in her kitchen and, unknown to me until it was too late, in front of her housemate Jenny! She asked if she could be next, but when I offered she declined. I ended up upsetting Fliss (as she liked to be called) in the process, which her drunken state enhanced into floods of tears. I apologised profusely, but ultimately I needn't have bothered: she couldn't recall anything about the incident the following day (worryingly, she only just remembered our time on the table!).

Fliss was about five foot six, a 34B, had long blonde straight hair, a chin that was a bit on the small side and incredibly small ears that would have looked better on a guinea pig. In typically male fashion, I would rate her a six out of ten. Still, she was a good laugh. But she was a flirt, very sociable and liked to drink and party. And she was very ambitious. She would often go out on business lunches and meals with other men. I was convinced that she would be prepared to sleep her way to the top. Not the ideal partner for someone lacking in confidence and with a fear of things that he could not control. Our relationship developed quickly from casual sex to 'going out' properly. I don't know what she saw in me really, as I showed no sign of having the same ambition and we were forever arguing. Still the sex was pretty good.

"Why don't you move some of your stuff here?" she asked. We had only been going out for about three months.

"Isn't that a bit soon?" I replied.

"It's no big deal," said Fliss. "It's just a convenience thing. I mean, you're here most of the time anyway."

Reluctantly, I agreed. A few clothes was nearly all that I owned anyway, so it did seem more than just a big deal. It was nice for the first few weeks. But then I hit a problem: I really started to care for her.

"What's she like then?" asked Jim, in his usual not really listening manner. Jim was my best friend. We had become good pals at university. I had dated his sister for a couple of months, a convenient fact when it came to any cussing match between Jim and I: there's nothing really that he can say when I start to talk about what she looks like naked and what she was like in bed.

"She's okay," I replied. "I mean, I like her as a person. I wouldn't say she's the most amazing girl to look at, but she'll do. You'd do well to get her."

"I'm going out with a model at the moment," he said, giving a smug smile.

"Really?" I asked, surprised.

"No, not really," he replied, bringing the conversation back down to reality. "But there's this model I like."

"How do you know her?" I asked, foolishly.

"My mum gets this catalogue that she's in," he began.

"Jim," I said, interrupting, "I want to tell you about this girl, not discuss some weird fantasy you have about some model in a catalogue."

"But it's getting to me," he went on. "I think I may have a problem."

"Go on," I sighed, knowing that this conversation wasn't going anywhere.

"Well, she models the older women's underwear," said Jim. "I think I've got a thing for older women."

"Don't worry about it," I replied. "You'd probably feel differently if you could see her in 3D."

"They're curvier," he continued. "I think that's what is doing it for me. All those other models, they're like sticks. I reckon they accept that when they hit fifty they're going to have curves, so they don't bother picking models who don't."

"There are curvy models that are younger," I said.

"Problem is," said Jim, "it's the fashion designers: they're either women or they're gay. It's a feminine trait, fashion. So the models they choose aren't chosen for their sexual appeal."

"Maybe," I replied. "And maybe gay men are trying to make heterosexual men fancy women who look like men. And after a while, we won't mind whether it's a girl who looks like a man or it's a man! Maybe it's a big plot by the gay community to convert more and more men to homosexuality!"

I should add that it was around 10 o' clock in the evening and the beers had been flowing for three hours.

"Someone tried to convert me the other day," said Jim. "I was in the gym, and there was just me and two other guys. One of them left and the other turned to me and said, 'At last, I've got you alone!' and winked at me."

"What did you do?"

"I laughed nervously," he replied, "and got out of there as soon as possible."

"Good place to hang out if you're gay," I said. "Just imagine if you could go to the gym and in the changing rooms there were lots of naked women!"

"Or prison!" he exclaimed. "If I was gay, I'd get myself locked up for something and pretend I was this nervous little thing and end up being anybody's bitch! It would be great!"

"I'd be careful about suggesting all gays go to prison," I replied. "So what am I going to do about this girl?"

"Just use her," he answered. "Have fun. You're still young. What does it matter? Who cares?"

"I can't *use* somebody," I said. "It's wrong!"

"Everybody uses everybody else. She sounds like she uses people all the time."

Part of me saw the wrong in it. Part of me saw that maybe I should just do whatever I please. I liked the idea of being a spirit. But I liked Fliss as a person. Looking back, I know now that I was starting to love her. With this loving came caring; with caring came fear; with fear came anxiety; with anxiety came my little disorder. Subconsciously, this began to scare me. I sat back in my chair and thought about it long and hard: so what if I used her? She would go off with some other guy for her career, I'm sure she would. I don't want the hassle of caring for somebody.

"I'm going to get another round in," said Jim, and off he went.

I was staring into my glass, wondering about Fliss. Was she the one for me? Or was it just convenient. We did get on pretty well, despite the fact we had nothing in common. I loved the way she would blow out when she found something funny, or the way she would make her bottom lip stick out when she was sad; our relationship was hitting that point where it's the little things that you notice about each other, things you wouldn't have really spotted at first, that began to appeal to you more. But I didn't want to be caring about someone like this. I didn't want all that going on in my head. So I did a bad thing.

Caroline was her name. She came and sat next to me whilst Jim was getting the round in. She asked me if I was single. I didn't even hesitate.

"Yes," I replied. "You?"

She had long straight brown hair, was very tall, sexy looking, but with a big hooter. It didn't look out of place on her, though, and I was immediately attracted.

We went back to hers that night. When my phone rang, I didn't pick up and then I put it on silent in case Fliss tried again. I had the audacity to text her to let her know that I was fine, had a great night, was thinking of her, etc. The next day I felt pretty shitty, but I put it to the back of my mind. So what, I said to myself. I'm my own man.

"Are you okay with me?" asked Fliss a couple of days later. "You're very quiet at the moment."

"I'm fine," I replied. "Just got a lot on my mind at the moment, that's all."

"Like what?" she said, sitting down next to me and putting her arm round my shoulders.

"Just work," I lied.

"Oh don't let a silly thing like that bother you," said Fliss. "Listen, maybe one day we'll have a family together and I'll be the one out working while you stay at home bringing up our kids!"

I sighed.

"Hey," she cried, "don't you like the idea of us having kids together?"

I smiled.

I never saw Caroline again. But I did see Emily. I wasn't one to go for the older woman, but she had that sophistication and experience that paid off in the bedroom. The sex was fantastic, but she was nearly fifty and had a bitter twist to her attitude; I couldn't see it being long-term.

"You seem very distant at the moment," said Fliss.

"I'm fine," I shrugged.

"I wish you would tell me what's going on."

"I told you," I replied, carrying on with the lie, "it's just work."

"Okay," she began, a warm gentle tone to her voice as she cuddled up to me, "you're going to have to tell me all about it even if I have to beat it out of you."

"Fine," I sighed, putting my book down. I tried to think of something. "It's just that … I feel that … that I should be so much more than I am."

"What do you mean?"

"Well, remember when you're a kid and you talk about what you want to be when you grow up?"

"Mm-hmm."

"Well," I continued, "I didn't ever say, 'oh, I'd love to be a tax accountant! That would be so much fun!' But here I am, a sodding tax accountant. I've got no interest in my work."

"So what did you want to be?" asked Fliss. "You could still be it, you know."

"I wanted to be an astronaut."

"Oh."

"So I could play with my Action Men up on the moon – it would have been so much more realistic."

"Well," she said giggling. "I suppose that's probably out of the question."

"I don't have them anymore anyway.," I replied, smiling. "I chucked my toys away years ago."

"Oh," said Fliss. "Well, I guess it's definitely not going to happen then."

We both laughed and she cuddled right into me, falling asleep on my chest as I lay there wondering what the hell I was doing with her and, moreover, what I was doing *to* her.

I never saw Emily again. But I saw Kerry; and then Tanya; and then Sarah; and then Jane. I kept Fliss at a distance emotionally, a skill that I had learnt from my Dad. She was getting more and more upset by my behaviour. I knew I couldn't go on like this. So I told her. I told her about all of them.

"Aren't you going to say something?" I said.

She continued to just stand there, her bottom lip quivering, her eyes staring at me, looking for an answer.

"Why?" she asked, eventually.

"Because," I said shrugging my shoulders. "I felt trapped. You were moving too fast."

"You could have said something!" she shouted, suddenly becoming animated. "If you didn't want to be with me, you could have told me instead of going round shagging a bunch of slags! Who knows what illnesses they've given you! And what have you given me? You selfish bastard!"

"I haven't got any diseases," I replied, patronisingly. "And anyway, you didn't exactly hang around before getting me into bed."

Wallop! You could hear the sound half way down the street as her palm caught me perfectly on the cheek.

"Get out!" she cried, banging her fists into my chest. "I hate you! Get out!"

So I left. And she left: she left me, the firm, moved house, everything. All of my clothes were returned with various rips and tears in them. But I didn't get angry – I deserved everything she'd done to me and more. I found out later that she was so in love with me, but didn't want to tell me too much. She was not as career oriented as I had thought; she gave up a good job just to get away from me.

My illness was making me into somebody that I didn't want to be. I didn't want to hurt Fliss. I had been selfish. I had chosen a way of life where I didn't care about anyone or anything. That's not who I am. I would rather have my debilitating condition than be like that. I was ashamed. More than that, I hated myself.

CHAPTER FOUR: MY PANTALAIMON

But I had second thoughts: maybe I could be the not caring type as long as I didn't hurt anyone. I could be like a rock, an i-i-island, like in that Simon and Garfunkel song. As long as I didn't let anybody in, I couldn't be blamed if they got hurt. And for all the pain I caused her, once I had stopped feeling so guilty, I realised that finishing with Fliss was like a huge weight being taken off my shoulders. I felt revitalised. I had no worries, no one to perform rituals for except me. But I cared little for myself, so it became easy to ignore stupid thoughts. 'You'd better look at the bloke opposite you on the train four times or you'll fall under a train', my random mind told me. 'So I fall under a train!' I told myself. 'Who cares?!' Ignored and neglected, the troublesome thoughts and the suggested evasive tactics were pushed from the forefront of my brain to huddle up in some dark corner of a cave deep inside of my head.

"You seem so sure of yourself", people would say; "I admire the way that nothing ever gets to you"; "I wish I could be more like you", etc, etc. And I felt good. It mattered not that I had this dark, odd secret. I feared that it may come back one day, but I did not show that fear and began to live with it.

With nothing to obsess about, there was no urge to act compulsively. Let me be what I must be and God would be my judge. Two fingers to stupid thoughts and feelings. Cause and effect shared a logical connection and there was no imaginary set of laws made by a petty, irrational, spiteful legislature. But it's easy not to care when you have nothing to care about.

Then *she* came into my life.

It was my birthday and a few of us went to the pub for our lunch hour. It was a day much like any others, but then that's how most of the crucial days in your life begin. She had joined that day. I could not have asked for a better birthday present! She was beautiful, of course, but there was something else there: a sweetness in her eyes, a genuineness and wisdom that surpassed her mere twenty one years on the planet. But also an innocence that I felt this sudden desire to care for. I wanted to protect her. I wanted her to be mine.

"Everybody," said John, one of the audit junior managers, "this is Tiana." Pretty name, I thought. Very appropriate. I tried to work out where she was from – I have always had a knack of telling someone's racial background, expertly separating my Patels from my Khans. But it was difficult with her: her skin was a light olive colour, her eyes were so dark they seemed to have no irises, just a large pupil; the name sounded Italian; her features could be Mediterranean, or possibly Middle Eastern. An enigma, although unquestionably beautiful. And with a huge pair of boobs, the kind that could end a famine! Then she looked at me. It was only briefly, but it felt like ages. She saw me staring curiously at her. I felt a bit silly and wanted to apologise, but was too nervous. Deep down there was something there that I had never felt before. I knew there and then that she was the lady I wanted to be with for the rest of my life. That sounds a bit far-fetched, considering I hadn't even heard her speak and knew nothing about her. But words are only one part of communication: there's body language too, and the eyes say so much. And her eyes said it all.

"Wow", said Frank, one of the guys I worked with. "So who do you reckon is going to bed her first?"

"Shut up!" I said, snapping.

"What's got into you?" he replied. "Since when did you get so serious?"

"Not every girl's a slag," I said.

31

"Not on the surface," he answered. "But if you scratch for long enough and deep enough, you can find the slag in them." Frank fancied himself as a bit of a philosopher.

"Okay," I said, turning to him. "So your Mum is a slag, is she?"

"Probably," he said, shrugging. You had to admire his stubborn commitment to his theories, no matter how hurtful the conclusions.

I was just about to ask him what he thought of my Mother, but the conversation came to a halt as she sat down beside me.

"Hi," I said. "It's my birthday. I'm 25." Wow! I was such a smooth talker!

"Oh," she said. "Right." Not much of a response, I thought. A silly idea entered my head that maybe she was thick or slow or something. I quickly dismissed it.

"You're not a strip-o-gram, are you?" I said, trying to be witty. What the hell had I just said?! I'd only had one pint and already I was talking crap! But it wasn't the alcohol that was affecting my ability to converse. My senses were paralysed by something stronger than alcohol. My hands were shaking. She looked at me and laughed uncomfortably.

"That's Mark," said Claire, raising her eyebrows. "You'll get used to his weird sense of humour."

Again, she just smiled and looked uncomfortable.

"I didn't mean to be rude," I said, trying to dig myself out of a hole. "It's just that it's my birthday and you look like you could be one … I mean, you're attractive … I'm not improving this situation, am I."

Claire shook her head at me. "He *always* chats up the new girls!"

You bitch!, I thought. If I hadn't completely cocked things up already, giving her the impression that I was some kind of a slag definitely would have done!

"So what have HR got planned for you for the week?" asked Claire.

And that was it! Our first conversation over with! Tiana spent the rest of the time talking to Claire. I tried to join in, but could not think of anything to say. I got a "see you later" out of her as she went, but that was it. That Claire was such a bitch, I thought to myself. I expect she fancies me and tried to ruin my chances with Tiana on purpose. Or maybe she fancied Tiana! There was never any logic to my mind-ramblings.

I did not see Tiana for a good week or so. She was on a course up in Birmingham. I couldn't stop thinking about her though and I had to suppress my joy when she appeared at my desk one morning.

"Hi," she said. She was wearing a knitted pink skirt and had her hair in a pony tail. Tiana was blessed (or, as she would say, cursed) with big boobs and I couldn't help looking right at them as I turned towards her – they were at my eye-level, after all. I quickly turned and looked at her face, hoping she hadn't noticed – she had, she told me years later. I remember a feeling of anxiety run through me, a feeling that I hadn't had for a while. But my new-found confidence quickly brushed it to one side.

"Oh, hello," I replied, trying to keep my cool. "How are you getting on?"

"Good," she said, smiling and shrugging her shoulders. "I've just been on a course."

"What in Birmingham?" She nodded. "Learn much?"

"I learnt that all accountants are piss-heads!" she replied. I laughed, nodding my head in agreement.

"It's the only way we can cope," I joked. "Have you been given much work?"

"Bits and pieces," she answered. "Why – do you have anything I can help you with?"

I seized the opportunity: "I could show you how to put a tax computation and return together!"

"Sounds like fun!" she said, enthusiastically.

"Oh, I wouldn't go that far!" I replied.

"I'm a bit busy for the rest of today," she said. Ah, playing hard to get, I thought. "But I'm free for the rest of the week."

"Okay," I said, trying to sound nonchalant. "Do you want to come round tomorrow morning?"

"Mm-hmm," she replied, smiling. She gave a little wave and off she went. Was that flirting? Would she have done that had I been a manager? Or a girl? I hoped not. She was so hot!

That night I thought of things that I could say to her. How should I act? Nonchalant? Hard to get? But I didn't want to seem like I wasn't interested. I lay there trying to think of some clever lines. Nothing came to mind. I went downstairs and put the TV on. Nothing much on. I turned to Channel 4 to watch the news. I turned the volume up. Another murder. I turned the volume as high as it would go and said in my head, "That will *not* happen to me!", the emphasis on the 'not' at the point the volume was at its loudest, going back down again on the 'happen'. But I didn't get it quite right. The thought nagged at me: do it again; do it again, or it *will* happen to me. I did it again.

Better! No. Not quite right. I did it again. And again. The door opened.

"Turn that down will ya." Nigel, my housemate, walked in with a bag of chips under one arm. "I can 'ear it half way up the bloody road!"

"Are you not round Shelley's tonight?" I asked.

"I'm going round later," he replied. He sat down in the armchair in the corner of the room and unravelled the bag.

"You should be a right fat bastard by now, the amount of crap you eat," I said.

"'snot about what you eat," Nigel replied, stuffing a handful of chips into his gob. "It's all to do with exercise."

"I see Alice is still causing your problems," I said, pointing at his belly.

Nigel was the most incredible eater that I had ever seen! He was a bit plump, but nothing like what he should have been, considering the amount he would eat. I was convinced that he had some kind of parasite living in his belly that was helping him consume all this food and stopping him putting on all the weight. I called this little parasite Alice and even gave them a whole back story, a real love affair: they had met at a Chinese restaurant across the buffet; it was love at first sight as Nigel took a spoonful of the sweet and sour that the young Alice was bathing in and let her slip down inside his throat where she would live for the rest of her days, safe with her man.

"What are you on about now, weirdo?" he responded. He didn't find the whole Alice thing very funny. "You're home early."

"Do you have any good chat-up lines?"

"Loads," he said, scoffing his chips.

"Give me a line," I asked.

"Try this," said Nigel, putting his chips to one side. "You go up to the girl and say, 'I betcha 50p I can make yer tits wobble without touching 'em'. Then she says, go on then. Then you grab 'er boobs, wobble 'em and give 'er 50p!"

"Brilliant," I replied. "That'll really work. And I can really do that at work too without any repercussions job-wise." Nigel shrugged his shoulders and carried on eating his chips.

He wasn't anymore help that night. I decided that I should just be spontaneous.

It was ten o' clock and she still hadn't arrived. What should I do? I couldn't phone her – that would look desperate. I needed the toilet too, but didn't dare leave my desk in case she came round in my absence. I cleared my throat. It didn't feel right, so I did it again. And again. A thought came over me: I had not done this kind of thing in a long time. Was my weirdness coming back?

"Got a sore throat?" Tiana appeared next to my desk. Shit! I needed to clear my throat one more time. And it needed to be the loudest. I had an idea: I cleared my throat really loudly, pulling a silly face at the same time and staring at her.

"Yes," I eventually replied.

"You're strange," she said. I felt a bit silly.

"And you're late!" I answered, smiling and trying to move my brain on.

"Sorry," she said, sticking her bottom lip out. "I had a few things to do for someone else." A wave of jealousy ran through me.

"Right, well let's get started."

Tiana sat down and I noticed it: a cut in her skirt that could reveal too much if looked at from the wrong (right) angle.

I'm sure she noticed my eyes almost pop out of my head! (She did – she told me later.) I managed to keep myself together as we spent the next two hours in each others' company. I showed her how to put a computation on the system and she showed me her belly-button ring and I fell completely head over heels for her. I showed her how I could wiggle my ears and she showed me the lotus position. I told her about my uni' days and she told me about her first two years and how she would be going back for her final year next August and my heart sank, but I tried not to show it. And I told her that I had been in a relationship a little while ago, but was now single and she told me about her boyfriend and you could hear the thud as my heart hit the floor.

I plucked up the courage to ask: "How long have you been together for?"

"Oh not long," she replied. My heart clambered up to my knees! "We get on so well." Another thud. "Bit too well, really." Right up to my waist! "We're more like mates." My heart was almost back to its starting position! "But he's so hot!" Thud.

"Great," I interrupted, trying to change the conversation before I needed to go into a handstand to let gravity work its magic on my most vital of organs (or maybe second most, with my brain coming in at third place for having too many faults). And that was that. The rest of the time we concentrated on the work. I tried not to show it, but I was feeling absolutely gutted.

A few weeks went by and nothing much happened. We saw each other round the office, chatted every now and then, but not much else. I couldn't stop thinking about her. I kept wanting to just go up to her and grab her and kiss her; but I decided that probably wouldn't be the best way to go about it. I thought about ways to ask her out, but never got round to it. I would purposely pull certain poses near her to show off my biceps or bum (apparently I've always had a nice, firm bum, if a bit on the hairy side, but that makes it nice to stroke – not my words!). Or try to say something funny when she was nearby, hoping she'd overhear and think what an amusing guy I was. And when another bloke was talking to her or sitting next to her, I'd be so jealous. Most of all, I hated if another guy made her laugh. It grated on me. I wanted to go over and say, 'that may have been funny, but I'm funnier aren't I?' I let my emotions build up inside of me with no outlet: passion, frustration, desire, loneliness, anger … Love? Possibly. The obsessive and the compulsive sides of my personality aren't restricted to my OCD – the two don't always gang up on me to complete the disorder. I can get obsessive about things I really like – not to any psychotic degree (purely neurotic, to use the medical terms), but I'm certainly more easily infatuated than most. Passionate – that's probably a better word! Sounds less freaky than obsessive. And the compulsive side can be quite liberating: often, if I feel like doing something or saying something that needs to be said, I do it or say it. It's a kind of leap before you look approach. Dangerous, maybe; reckless, probably; inappropriate, definitely. But I'm waffling.

Then came the annual conference: once a year the whole office would get taken out for the day, culminating in a dinner and dance in the evening. The morning would consist of some big cheese harping on about how bloody wonderful the business was, how well we were doing, how awful our competitors are and how we are one big happy family! It's at times like this that I wished I had Tourette's instead – at least that way I could get away with heckling. "Lying bastard!" or "Where are our bonuses then?" would be my choice of uncontrollable shoutings. The afternoon would involve team-building exercises, which were surprisingly good fun considering we were all sober and surrounded by accountants. The evening would involve a dinner and a dance and it was this that would provide the epicentre for the office scandals and rumours. This year was my turn to start a few!

On this particular occasion, we took a trip on a boat down the Thames to the Millennium Dome. After listening to them waffle on all morning and trying to suppress my desire to compulsively shout out a phrase that would include the words 'lying' and 'bastard', we stuffed our faces at lunchtime and in the afternoon carried out a team building exercise involving various drums. The idea was to come up with some two-minute piece involving all of us banging away. We were crap, but it was good fun. I managed to get the biggest drum. All day, I had been trying to get closer to Tiana, but with no luck. This obnoxious ginger-haired dick called Ricky had some how managed to sit next to her all morning, then at lunchtime and even got into her group for the drumming! Spawny git is the expression, I think. I couldn't help watching them, checking Tiana's body language. She was laughing far too much for my liking, although she has always laughed readily. But he was a tactile little bastard and would keep putting his arm around her shoulders and squeezing her. It was fast becoming clear to me that Tiana was a flirt. It's a typical trait of somebody with OCD to be a bit insecure and it takes a lot of reassuring before I can really feel comfortable that a woman would want me and just me. This little characteristic of hers would cause me great amounts of grief in the next few months.

Evening arrived and we were all in our D.J.s and posh dresses for dinner. They did their typical routine of arranging who sat where on each table, with the result that you were forced to make conversation with some boring colleague who you'd always tried to avoid in the office and had nothing in common with. The presence of alcohol helped us all: other people became more relaxed and I became even more inappropriate, which stopped them talking to me for too long. As bad luck would have it, this Ricky bloke was on our table. At least he wasn't with Tiana and this way I could keep my eye on him. To show just how annoying this guy was, I provide below a sample of his conversation. He is responding to my mentioning that I used to do martial arts when I was younger.

Ricky: "There's no point in it."

Me: "Why do you say that [you silly tosser]?"

Ricky: "I'll tell you a story. A few years ago, there was the best kung fu expert in the world and the greatest karate guy and they were in this bar together."

[Bullshit alert! What is the likelihood that these two people were hanging out together?! Moreover, there are no such titles! It is at this point that all respect for him (which was not very much) left me.]

Ricky: "This bloke starts on them. They go to fight him. He pulls out a knife. Both of them end up dead. Can't defend yourself against a knife." He winked at me and sat back in his chair as if to say, that is that, it's a fact and there is no answer.

I didn't respond. There really is no need to respond to something as ridiculous as that. I shook my head in disbelief and turned to talk to the chubby boring old guy with halitosis sitting next to me.

The dinner continued uneventfully for the most part, except for one small incident which did nothing to harm my chances of never going any further in the firm: someone had decided that flicking bits of tissue and left over food (I'm talking peas and that kind of thing here, not a steak or curry sauce, for example) through fingers in the shape of goal

posts would be a good idea. Foolishly, I joined in, flicked a boiled potato at the person opposite, missed by miles, knocked over a glass of red wine, spilling it all over the nice white dress of the office managing partner. 'Idiot' is not the exact phrase she used, but that's the polite equivalent. I caught her give me a couple of glances a little later that spoke volumes of how I would never be a partner in that firm. I tried giving a look back that said, 'don't want to be a partner in this shit hole'.

As soon as the puddings came, I scoffed mine down, finished my sixth glass of wine and made my way over to Tiana, sat down next to her and indulged in talking absolute crap.

"How was your meal?" I asked.

"Okay," she replied. "I'm not overly keen on this nouveau cuisine crap, to be honest. I would have preferred a nice curry or some Chinese."

"I'll remember that," I said. "We can go for one on our first date."

"Bit presumptuous, aren't you?" She laughed. "I've got a boyfriend, you know – that might get in the way."

"Well I'm sorry," I answered, "but I'm only paying for yours – he'll have to buy his own."

She laughed again. "You're mad! And drunk!"

"Aren't you, then?" I asked.

"I guess I must be," she replied, "otherwise I wouldn't be talking to you!" She was smiling, so I assumed she was just playing.

"Drink some more then," I said, "then you might want to do more than just talk."

"Hey, cheeky," she responded. "I've been warned about you."

"By who?" I cried.

"Claire – she says you chase women just to get them into bed, according to her."

"Rubbish!" I said. "She doesn't even know me that well!"

"To be honest," she whispered, leaning towards me, "I reckon she fancies you."

"Never in a million years!" I cried. "Anyway, how was your meal? Have anyone decent on your table?"

"Oh, there was this right 'moaning Minnie'," she replied. "She'd forgotten to request a vegetarian meal, then claimed no one had mentioned it to her, blah, blah, blah!"

"Vegetarians are so very wrong," I said, sighing. "They're harming future generations."

"How d'you work that one out?" asked Tiana.

"Well," I began, ready to go off on one, "if you look at herbivores, like your average cow or sheep, they have eyes on the side of their head."

"What just on the one side?" she interrupted.

"Don't be silly," I said, smiling. "I'm making a very important point." She pretended to look serious. "So if a nasty carnivore is creeping up on them they can see behind them and make a run for it before they get eaten. Carnivores on the other hand, their eyes point forward so they can focus on their prey. Now humans, they have eyes that face forward."

"Not all of them," replied Tiana. "What about that Martin bloke on the second floor."

"Ah," I said, chuckling, "that might well prove my point! You see, humans are meant to eat meat. If you just eat vegetables, eventually your eyes will move to the side of your head. Not you, but your descendants. By my

calculations, the signs will be there by the time your great grandchildren are born!"

"So Martin's great grandparents were vegetarians?"

"Possibly," I answered. "Or there's a sheep going back somewhere."

"One problem," said Tiana. "For your theory to work, it would mean that vegetarians would be worried about meat-eaters creeping up behind them and taking a chunk out of them. I don't reckon they do that."

"Well let's start now!" I cried. "Where is she?"

"Over there," replied Tiana, pointing at a middle-aged, pompous looking woman. "But don't … !"

Too late! I was out of my seat and creeping up behind her; as I got within a foot away I suddenly pounced on her, gently biting her shoulder! She jumped up screeching!

"What the bloody hell are you playing at?!" she cried, turning to me and waving her arms about.

"Oh, I'm so sorry!" I said. "I thought you were someone else."

"Who?" she cried. "Who do you possibly know that you would want to bite their shoulder?"

"I'm really sorry!" I repeated and walked swiftly back over to Tiana. "I'll be more careful who I bite next time!"

She was fuming! I grabbed Tiana by the hand, who was in fits of laughter, and pulled her away.

"Let's dance!" I whispered to her.

"Yay!" she said and we ran over to the dance-floor.

We danced like crazy for the next hour: we disco'd, swung to 'Stuck in the Middle with You' (the one from *Pulp Fiction*), played air guitar, hand-jived, did the YMCA (at which point I wondered whether Tiana might be dyslexic as her 'c's were back to front and she kept getting the 'y' and the 'm' round the wrong way), all the usual floor-fillers, then we went to one side and collapsed in some chairs, exhausted and sweaty.

"You dance pretty well for a bloke," said Tiana.

"Do you want to see my moonwalk?" I asked.

"Okay," she answered. "If you've still got enough energy left."

I jumped up, pulled my trousers and pants down below my backside to reveal my hairy behind and walked up and down for a bit. Tiana was laughing hysterically.

"You're mad!"

We spent the rest of the evening together, telling each other funny stories, going for the occasional dance and generally being silly. Then came midnight and it dawned on me: I'd missed my last train home! Well, the truth is I knew what time I had to leave and let that time pass by without worrying about the consequences. My logic was that it was worth spending another few moments with her even if it meant being homeless for a few hours.

"What do I do now?" I cried. "I'll have to sleep out on the streets!"

"Don't be silly," she said, looking at me mischievously. "You can come and stay at mine!"

I wasn't expecting that and even with my Dutch courage I couldn't conceal my nerves at the proposition.

"Erm, yeah," I stuttered, "definitely, okay. Okay."

So we did: we left there at about one o' clock and made our way across London to where she lived in the Docklands. It was a really upmarket area. Tiana rented a room in the house. There were two lads that also lived there, but they were hardly ever in so she had the house to herself most of the time. Her house was on the top floor. We had a pint of water each then went upstairs to her room.

"You're on the floor," she said.

"Of course," I replied, smiling. "I'm a gentleman."

An hour later, we were lying in each other's arms, sharing that moment straight after sex where nothing else matters, everything is wonderful. I always feel like I can take on the world after sex, as if I can do anything, but as long as I can leave it until tomorrow.

"Ever wondered how lesbians know when to stop?" I asked her.

"Stop?" she replied.

"Yes," I said. "A man and a woman – or a man and a man – know when to stop because the bloke comes. And he can't carry on after that. At least not straight away. Two women on the other hand."

"Well," said Tiana, "they stop when the woman comes."

"No: women can keep coming. So they can go on forever."

"Maybe it just fizzles out then," she suggested.

"Maybe," I responded. "Sounds like a bit of an anti-climax."

"Why don't you ask a lesbian?"

"Don't know any," I replied. "You?"

"I could have a good guess," she said. "What about that Fiona girl?"

"Yeah! I thought that too! I'll ask her when I next see her!"

We chatted like that for a good hour or so more, never mentioning her boyfriend once. I didn't want to ask. I didn't want to think about him and spoil this wonderful moment.

She acted strange when we woke up the next day, or later that day, should I say. Maybe she was just tired, but she didn't really want to say anything to me. No offer of breakfast, no goodbye and see you soon. Maybe she was feeling hung-over. I said goodbye, kissed her on the cheek. She didn't offer to show me out. I guessed that she was feeling guilty.

Me on the other hand, I had mixed emotions: I was glad we did what we did and I was sure she had enjoyed it as much as me – at least she sounded like she enjoyed it; but I felt confused by her lack of interest in me when we left.

The following week when we returned to work, she never said much to me. A polite 'hello' and that was it. I e-mailed her and got no response. I tried again. And again. Finally, she replied: "Just leave it alone." And that was it. So I left it alone, feeling desperately gloomy. The usual insecurities hit me: had she not enjoyed it?, does she prefer her boyfriend?, did she do it just to satisfy me? But it didn't seem that was the case straight after it had happened. I was confused.

I left it alone for weeks.

It was a Friday lunchtime and everyone had a little too much to drink, including Tiana. She gave me a certain look – an invitational look. We got back to the office and I e-mailed her: "How about it?" That's all I put. I waited. Finally, a 'ting': new mail. "How about what?" "You and me." "When?" "Now." "Where?" "The roof garden. I'll walk past your desk. Follow me after a couple of minutes."

A little while later, we were rolling around amongst the hedges and concrete high above the London streets. Weeks of passion released. Not the most romantic place, but this wasn't about romance: this was purely physical. Romance could come later.

I sat back down at my desk. The guy next to me was waffling on about some client and whether they should be paying tax under schedule A or schedule DV. I couldn't give less of a shit if I tried. I wanted to shout out, "I've just had great sex with a beautiful woman in the London skies." But I decided against it and settled for a smug grin. Even when he asked me why I had a leaf stuck to the back of my shirt, I managed to hold back.

"What now?" I asked, as we lay there together. "What are you going to do about him?"

"I'm going to tell him," she said. "Soon."

"When?" I insisted.

"After Christmas," she replied. "Not before. It wouldn't be fair."

So the Christmas parties came and I had to pretend we weren't together. I had to ignore it when other blokes would put their arms round her or kiss her on the cheek. Tiana being Tiana, she would flirt back, always stopping short before they went too far. I began to feel anxiety building up in me. Tiana has always been so much better at hiding her emotions and my insecurity made me doubt whether she was sincere. But the more merry we became, the more difficult it was to hide our feelings, especially for me. At the tax department do at the Spanish tapas bar, *Macarena's*, I pushed my luck with her. Sitting next to her, eating a chocolate gateaux, I lost my appetite and pushed it towards her. "Here," I said, "you like to have your cake and eat it too." She didn't talk to me whilst we remained seated. Then she went over to a far corner of the room and started dancing with some blokes, so I followed. We argued. She told me to stop being so clingy and to just enjoy the evening.

I accused her of being too flirtatious. She told me that it didn't mean anything and couldn't care less if I wanted to flirt with another woman. She moved to the other side of the dance-floor, bottle in hand, a smile across her face. I knew it was fake, but couldn't help but be irritated. I stormed over, pushed a couple of people out of the way, took that bottle and chucked it across the floor; she told me to "piss off and leave her alone", so I decided to pick up a chair, throw it at the wall, and kick a table, breaking my toe in the process (it still crunches in the Winter if I move it after a long time of it being motionless!). The bouncers surrounded me. I felt the urge to throw some punches, but the urge left me and I surrendered to an octopus of arms, dragging me, lifting me and chucking me into the streets. I waited for a while, but she never came out.

We made up when we were sober. And she never made me apologise when Ricky got a little too close to her at the main Christmas party and I took the opportunity to grab him and throw him over a table. She was beginning to understand just how frustrated and upset I was. Plus, I think she was getting a little annoyed with him too.

"You will finish with him after Christmas," I pleaded.

"Look," she answered, "let me do it my way."

But I didn't. Christmas Eve came and I became impatient. It was something that I could have controlled had I not had eight pints of beer. I rang her mobile. A man's voice picked up! I hadn't anticipated that! I hung up. "Shit! SHIT! SHIT!!!" I said, with increased ferocity. Why did I have to do that?

I spent the next five or so minutes fretting and hoping I hadn't blown everything. Then the phone rang: Tiana.

"I've done it!" she exclaimed. "Are you happy now?! I've told him everything on Christmas Eve! He's gone! We'll be together! Are you happy now?" she repeated, bursting into tears.

"I'm so sorry," I said. "Thank you. I won't let you down. Never."

So we finally became an item. Our official starting date was 1 January 2001 as that's the date we next met. That was the first time we could kiss in public without a sense of guilt or betrayal. I felt like a heavy weight had been lifted from my shoulders.

I was in love.

But love implies caring deeply for somebody. A by-product of caring is worrying. To worry could lead to anxiety. I knew all this. But I would be damned if I would let it take away the most beautiful wonderful woman that I had ever met. So the door in my brain swung open, the guard retired, and OCD prepared itself to stroll back in, with its stupid smug grin and arrogant swagger. But he didn't come in just yet – he had a long walk there first.

CHAPTER FIVE: COUNTDOWN TO ARMAGEDDON

The next six months were some of the best we've ever had together. We partied, we dined, made love, had sex, learnt so many brilliant things about each other, both spiritual and physical. It was my 26th birthday that Summer and she made an effort to make it the best day ever for me in a way that nobody else ever had. It was a Friday morning and we had arranged to take the day off work under her instructions.

"Where are we going then?" I asked her for the umpteenth time.

"Look," she replied, "I haven't given in and told you yet; what makes you think I'm going to tell you now?"

"Will I like it?"

"You better!"

And I did: we went to Twickenham first for a tour of the stadium, including going into the changing rooms and through the tunnel leading to the pitch; then we were back on the tube and up the London Eye, despite Tiana's fear of heights (she tried not to cry, bless her, but she did it because she knew how much I wanted to); then back on the tube and off to Islington for a meal at a Korean restaurant; then back to her house and a perfect finish for a perfect day.

"That was the best birthday I've ever had," I said to her as we lay together in bed. "Even beats the one where I got a BMX Burner!"

"Woah!" she replied. "That's pretty damn good then!"

"Yep," I nodded. "Guess I'm going to have to do pretty well to beat that for your birthday!"

"Oh, it's very easy," she answered. "As long as you've got a spare couple of grand, it shouldn't be a problem."

"Oh," I said, chuckling. "I've got it in the bag then!"

We discovered so much about each other those first few months, as you do when you fall in love. She could be so loving and gentle. She has always needed several cuddles a day, to be told that she's loved and to be kissed as often as possible (between breaths if she had her own way). Tiana is the most loving, gentle, kindest lady I know, which makes her very easy to love and to kiss and to cuddle. She's very sociable too, and loves to go out and meet new people, try new experiences and generally have fun. Her parents had brought her up like that. She is my antithesis in so many ways. But it took me a long time to understand all this. None of it came naturally to me and never before had I to try and understand why some people are like this. I was cynical of it, I guess, always thinking that there was a hidden motive in it, that she was keeping something from me. I would often feel slightly anxious when we were out together; even more so when she was out with her friends and I was at home. However, as much as she liked drinking and partying, she liked me more. I knew this deep down, but I was not secure, had never socialised much and I would easily lose sight of the real picture, fretting that she was up to no good behind my back. I had never had many friends and was not comfortable with socialising. She showed me more than enough loving to explain why I was so head over heels for her, but her way of life made a perfect breeding ground for somebody as pathetic and insecure as I was to develop full-blown OCD.

For all my worrying and stupid questioning, Tiana remained blissfully unaware of the impact that all this was having on my brain. There was only one really bad argument in all that time and I don't think it was entirely down to my paranoia. She had planned to meet up in London with one of her girlfriends from university. They were meeting in a Wetherspoon's pub just next to our office. Tiana asked me if I wanted to come to the pub, then they would go and do their thing in Covent Garden. I agreed. This other guy from work, Malcolm, joined us. The conversation was going well and the alcohol was flowing. They stayed far longer than they intended and by 9 o' clock we were all suitably drunk. Then her mobile rang, she looked at me strangely, stood up and walked outside. I tried to ignore it for a bit and carried on talking with the other three, occasionally looking round to see what she was doing.

Eventually I went outside to listen. All I caught was, "I love you!"

"Who's that?" I asked. I grabbed the phone from her. "Hello?" The line went dead.

"Hey!" she said, grabbing it back from me. "Hello, Paul? Paul?! He's gone, you idiot!"

"Who the hell was that?" I demanded.

"My mate from uni'", she replied. "You get so bloody jealous!"

"How would you feel if I was telling some other woman that I loved them?" I retaliated.

She stormed back in the pub, sat down with the other two and pushed the fourth chair away. I grabbed her arm and tried to pull her up on to her feet, asking her to talk to me about this. She came off the chair, falling heavily on her knees!

"Come outside," I cried, ignoring her fall and continuing to pull her arm, "we need to talk about this properly!"

"No!" she shouted, tears welling up in her eyes. "Just piss off and leave me alone! I've come here to be with my friend! Just go home!" I let go and she got back to her feet.

"I'm not leaving it like this!" I shouted, and proceeded to try and drag her outside, but she fell to her knees again! I tried to help her up, but was grabbed by several arms and – as was starting to become a theme – physically thrown out of the pub! They locked the door after me. I stood outside, banging on the window. "Hey, let me back in, you bastards!"

I gave up and stood outside, staring through the window, looking at her laughing with her friends, ignoring me. I couldn't believe she could be such a bitch!

I sat on the ground for what seemed like ages. Finally she came out and walked straight past me. I followed her.

"Please talk to me," I pleaded. "I'm really sorry. All I want to know is why you're telling another man you love him!"

They hailed a taxi, got in and slammed the door in my face! I banged on the door and chased it as it drove off. And that was that!

I stood there, not knowing what to do or what to think. I texted her, telling her how much I loved her and please don't do anything silly. She texted me back a little while later: "You really piss me off. But I love you too. Trust me." So I did.

Thoughts went through my head as I made my way back home, horrible images of Tiana in some big orgy or lying on the street somewhere, raped and lifeless. "That does not happen," I would say in my head, over and over again, counting the number of times, tapping something each time I said 'not'. I tried ringing her but got no answer. I left it – I had to show I trusted her.

I got a text at about four o' clock in the morning as I lay in bed, eyes wide open, performing my rituals: "I'm back home safe. Don't worry. I was good. Let's talk tomorrow. ☺."

I rang her back there and then and we talked and we made it up and we both apologised and accepted that we'd both been absolute idiots and we loved each other more than two people had ever loved each other before. We would say that we were both carved out of the same block of life and were always meant to be together.

Thankfully, that was by far the worst of any arguments we've ever had.

But there was something else hanging over us like the sword of Damocles: she would be going back to university in September and we would be forced to only see each other at the weekends. As the time came closer, I became more and more anxious. Then she dropped a bombshell: she would be living with Simon, a model and a good friend. She had promised him they would live together long before she had ever met me. I asked her if they had ever gone out.

"No," she replied. But there was something in her response that made me probe further, something more than just an OCD urge. Finally, she admitted it: "I slept with him once. It was just a silly one-night stand and it was before you and I had started sleeping together." "How long before?" "About a month." About a month!!! That was all! I began to wonder what kind of girl this was!

But I knew she wasn't a slag. She had been stuck in a rut for a year or so. Ed was there and she liked him, but never enough for a relationship. Then I was there and she liked me and more than enough for a relationship. So there we were.

"How would you feel if it was the other way round?" I asked in one of my many attempts to get her to change her mind.

"I'd trust you," she said. And I know she would have done. So that was that. She was not going to budge and the more I pressed, the worse I was going to make it. Tiana could be incredibly stubborn when it came to her independence. She would live with him just to make a point, if she had to.

So I decided to grin and bear it.

During all of this time, my symptoms were usually mild except for the odd hiccup and could be ignored for the most part. But they were like a simmering pot and with a sudden adjustment in setting would boil over. I did the occasional checking doors and things; I counted the amount of times I would use certain 'key' words in sentences; sometimes I would repeat whole questions. The worst I would do is ask about other blokes: "Did anyone chat to you last night?"; "Have you ever been out with him?"; "Have you ever got off with him?" And sometimes I'd have to ask the question four times. It wasn't that I was jealous and I didn't think she'd done anything; I just felt a compelling urge to ask, and often it didn't feel right until I'd done it four times. I wasn't overly interested in the answer. But sometimes the answer wasn't as definitive as I would have liked. "No, I never got off with another bloke last night!" She could have kissed him though, not necessarily snogged. Perhaps she had a different definition of 'get off': "What do you count as 'getting off' with somebody?" I could drive her mad with these stupid questions. Tiana thought I was just jealous. I didn't tell her that it was a compulsion; nor that I was beginning to develop an obsession of her with other men. A horrible obsession of her cheating on me. Or worse.

Every so often, I would be introduced to another of her many 'best friends'. Kim was one of these so-called best friends. She was very short and tiny with it. She looked like a large hobbit. We met in a pub one evening.

"So, you're the famous Mark, are you?" she asked.

"Infamous," I replied. I leaned forward and said in a threatening voice: "so just watch yourself." Kim looked a little taken aback. "Hey, I'm only joking!"

"Okay," she said, half-smiling but looking a bit unsure.

"Sorry about him," interrupted Tiana. "He can be a bit weird sometimes!"

"It's nice to meet you and find out you're not handicapped!" I added, trying my best to get a laugh.

"What?!" cried Kim, looking at Tiana in amazement.

"Well, Tiana's got a picture of you and a few others sitting round a table in a pub," I explained. "Your tongue's hanging out to one side and you're cross-eyed. You looked like you had a mental problem!" I could see that this wasn't going very well. "I think you were all very drunk at the time."

"Oh, yeah," she replied, putting on a false smile.

The conversation went down hill after that. She didn't really say much to me. They spent most of the time talking about going to Spain for a week with another of her friends. I didn't like the sound of that.

"Why did you say that?" she asked later that evening.

"What?" I replied, knowing exactly what she was talking about.

"You know!" she cried. "Why did you say she looked like a spastic?"

"I thought it would break the ice!" I said. "I didn't realise she didn't have a sense of humour."

"You've got no sense of what you should and shouldn't say," she replied. "You don't go round calling people spastics, especially if you've never met them before. Kim is really sensitive. She'll be going on about that for ages now."

"I didn't call her a spastic, I was just joking about her pulling a funny face. You're not going on holiday, though, are you?" I asked.

"Yes, probably," replied Tiana. "Why, what's wrong with that?"

"Well," I replied, "bit expensive isn't it? And anyway, you've got a bloke now. You don't need to go on girlie holidays, do you?"

"I'm not going to stop going on holiday with my friends," she answered, "just because I've got a boyfriend. I need a break before I go back for my final year. I need to get a nice tan and enjoy myself, to relax and let my hair down. This next year is going to be the most important of my life!"

"Well, why don't we do something together?" I asked.

"I can't afford to go away with you as well," she replied.

"Well what about instead?" I suggested.

"You're pathetic at times," said Tiana. "I'm going to go away with a couple of friends and that's all there is to it."

And she did. They arranged a holiday for a couple of months later. She looked up 18 to 30s holidays! I couldn't handle that!

"That's for a load of single people!" I pleaded.

"Don't be silly!" she said. "It's just a cheap young people's holiday! And I'm not going to do anything anyway! They do lots of fun events for young people! Just trust me, will you?"

I did. But I'd seen those kinds of holidays on *Ibiza Uncovered* and similar programmes: a load of young girls and lads would play games that involved drink and quasi-sexual encounters (and some non-quasi ones too!). And in the evening, she would get drunk, maybe forget what she was doing, where she was, who she was with. She could wake up the next day in another man's bed. Or worse. Ideas filled my head, ridiculous ideas of what could happen.

"I don't want you to go," I pleaded for the millionth time. But to no avail.

It was about a month before the day of her flight and we were watching a film on her bed. I coughed. Once. Twice. Four times. I was counting. I had a tickle in my throat. But not every cough was necessary, at least from the point of view of my throat; but I suddenly found myself in a repetitive pattern of coughing until it 'felt right'. But then the feeling that something was not quite right came back again. Thirteen was a bad number, so I avoided that. Sixteen came up. Soon I had counted out nearly thirteen sets of four, so I made sure I went over that. And Tiana began to get annoyed.

"Stop coughing," she said. "Go and get some water or something. It's really annoying!"

So I stopped. For a bit, anyway. But then I wasn't sure whether I had coughed enough. So I waited until she went to the toilet for a break and took the opportunity to cough some more. Then I annoyed her by coughing when she got back, so I went to the toilet and coughed some more. By the time the film had finished, I had completely lost count, had no idea what the story was about and had really annoyed Tiana. Eventually I stopped coughing for long enough to break out of this strange pattern of repetitive behaviour. And half an hour later I felt silly and confused. Why had I done that? I know I carried out some strange behaviour at times, but never quite so strange as that. Never quite so compelled to carry such a routine out. And why coughing?

The strange coughing behaviour continued: on the tube, I found myself having to cough four times at each stop to make each one 'safe'; I counted the days I was doing it for. I had coughed eleven days in a row by the 13th August. I couldn't stop that day, so coughed on the 14th too. But then

I wasn't sure if I had gone 12 days or was it 13? So I coughed for 16 days in total, then swore that I'd stop. But I didn't.

One night, Tiana was out with one of her friends from work. I was staying at her house that evening. She would be coming back later, or so I thought. I began coughing. But hard, as though I was trying to cough something out of the back of my throat, though there was nothing there to cough out. I watched TV for a while, then tried reading. But the programmes and the chapters were broken up by coughing fits. I didn't need to cough, I just felt the need to start coughing hard, really wheezing, louder each time. Then that would be my last. But it wasn't.

The phone rang. It was Tiana.

"Olivia is really ill," she said. "We're in a taxi and I'm taking her home."

"What's the matter with her?" I asked. "Alcohol?"

"Yes," she replied. "She was downing Tequilas but she couldn't handle it. There was us and a couple of blokes we met."

"What blokes?" I cried.

"Oh no one," she answered. "Just a couple of blokes we were chatting to. Just having a laugh with. Don't worry, it wasn't like that. Anyway, I've got to stay with her in case she chokes on her own vomit."

"Are they with you?" I asked.

"Who?" said Tiana.

"Those blokes you were with," I replied.

"No! Of course they're not!"

"Are you going to come back here soon?" I said.

"No," she answered. "I doubt it. I'll be back early tomorrow morning though."

After falling back into a coughing session, I finally fell asleep about three in the morning and slept until she came in the bedroom door seven hours later. I never said anything about my strange behaviour. I was embarrassed by it and anyway I was far too busy bombarding her with stupid questions.

The following Monday I went over to her desk and waited for her to turn up so we could go to lunch together. I wasn't spying, I just noticed an e-mail from some bloke called Jeff entitled 'Friday night'. I opened it and caught something about meeting up again; I didn't have time to read it all before Tiana grabbed the mouse and turned it off.

"What are you doing?" she cried.

"Tell me who the hell Jeff is!" I demanded. "Is he one of the blokes from last Friday?"

"Yes," she replied. "How dare you look at my inbox!"

"Why is he e-mailing you?" I asked.

"Because I gave him my e-mail address!" said Tiana. "He's just a friend!"

I went mad! We argued for days. On the one hand, I wanted to know why she was giving her e-mail address to strange blokes she meets in nightclubs; on the other, she wanted to know why I was reading her e-mails (like that was just as bad!)! After a few days, it was obvious that she was much better at keeping up a bad mood than I was, so I eventually decided to put the argument to an end and apologised. She forgave me! I felt the urge to say I was only apologising so we could move on and start talking again, but decided it was probably best not to. Tiana can be incredibly stubborn at times and I learnt at an early point in our relationship to back down sooner rather than later.

And the holiday came. They were two hours ahead in Cyprus, so when they went out in the evenings at seven o' clock it was nine there; when she finally got home at eight in the morning, it was six our time. I had not slept much. I phoned her one of the nights and she accused me of checking to see whether she'd pulled or not. I didn't go to work that week, feeling anxious all over, my throat sore from coughing, my head aching from anxiety. I stayed at home in bed, alone with my thoughts. I entered my own private hell. My mind was left to wonder; my imagination ran riot. Images of sexual encounters: topless dancing; snogging in the corner of some nightclub; lying in the kerb, her knickers by her ankles, her friends round her laughing; her in the middle, two different men either side; continual images over and over again and nothing to break the flow. The days were easier: the sounds outside, the television, the occasional calls from friends, relatives and colleagues, it all helped me get a sense of perspective and reality. But then the nights would come again and any idea of normality would leave with the sun. Each day, I was getting progressively worse and becoming more of a recluse.

By the fourth day, I had enough of my wits about me to know that I had to get out of there and find myself some company. I went to stay with my Nan for a few days, just until Tiana got back. She lived on her own and would get incredibly lonely with only the TV as company. My Mum would visit as often as she could and there were plenty of neighbours near by. But what she really missed was living with somebody, cooking for them, doing the washing, just having a reason to get up in the morning. She spoilt me whilst I was there! And we had some fascinating conversations. There was one in particular that I remember clearly to this day.

"Of course success wasn't easy to come by for your uncle John," she said. "He was a very nervous lad, although you couldn't tell it now. He had to work hard to build up his confidence enough."

"What was wrong with him?" I asked.

"He had a sort of a nervous 'tic'," she replied. "He would have to tap things a few times."

"Like what?"

"Well," she continued, "he would come into the front room and just stand there looking worried; then he might go up to the television set or a table and just tap the top of it a couple of times. Then he'd walk away; but sometimes he'd come back and do it again."

"Why did he do that?" I asked, pretending to have never come across such weird behaviour. As you'd expect, I was curious to find out more.

"We took him to the doctors about it. The doctor said it was just a phase that he was going through. That he would grow out of it."

"And did he?" I said.

"Eventually," she replied. "He was always a very nervous boy, though. And it took him a long time. It wasn't until he was about fifteen and started to get lots of friends and go out more. That's when it seemed to go away. And when he was in the middle of something, like his music; something where he could focus his mind. It was when he was feeling worried about having to go somewhere or sit an exam."

"Did you ever ask him why he did it?" I asked.

"Yes," she answered. "But he didn't really answer me. He said he didn't know."

I felt sad for my uncle, but glad that there were other strange people in my family that suffered too. Did this mean it was genetic behaviour? But I put it down to coincidence. I wanted to ask him about it, but we were never close so it would have seemed a bit strange. Plus, he might have got over it years ago and probably wouldn't want it being brought up again.

As well as all of these fascinating conversations, my Nan and I would sit and do puzzles together or go for walks; I enjoyed just helping her round the house and in the garden. I know she felt enthused to have me there and she definitely helped me in a way that she would never know. My OCD was back on the retreat and the time began to fly by before Tiana was home. We continued to text each other and speak every day on the phone; but now it was more positive, with me being genuinely wanting her to be having a good time and enjoying the break. I was keen that she felt refreshed in time for her final and all important year and that I didn't spoil this for her.

When Tiana finally returned we cuddled and made love and laughed and joked endlessly for a whole week! She burst out crying at one point. I got jealous, thinking maybe she had something to confess, but I didn't accuse her of anything. She admitted to missing me and not enjoying being away from me for so long. Apparently, she even cried a couple of times. I accepted that, believing her. And the next three weeks were fantastic.

Then she went back to university for her final year, a vital year. A year of separation during the week and seeing each other at weekends. A year of her living with another man who she'd once slept with.

It was the year my mental illness first dominated my life.

CHAPTER SIX: A VOYAGE OF SELF-DISCOVERY

"It's only a year," said Tiana.

"Not even that," I replied. "October to July inclusive – that's ten months. We can handle that!"

"Of course we can!"

Little did I know how hard it would be. I had my last set of tax exams to take that November, so this would help me keep my mind occupied, I thought. During the week, I would get up at six, walk the half hour journey to the train station, get on the train and study, get to work, go to the gym at lunchtime, on the train by six, home by half seven after a long walk back, make dinner, eat, wash up, study until half nine, talk to Tiana (not for the first time that day – I never used to count this though), go to bed at about eleven, read and fall asleep. On a Friday, one week I would get the train to see her in Bournemouth and leave again on a Monday morning; the next week she would drive to me, get there on a Friday evening and leave on a Sunday evening. Monday, the anxiety would begin to build up, gradually increasing and peaking on a Thursday night; Friday, it would decrease measurably as I knew I'd be seeing her again that evening. Saturday, I would be virtually anxiety free; Sunday it waited at the door for me to let it in that next morning. The period from October to July followed a similar pattern to the days. I had finished studying by November, but this only freed my mind up for more stupid thoughts.

My genuine cough had come back again around October. I would count the amount of coughs I did all day. Then it became a case of counting from day to day. Of course, I lost count numerous times and had no idea of how many I had done, nor when I had begun to count. But that didn't really matter; what really mattered was that feeling that something was wrong, that I had to avoid certain numbers like the plague: those that were divisible by thirteen were 'bad' numbers; those divisible by four were 'good' numbers. If I tried to stop myself, my heart would beat faster, I could feel myself tense up. My mind would think of nothing else, but 'correcting' the error. People would ask me why I was so quiet, what the matter was, why I looked so worried. I could hardly say, 'I'm not sure how many times I've coughed.' People would think me mad.

Tiana didn't really notice my coughing. Looking back, she probably didn't see much of it as I would be less anxious when I was with her. It was my fellow commuters, clients and colleagues that would suffer from my strange behaviour. No one ever said anything, but you could see in their eyes that they thought me a little odd at times.

Eventually the cough went away in time for my exams. They went okay, not brilliant. I was pretty sure I'd passed.

Despite the emotional hardship, we had some really lovely times too. I remember one fresh November evening arriving back at her digs after enjoying a nice Indian meal, the hot spices warming our bellies and pints of Cobra providing us with beer coats.

"Brrr, it's cold in here!" said Tiana through chattering teeth. "Let's put the heating on."

"Maybe we should make our own heat," I whispered in a corny fashion.

"Not from the curry," she replied, patting my backside.

"Hey!" I cried and picked her up, put her over my shoulder and made my way to her room. Bursting inside, I managed to wallop her head on the door frame!

"Ah!" she shouted. "You idiot!"

"I'm really sorry," I pleaded, putting her down and trying to rub it better.

"Get off you buffoon!" she said, her bottom lip quivering. She walloped me on the arm.

"It's okay, it's not bleeding," I said, trying to cuddle her.

"No thanks to you," she replied, and gave me another wallop for good measure.

"Hey," I cried. "Stop that! You okay?"

"I will be," she replied. "Luckily I've drunk enough to not feel too much pain."

"Shall we put it in a sling for you?" I asked.

"You don't put somebody's head in a sling!" she giggled. "Silly!"

"Yours could," I replied. "It's such a strange shape!"

"Oy!" she cried, chuckling some more. "You're head is like a big baked bean!"

We laughed and mocked each other a little more as we got undressed and climbed into bed.

"Oh, hang on!" I said, suddenly remembering. "I nearly forgot!" I rushed out to the kitchen and grabbed a bottle of port that I'd bought earlier. I took a couple of glasses and a bottle opener and went back to Tiana's room. She was putting on a CD.

"Let's get drunk!" I bellowed in a stupid voice.

"We're already drunk," replied Tiana.

"Okay," I said, "let's get more drunk!"

The sound of Nat King Cole came out of her stereo: "There may be trouble ahead/But while there's moonlight and music and love and romance/Let's face the music and dance!"

"What's this?" I asked. "This isn't that usual R&B crap you normally play."

"It's my swing CD," she replied, and started to sing: "Before the deediddlers have fled/before they ask us to da-da-da/and while we still have the dee-d-chance/let's face the music and dance!"

I laughed. "You don't know the words!"

But that didn't stop her! She danced and frolicked around the room, making up half the words while I stood there laughing at her silliness! I unscrewed the bottle and poured the port into the glasses. Tiana snatched a glass away from me in mid-verse and downed the lot in one go! Then she carried on trying to sing. She has a beautiful voice but a complete inability to remember words to songs.

Next it was my turn as Dean Martin took the floor singing about "when the moon hits your eye like a big piece a [pizza? – never could work it out] pie that's amore", etc. I put on my best crooning voice, much to Tiana's amusement.

Then it was a duet! I was Frank and she was Nancy and we were both singing something stupid.

And the next eighty minutes went on like that, the singing broken only by the sipping of port and the occasional nonsensical chatter! There was a bit of pretend anger from me when she dared to skip the *Wichita Lineman*! "Pure sacrilege!" I cried; "Pure crap!" she responded. Glen Campbell would turn in his grave (actually, I'm not sure if he's dead yet – apologies, Glen, if you're not!)! Oh, and Nancy Wilson's *Wives and lovers* got Tiana's back up a bit.

"No way I am ever going to be like that!" she said in reply to the anarchic lyrics.

"You'll do as you're bloody well told," I cried, pretending to be severe.

We struggled our way through *Wild is the Wind* and finally came to a halt. The CD ended, we looked into each other's bleary eyes, half-tired, fully drunk, and kissed and made love. And slept in each others arms, not moving till midday (quite a feat considering Tiana's inability to keep still for more than a minute most of the time). We were so very much in love.

One of the things I liked best about Tiana was the fact that I could talk utter shite with her and she'd love it. I would tell her silly things, like how if someone has a moustache for too long eventually the lip underneath wears away until there's nothing left. That they can't shave it off otherwise they'll just be left with a set of gums and teeth below their nose. Or I would tell her bits of trivia about the natural world.

"Do you know a squid communicates by changing colours?"

"Really?" she replied.

"Yes," I continued. "I saw this documentary where this squid had this 'chick' squid on one side of him and a group of 'lads' the other. The side where the guys were, he would be all pale, nothing much going on: 'hey dudes, what you up to? Me? Ah, just chillin'.' But on the other side, where his love interest is, he'd be vibrating colours of the rainbow, really showing his moves to this hot stuff, like, 'hey pretty lady, how do you fancy going out some time for dinner? Do you like shrimps?', really going for it!"

"You come up with some crap!" she said, laughing.

"All true, all true," I answered. "Just ask Sir David."

I took a good month thinking about it – about asking her, you know, the big one! We'd only be going out for ten months when I first started to toy with the idea, but we got on so well and were just so in love. I wanted to show how committed I was. She'd dropped the odd hint, letting me know her finger size ('M' for mother or marriage or mine) and what her ideal ring would look like – a gold ring with a sapphire surrounded by diamonds – so I knew it wouldn't freak her out or anything. Yes, we were still young – I was in my mid-20s, she was 21 – but what does that matter when you're in love and you know it's going to be forever? Tiana was one of these people that had her whole life mapped out from an early age, she was so organised and meticulous: she would go to university, get her degree, be single and party for the first two years, work hard for the third, meet the man of her dreams when she was, say, 21, settle down, marry when she was 24 and have her first kid when she was 26. "I'm just waiting for the undertaker to come round one afternoon and measure me up," I sometimes say to her, joking around. "But you're going to change shape and size when you get older," she would reply. However, between you and me I wouldn't mind betting she's done all the calculations to work out how big I'll be by my age of death (which she has also probably worked out!).

After a month, I realised that it was a no brainer: I would be with this girl for the rest of my life, period. I never wanted to be without her and I was sure she felt the same about me too. And so what if the only ring I could afford was from H. Samuels. After all, it's the thought that counts.

She was staying at my house that weekend. We went out for a meal. I tried not to give anything away, but she told me later that I was so quiet and nervous she was thinking, something's up here. I didn't actually pop the question until we got back to my house.

"Sit down and don't turn the TV on!" I said. So she did and she didn't (if you see what I mean). I went into the kitchen and opened a bottle of wine (nothing special, just some £5 bottle from the supermarket). I poured us a glass each and gave one to her. I put mine on the table next to the settee where she was sitting. Then I got down on one knee, pulled out the ring and:

"Will you marry me?"

She didn't even look at the ring, she just grabbed me and started crying! She hugged me so hard! Then she sat back, looking at me, smiling, sniffing, tears running down her face, then hugged me again!

"Erm," I interrupted, "I don't mean to be persistent, but have you got an answer?"

"Yes," replied Tiana, smiling, laughing and crying. "Of course, yes, silly!" And finally she looked at the ring: "It's perfect!"

That week, all she seemed to do at university was show off her ring to her friends and talk about her wonderful fiancé. We were both on cloud nine! When she went out to the local student nightclub I didn't feel the same anxiety I'd usually get. When the phonecall came at half two in the morning, all she could do was tell me how she'd talked about me to everyone and showed off her ring and how much she loved me and cry even more. I felt no urge to question her, no anxiety at all. I wanted to hold her so much, but to hear her happy voice was enough.

But the high was brief and the anxiety came flooding back into my head. June seemed so far away, the days were shorter, darker and much colder. My OCD was about to reach new heights.

Tiana would wear this red and white striped rugby shirt. It became the shirt that she would wear when the image of her being sexually assaulted would come into my head. An image that would involve a gang of men and then me running to save her, knocking them away and taking her to safety. I would have to play the image in my head in a certain way to 'neutralise' the image. It would have to be just right or I would have to start it all over again. Then every time I caught sight of something that was red and white in colour, I would need to look at it four times and move on. I would be walking from Waterloo station across the bridge and would be staring at traffic cones or warning signs. I'm sure people would notice, but I tried to avoid their stares, which wasn't too hard when caught up in this strange locked up world. In reality, it was a red and white shirt; in my head, it signified danger.

"Do you ever do strange things?" I asked Tiana one night.

"All the time!" she replied. "What like?"

"Well," I said, feeling a bit foolish and not wanting to freak her out, "like check your front door when you know it's already locked; or the cooker, even if you haven't used it all day."

"Sometimes," she answered, and I felt a strange sense of relief run through me. "When I eat grapes I have to put one in either side of my mouth."

"What happens if you don't?" I asked, excitedly.

"Nothing," replied Tiana, as if slightly confused.

"Do you not think that something bad is going to happen?"

"Kind of," she said, "but I know it's not and that it's just a silly thought going through my head."

"Sometimes I get that," I continued, "but I can't shake off the feeling that something awful will happen if I don't carry out this strange behaviour. It nags at me."

"You dwell on things too much," she answered. "Just ignore it and get on with something else."

"But I can't do that," I replied. "It can overwhelm me."

"Don't let it," she said, matter of fact like. "It's only a silly thought."

Then she changed the subject. I wanted to continue, but she didn't really seem to understand what I was trying to say, nor how difficult it had become. So I kept quiet and tried to follow her reasoning. There was a lot of sense to it, but I needed more than just words.

Anyone with OCD knows how difficult it can be to talk about. When you do pluck up the courage, the other person never understands just how serious your problem is. They either don't get it at all or, like Tiana, think it's just a little idiosyncrasy that lots of people have. So we tend to keep it to ourselves. It's no wonder that it took so long to be identified as a disorder in its own right.

Then came Christmas Eve and I fully developed what was to become my most debilitating habit: the repetition of phrases in my head. I had done it before, but nothing like to the degree that it soon reached. Tiana was staying with me that evening, then we would go to her Mum's for Christmas the next day. We popped in to see my Mum before we went to Midnight Mass. I wasn't the religious type, but Tiana has always gone to church on a reasonably regular basis. We were indulging in small talk, something about what was on that evening, about some girl that got raped in a soap opera. Then I said the phrase in my head, just once to ensure it would never happen to her: 'Tiana is never raped'. But then I seemed to hear, 'Tiana is raped' in my head. So I repeated myself: 'Tiana is never raped'. And each time I thought I'd said the opposite, I had to repeat it again. Soon I wasn't listening to anyone else in that room, I was simply repeating the phrase over again in my head. And it went on right into Midnight Mass until we finally got home and went to sleep. It would go by the morning, I thought. I won't do it after that.

But I did, of course.

Christmas came and went. We had some really nice times and I enjoyed spending time with our respective families. New Year's Eve was spent with her Dad, a nice quiet guy, very clever, laidback and fun-loving. I made my New

Year's Resolution: no more of this silly behaviour and at midnight I was feeling very positive about the future. I broke this resolution by late afternoon of January 1st.

As winter set in, so did my OCD. It took a hold of me and my loneliness during the week and I was completely debilitated at times. Whether at work, on the train, or at home, when it set in I was completely locked in to a pattern of ritualistic behaviour. I was aware of what I was doing, but too caught up in my head to do anything about it.

That first moment of the day, when waking to the sound of the music on my radio alarm clock, was always the best. I didn't feel any anxiety; rather, I felt optimism, like I could do anything and it was those moments back then that gave me hope that one day I might be okay. That and my beautiful fiancée. But the anxiety soon set in and I found myself caught up in that vicious thought process. Practically living on my own (as Nigel was never in), there was no one there to help me break out of it. I would not be talking to anyone until I got to work. If I was lucky, I'd manage to fall asleep on the train and break out of the strange pattern of mental behaviour. But that was after the arduous, debilitating process of getting ready for work and walking to the station.

Shirts could be taken off and put on four times in a row; the door checked several times, maybe after walking back to the house when I was a good ten minutes into the journey; walking through subways (which represented a hidden world of danger and set off a great deal of anxiety in me) a certain amount of times, trying to make out to people that I walked past that I had forgotten something by muttering 'damn', sighing and walking back in a hurry, then turning round again with an 'oh leave it' gesticulation. My behaviour was getting very strange. On the train, I would sit down and stand up a certain amount of times until it felt right. I would read a book to try and move my mind onto something else, but lines would need to be read several times over, especially if they mentioned something about rape or murder or some other anxiety raising obsession-related statement. I remember reading the same page over and over again – not actually reading it, but running my eyes over the page – this lady opposite looking at me strangely; but I was feeling too anxious to let her discovery of my weirdness stop me. The world around you becomes an insignificant background, like a television, when you're in the thick of a ritual.

At work, I would try to occupy my mind: if I kept myself busy, I could cope and by early afternoon I would be wondering what the big deal was. But I would often get stuck in a pattern of ritual behaviour that would take up most of my day. My behaviour would include ensuring certain key words appeared a certain amount of times when talking to somebody or writing an e-mail, clearing my throat four times in a row, gulping in a strange manner so that I could really feel the tongue and tonsils rub against each other, and other strange behaviour. My job required me to charge my time for each quarter of an hour, so I would need to try and hide this time some how. Inevitably, I was spending too long on particular pieces of work. Things would not be done in time and we would overrun on costs. Consequently, people began to give me less work, I had more time on my hands and the rituals became more frequent. However my day went, I would be dreading the journey home. By the time I was on the train my disorder was raging. My only escape was to fall asleep. I would wake feeling momentarily optimistic, but it did not take long for the walk home to convert me back into a mentally debilitated moron.

Then came the evenings. Concentrating on cooking, washing up and doing bits round the house would help. But there would be times where I would fall into the ritualistic behaviour, leaving food cooking for certain periods of time, even if it meant burning it or undercooking it, or having to iron a certain number of items of clothing, even if I had to re-iron a pair of trousers or shirt or iron a pair of pants or socks. I would speak to Tiana before I went to bed, trying to pull myself back into the real world. But as soon as we said goodbye I was straight back into the hell that is OCD. The last thing I would do is pray. I inevitably got that wrong, leaving on a message that wasn't said properly so would have to be repeated, sometimes several times over. It is lucky that time is not a constraint for God otherwise he would never get a chance to talk to anyone else. Then I'd turn the lights on and off until it felt right. Finally, I'd go to sleep and hope for a quiet night.

The hardest evenings were when Tiana would be going out drinking with her friends. Every Tuesday, she would go to a club where it was student night and the drinks were therefore very cheap and she would set out to get absolutely bladdered. I would ensure that I knew who she was going with to see if they could be trusted. All of them could be, except this one girl, Melissa, who was crazy when she was drunk: she would run out into the road, laughing and screaming, or swipe blokes' drinks away from them, walk off and laugh, or tease guys sexually. She was a nightmare! When she was sober she was a quiet girl, but with a drink inside of her she turned into the epitome of a ladette. Luckily, Tiana only went out with her when there was a group of them.

On a typical Tuesday/Wednesday night I would wake at around one o'clock in the morning and look over at my mobile. There were no messages. Still, it was early and the club wouldn't shut until two. I tried to get back to sleep. I was not even sure why I had woken. Whenever she was out, my body clock would tell me to wake in the early hours to see if she had got back safely. I reassured myself that she would still be at the club dancing with her friends. There may be other men dancing round her, but I trusted her. I said to myself, "Tiana is never raped or murdered" four times over in my head, just to make sure she would be okay, then I closed my eyes and tried to get back to sleep.

Two o' clock came and still there was no sign of her. I was wide awake by that point, various lines having been repeated over and over again, possibly hundreds of times by then. If it finished at two, no doubt she would finish her drink and then eventually be asked to leave. Say, ten past two. There would be a queue for coats, then it would take time to get out of the door. Say, two twenty-five. Then she would walk home, the long way round in order to avoid the park and the woods, which would take another ten or so minutes. She might get herself a cup of tea before she went to bed, but probably not. I decided not to include that. By the time she had got in and climbed into bed it would take, say, ten minutes maximum. That would make it quarter to three in the morning! I looked over at the clock: five past two. I repeated a sentence in my head four times, then closed my eyes and tried to go to sleep.

Each passing minute seemed like hours. My mind was working overtime, thoughts going through my head over and over again, terrible thoughts of her giving blow-jobs down dark alleys, or, worse, horrific images of rape. I tried to control them, but it felt like desertion. I imagined myself arriving at the scene and saving her from would-be perpetrators. Finally, at half past two I phoned her. It rang for a bit then went on to the answering machine. I cursed myself for phoning and her for not picking up. I tried again. Then sent a text message: "Couldn't sleep! Wondered if you were back yet! Thinking of you: I have a boner! Wish you were here!"

Finally the phone rang! It was twenty to three.

"Hello, Mister Worrier," said Tiana. She sounded drunk, but not out of control.

"Hi," I said, trying to sound sleepy.

"Why can't you sleep?" she asked.

"I don't know," I replied. "Did you have a good time?"

"Yes," she said enthusiastically. "I danced all night and now I'm knackered!"

"How many boys chatted you up?" I felt compelled to ask.

"Hundreds!" she said, sarcastically. "None! Mister Paranoid!"

"Why not?" I said. "What's wrong with you?"

"You should get some sleep," she said, ignoring me.

"Are you at home?" I asked.

"Yeeees," she said in a 'fed up' tone of voice.

"I just like to know you're safe," I explained.

"Go to sleep," she said. "I'll speak to you tomorrow."

"Today," I said. "It's already tomorrow."

"Goodnight," she replied, laughing gently. "I'm going to sleep!"

"Bye," I said. The phone went dead. I looked across at the clock. Three and a half hours left to get some sleep. I sighed and fell asleep as soon as my head hit the pillow.

This routine went on for several months. At weekends, I would see her and we would have a great time. But then Monday would come around and I would spend another five days feeling paranoid and missing her. Friday nights were such a relief. The anxiety of the week backed down and along with it went the rituals. Saturday was almost 'weird behaviour' free, but the peculiarities would come flooding back on Sunday as Monday was preparing to rear its ugly head. I was becoming consumed by the disease, almost a vegetable on occasions. Like any professional sufferer of OCD, I became an expert at hiding my strange behaviour, but it became so influential and pervasive that it proved more and more difficult to avoid raised eyebrows and confused looks.

Once, OCD provided me with quite an amusing situation. I was in a bar after work and looked at this lady. She was in her mid-forties and reasonably attractive, but I was in no way interested, of course. However, I felt the urge to look at her again and again. Inevitably, she came over and started talking to me. I was polite, tried to avoid giving her the 'come-on', but was sure to not give her the wrong impression. When the time was right I slipped in the fact that I had a fiancée whom I loved so much and couldn't wait to marry. That worked a treat. If OCD had been a real person, I would have given him a dig in the ribs for that little trick.

Maybe I should have tried harder to speak to Tiana about all of this at that time. She was a smart girl and would have probably understood. But she needed to concentrate on her studies and did not need my problems making it more difficult for her. She worked so hard that year, partly for her own satisfaction, but a big incentive for her was to do well for us and to get a well-paid job so we could have a good start in life. I needed to be strong for her – she needed to be able to lean on me during this time. I needed to be a man and didn't want to fail her. And if I wasn't coping well, there was no way that I could afford to show her by just how much. And where do you begin? I did not understand it myself at that point in time. All I knew was that whenever I got anxious and unhappy I would find myself carrying out these strange rituals that, once performed, would reduce my anxiety, but only in the short-run. Any relationship is hard when you spend so much time away from your partner, but when you have such a condition and your other half is the party-going type and not overly concerned about her own personal safety, then it is infinitely worse. Once she decided to stroll through the park with a couple of boys she met on the way home! She could be so reckless at times! Sometimes, she was so drunk that I could barely make out what she was saying. There were times when her and her flatmate would have friends round for a party; in a drunken stupor, she once told me how difficult it was when all her friends were getting off with blokes and she would have to sit there chatting. But she told me that she never cheated on me and I don't believe she ever did. I trusted her – it was only my OCD that didn't.

I remember one night her and Simon, her housemate, got back from a club at around two in the morning then decided to watch a film on her bed. I phoned her as I was inevitably still awake.

"Hi babe!" she said, drunk and excitable. "What's the matter?"

"I thought you were going to phone me when you got back," I replied.

"I was going to!" she said with a slight irritation to her tone. "Me and Si are just gonna watch a film together in my room."

"Why your room?" I asked, annoyed and feeling a rush of anxiety run through me.

"There's no video in the other room," she answered. This was a reasonable enough answer. But it would take a very relaxed, trusting, laidback individual to accept that their other half was lying on a bed, drunk, in the early hours of the morning, with somebody she'd slept with before and not be worried. At the very least, I knew as a fellow bloke he would be hoping that an opportunity might arise.

"Hey, come on!" I cried. "That's bang out of order! It's hard enough that you live with him without doing things like that!"

"Don't be silly," she said, "it's not like that!"

"How naïve are you?" I replied. I had to be careful – Tiana was not the type of girl that you should annoy at the best of times, but when she was drunk and tired her fickle and volatile nature could be particularly dangerous. "Please, I'm asking you, don't sit there with him. I can't handle it."

"Well," she said, sighing, "he's just gone. He could probably hear you! Thanks very much. Oh and don't call me naive!"

"Good," I answered. "He does show me *some* respect then. Thank you."

"Huh," she muttered.

I left the conversation going on long enough to be happy that he was not going to return and then said goodbye. By that time, she had forgotten all about it and had a loving tone again. The incident did little for my anxiety.

Deep down, I have always trusted Tiana. I think women are naturally far more likely to be faithful than men. From my experience, especially with Tiana, if they really love somebody no amount of good looks, muscles or money could get in the way of that. Women generally seem to have a deeper moral code than us men. Moreover, they have a stronger desire for romance, whilst our primary drive is far more basic.

The year carried on this way, getting worse as time went on and I began to worry if I would ever be normal (or as normal as possible) again. Then around April time my illness began to turn around and decrease considerably in its severity. Much of this could be put down to the fact that July was getting closer and Tiana and I would be moving in together;

much was as a result of my mind being occupied with the pair of us looking for a house, sorting out a mortgage and generally getting ready for this big event. Additionally, I had passed my exams, was promoted and was consequently getting more work to keep me occupied. However, the main reason was my big discovery, my moment of enlightenment.

It was a cold Thursday night in early February and I was randomly switching between channels, finding something half decent to watch. There was too much of this reality TV crap on. What I wanted was a good documentary. Finally I found one: a Mother and Father were sitting on a sofa being interviewed.

"She's behaved like this ever since she was a young girl," said the Mother. Something made me want to carry on listening, a feeling of familiarity – maybe the sympathetic but confused tone in her voice. "We didn't discourage it at first because her room was always so neat and tidy! What more could a Mother ask for?"

Then the picture switched to a young girl of around five years old in her bedroom. She was preparing to go to bed. She walked to the corner of the room and put her toes right against the skirting board; then she turned, counting her steps one to five, as she walked over to her bed and climbed in.

"Why do you do that?" said the unseen interviewer.

"I've just got to," replied the little girl. She was smiling, but in her eyes there was a look of dread so heartbreaking in such a young person. Nobody so young should know such fear. I was glued to the set, listening to her every word as she explained her daily rituals, keeping her room tidy, how nobody was allowed inside except her Mum. And I cried. Not out of pity, but a kind of relief. Maybe a realisation that I was not alone, not so weird afterall. The strange behaviour that I had so cleverly hidden from the world for all these years was not so personal to me. I had found empathy and the power of empathy can never be underestimated.

The programme then turned to a Mother washing her hands. The camera closed in on them to reveal the cracked, bleeding skin. She turned off the tap and began to dry them, but then stopped and washed them again.

"Just got to be absolutely sure," said a strained voice. The camera turned to the face of the woman. She looked to be in her late twenties. There was a look of anguish and pain on her face. Eventually she stopped and dried her hands.

"How many times do you wash your hands a day?" said the interviewer.

"Over a hundred," said the woman, blowing out and raising her eyebrows. "I try to wash them after touching anything."

"Anything?"

"Well … yes," she replied. "Pretty much."

"Why do you do it?" the interviewer asked.

"I just get this … feeling," she answered, laughing quietly to herself. "It's like a nagging feeling that I *need* to wash myself to avoid some catastrophe." She suddenly became very animated. "I don't understand it myself. I just have to do it. Otherwise… Sometimes I can spend two hours in the shower. I rarely leave the house and …" at this point she started to cry, " I haven't been able to hold my two year old son for months now! I'm so afraid I'll hurt him. He doesn't understand, the poor little thing. And neither do I! He used to run up to me, arms outstretched, smiling and giggling, hoping for a cuddle. I started to back off and he thought it was a game. So I would shout at him! Tell him not to try and touch Mummy! Now he doesn't come anywhere near me! He just sits there staring at me, looking confused. I hate it." She broke down in tears. "I hate it", she repeated in a muffled voice.

I discovered that I had obsessive compulsive disorder, or OCD for short. This was the first time I was able to put a name to it. And I wept with relief. Not the frustrated crying that I had done so often in my life, but crying in relief, knowing that at last I had an answer. What I now needed was a solution.

I looked through the *Mind, body and spirit* section of the bookstore. I was already late for work, so needed to hurry. I picked up a book on anxiety disorders and turned to the content page. Inside I found what I was looking for: obsessive compulsive disorder! Page 104 – bad number! Divisible by 13 – what should I do? I put the book back, then, realising my stupidity, I reached for the book again and turned to page 104. Words jumped out at me: counting, checking, cleaning (those bloody cleaners!), hoarding; anxiety; worthlessness! Excitedly, I read on: thoughts of hurting others, pain, inappropriate thoughts! I looked around to see if anyone was watching me – they weren't. The chapter went on to describe the symptoms and the medication available. Medication? But it ended too soon. I continued searching for another book and stumbled on one called *Locked Inside*. Something in the title appealed to me, a feeling of familiarity. I picked it up. The front cover read in bold red capitals: 'FREE YOURSELF FROM OBSESSIVE COMPULSIVE DISORDER'; I read the blurb:

> *Is your day filled with obsessive thoughts and repetitive, tiresome routines? Do you act in irrational ways to rid yourself of bothersome images? You may be one of the millions around the world suffering from Obsessive Compulsive Disorder.*

> *'Locked in' has been compiled by specialists and experts in cognitive neurology from around the world*

to provide you with guidance and understanding in overcoming this most debilitating of mental illnesses.

Included within are methods for treating OCD, recommended medication, examples of sufferers and their experiences of overcoming their illness and much more.

Without further ado, I made my way to the counter and bought the book. I suddenly felt better than I had in many years: a sense of hope entered me! I wasn't alone, I wasn't mad and, best of all, I could get better! That day at work I was more productive than ever! My rituals were few and far between and the nagging sensation of 'did I do it right?' did not hang around for long enough to bother me.

I got home that night, made myself a bowl of cereal and sat down on the settee, *Locked In* in my hands. Right at the beginning was a test to be carried out, asking questions like:

- do you have to keep checking that the oven is off?

- do you wash your hands even if you know they are clean? ("No!," I thought to myself.)

- do you avoid certain numbers?

- do you have to keep repeating an activity until it 'feels right'?

- do inappropriate thoughts come into your head, such as violent or sexual images?

I read through, marking 'yes' or 'no' accordingly. Then I turned to the results page, making a note of my score. Sixteen. I checked it against the total: one to seven was for those with minor quirks only and nothing to be bothered by; seven to fourteen, more than just quirks and should consider amending behaviour patterns, but not serious enough to warrant medical attention; fifteen or more: serious condition and medical attention should be sought. What should I do now? Should I see a doctor? I made up my mind to complete the book first, and then, if I felt I had to, I should see a doctor at that stage. After all, I was only just in the final category.

I must have read nearly a hundred pages that night before falling asleep. I was fascinated and so relieved. At last I was beginning to understand my condition.

"Tiana!" I cried, grabbing her by the arms and smiling gormlessly. "I've got something to tell you!"

"What?" she replied, smiling but looking slightly perplexed.

"I know what's wrong with me!" I said.

"I didn't realise anything was wrong with you," said Tiana, "unless telling bad jokes is a problem!"

"Remember I told you about the weird behaviour I do?"

"Yes," she answered, hesitatingly.

"Well it's something called 'obsessive compulsive disorder' or 'OCD'!"

"What that handwashing thing?" she replied, annoyingly. "I've never noticed your hands being particularly clean! In fact I've never noticed anything about you being particularly clean!"

"Bloody hand washers!" I cried. "No, not that! Well, yes, that. But that's just one type. I've got a different type: I have to check things all the time and count to certain numbers and avoid others! It's all rather weird! But it doesn't matter now: I've found this book which explains what's wrong with me!"

"Well I've never noticed anything wrong with you!" she answered.

"I don't try and show it," I replied.

"Everyone does weird things," said Tiana. "It doesn't mean there's something wrong with you!"

"No," I cried, "this is more than that! I've always thought these weird things and now I know what the problem is!"

"There's no problem," she insisted. "You just dwell on things sometimes, that's all. We all have funny habits! Just because you've read some stupid book that seems to have convinced you that you've got a problem … I'm sure if I read it I'd think the same!"

"You're not listening to me!" I said, feeling frustrated.

"Come on, let's not argue," replied Tiana. "I only get to see you at weekends and I don't want to spend the time arguing. What do you want to do this evening?"

And that was that. So I gave up trying to explain it to her.

I read the book cover to cover. Twice. And not because it was a better number of times than just once either. It was so enlightening; everything in it rang true! I knew what I had to do: change my brain's way of working and I would be fine! And I was. For a little while anyway.

CHAPTER SEVEN: SELF-DIAGNOSIS

I have obsessions and I have compulsions. Obsessions are intrusive, unwelcome, distressing thoughts and mental images. My obsessions are of death, pain, suffering, losing loved ones, family and friends being physically abused; rape, torture, murder. My greatest fears. When they enter my head, they become overwhelming and my anxiety hits the roof.

I am compulsive: I act off the cuff, wear my heart on my sleeve, put my ability to rationalise to one side and let my emotions take over. When obsessions enter my head, I try to exorcise them through the performance of rituals, which I am compelled to repeat over and over again: I check things, doors, cookers and other electrical appliances; I count, avoiding 'bad numbers', staying close to 'good numbers'; I repeat sentences over and over in my head; I ask the same question over and over again; I stare and blink; I touch certain items several times. The list goes on. Basically, I'm bloody weird!

Us humans, we're not rational, we rationalise. Our natural reaction to an event is an emotional one, based on instincts following millions of years of evolution. The brain is first and foremost an emotional organ. Rationality is a tool for us to make sense of our world; whether we choose to use it and the extent to which we do so is down to the individual. Us OCD sufferers, our rationality tool all too often is lost in a metaphorical shed.

I have a disorder. I know that now. We all have quirks and strange behaviours. It's our natural inclination to act instinctually that causes these. But us OCD sufferers, we have more than just quirky behaviour: our disorder is all consuming, overwhelming, completely and utterly debilitating. The hours I've wasted carrying out pointless rituals, using up valuable brain power on idiotic thoughts, would probably add up to years.

OCD sneaks up on you, takes you unawares. A silly obsession comes into your head, causing a small amount of anxiety, so you perform a silly ritual and the anxiety goes away. It even feels pretty good momentarily. You feel confident for a short time. But the obsession comes back stronger and it takes more of an effort in the ritual to rid oneself of that thought. And it comes back again, nagging away at you. You may be able to focus on some other behaviour, move the brain on, but then it taps you on the shoulder and gives you a little reminder: 'I'm still here, sunshine – you really ought to do something about this.' And you do. And it gets worse. That silly obsession that you dealt with so easily, that suppression of that anxiety, it's a snowball effect, soon to form an avalanche. It's that initial thought that's the time to quash it, to deal with it rationally. Not to perform a ritual, no matter how easy it is and how quick it takes to perform, because it's not easy or quick in the long run – it's downright hard and time-consuming. But the signs can be so easy to miss. You've got to anticipate the occasions. But it's so easy to forget to do when you're not in that OCD state of mind. The natural thing to do is to follow your instincts, act on your emotions, not to rationalise. If you can identify the signs and not follow your OCD-warped instincts and focus on something else, within a few minutes, half an hour at the most, the nagging sensation usually goes. If you give in, it'll be hanging around for a lot longer.

The brain is a complex organ. It's an amazing piece of machinery, built up over millennia. The core of the brain is where you carry out all the automatic actions, the instinctual stuff. Our species grew that part first. The more layers on top of that, the more powerful our minds have become. Parts of the brain enable you to learn new things, new behaviours, then – once mastered – passes the knowledge down to a part that deals with automatic behaviour.

OCD sufferers do not process information well. There is no automatic flow from what is in front of us to how we should react. We have a signal-processing centre made up of the *caudate nucleus* and the *putamin*. The former acts like an automatic transmission for the front, thinking, part of the brain. The latter is the automatic transmission for the part of the brain responsible for bodily movements. They work together to provide for coordination between thought and movement. With OCD sufferers, our thoughts get stuck in the *caudate nucleus* and cannot easily get out. If you were to see a scan of what is going on within the brain of a person with OCD whilst in the middle of an 'attack', you would see that the *orbital cortex*, the underside of the front of the brain, is working overtime. You could literally see the thoughts stuck there, going round and round and getting nowhere, leaving the brain to overheat.

Most people have difficulty understanding the conclusions of cognitive neurology: that thoughts are physical things. People seem to automatically differentiate between the physical and the mental. Maybe people don't like the idea that our thoughts are physical. It implies that our emotions, our personality and essentially our spirit or soul can all be located somewhere and occupy space. It implies we may not have a soul, as such, and people do not want to accept that. But how else would it work? If everything were physical, we would require thought to control the way we move, etc, so there must be the theoretical possibility that thoughts are physical. And science seems to back this up. We're just a physical, biological being, our thoughts being a tangible, chemical 'going-on' within the brain. It has implications for religion, ultimately: if the spirit can be located, if the personality can be altered depending on the chemistry of your brain, surely there is nothing within us to then leave us when we die and therefore no need for a Heaven or Hell; we die and our spirit dies too. Yet, despite this overwhelming proof, there are scientists out there with amazing brains that still believe in a god of sorts. This must be the ultimate proof that we're emotional beings, not rational thinkers! Or maybe it just means that rationality can only explain so much. I like to think it's the latter.

I read the book with relish. I studied every page. I got my hands on more books on OCD and cognitive neurology; I studied the brain, worked out what each part was for. I read fascinating stories of people who've suffered like me, but have come through the other side. I even sympathised with the attention-seeking, over-hyped handwashers. Then there were the hoarders, the general cleaners, the checkers and counters, like me. And there were some very strange and specific stories too: the bloke who feared that his underwear was too tight; the guy who feared battery acid had leaked from his car and spent the early hours of the morning scrubbing roads. All kinds of weird and would-be-wonderful-if-it-wasn't-so-devastatingly-painful people. I was enthralled! At last, I understood my problem and knew there was a way out!

No one is ever cured of OCD as such, but you learn to cope with it. That is far more of a brilliant goal than it sounds. The thoughts are still there, but you learn how to suppress them immediately and move on to more productive thoughts and behaviour. They have a minimal impact on your life and you spend the overwhelming majority of the time enjoying yourself and getting on with living, instead of being stuck in that glass room. But to achieve this takes hard work and no little effort. It is a constant chore and you should not allow yourself any let up. You should certainly never 'give in just that once' to get some momentary peace and quiet; that's when the trouble starts! It took me a long time from reading up on OCD to finally live a normal, productive life. And I sunk to the very depths of depression before doing so. Maybe to really appreciate happiness we have to drown ourselves in sadness. I hope not, but that's what happened to me. That's what it took me to reach my current state of happiness.

I watched documentaries and films on the subject too. I watched a documentary on Tourette's Syndrome and recognised their suffering as akin to my own. It is considered to be a cousin of OCD and many sufferers of Tourette's also suffer from obsessive-compulsive disorder. Luckily for me, I have never suffered from Tourette's, although my wife has often accused me of having Tourette's of the backside.

There are two films in particular that should be noted. One is a brilliant portrayal of the anguish and pain that we suffer; the other is a pointless, pathetic, glamorised, Hollywood pile of shit.

In *The Aviator*, Leonardo DiCaprio is simply brilliant and deserved an Oscar for his wonderfully accurate portrayal. The film tells the story of billionaire Howard Hughes, an incredibly talented man who excelled as a director of films, a businessman and, most importantly of all, in the aircraft industry. Ultimately, his OCD overwhelmed him, completely consumed him. He died a fearful wreck, lying in a bed in a room scared of contamination and surrounded by a world of rituals that he had imposed. As every good cognitive neurologist will tell you, assisting with the carrying out of rituals is one of the worst things you can do – it is completely counter-productive. His billions allowed for him to finance this lifestyle, particularly the helpers who were essential in carrying out these rituals. The biographies that have been written about him reflect the misunderstanding that OCD sufferers have had to deal with. There are a few that comment on his disorder from a position of knowledge. Then there are those that are completely clueless, not even attempting to understand his disorder, referring to it as an eccentricity or madness and of Hughes as an evil bastard, dismissing this crucial aspect to is personality.

The scenes during which his OCD reaches its heights are haunting and the credit for this should go partly to the director, the legendary Martin Scorcese. However, DiCaprio's acting was so accurate that you can't help but feel he is not alien to the disorder himself. The loneliness of being locked up in a room with only yourself and your thoughts, the anguish that fills you, the pain, the anxiety; it is written all over his face and in his body language. I looked at him and saw me. I had been there. I had been totally consumed. I recognised the pain and cried at the performance. Rumour has it that poor Leonardo immersed himself in the part so deeply that he began to develop OCD too. This may explain the brilliance of his performance. Either way, Mr DiCaprio, I take my hat off to you for what is, in my humble opinion, one of the finest acting performances of all time.

And then there is the romanticised pile of dog-shit that is *As Good As It Gets*. No doubt, some Hollywood executive saw the popularity in OCD as a fashionable quirky disorder amongst the rich and famous and took the opportunity to make a commercial film. OCD is portrayed as an amusing, extroverted way to carry on. The main character, Jack Nicholson, is obsessed with cleanliness, is angry, grumpy and downright rude; he eventually falls in love, sees the error of his ways and miraculously cures himself of the disorder. Nicholson had obviously carried out no research for the part and deserves an award for the most inaccurate, shitty acting ever. Basically, he plays Jack Nicholson being grumpy. It's pathetic and if ever you get hold of the DVD the best use you can put to it is for scraping your pet dog's shit off the pavement to be disposed of accordingly.

The glamorisation of OCD has continued in recent years, with several American TV series deciding to add a bit of eccentricity to characters by giving them a touch of OCD. Surprise, surprise, those attention-seeking hand-washers seem to have monopolised the character traits. And it's even managed to enter the UK's market, providing more of a comical element than a serious look at the disorder. Maybe it appeals to that large minority that have a touch of the OCD. For us serious sufferers, it's just damaging. Oh well. Ignorance is bliss, they say. Well maybe for the ignorant. For those of us in the know, ignorance is really bloody annoying!

Enough of my rambling! I have digressed too far. So what did I do with my new found knowledge? Initially, the discovery that I was not alone, not going mad and there were people and techniques out there to help me were enough. I spent the next few years showing little signs of a relapse. There were bad times, which I will elaborate on in the next chapter. But for the most part, they were good. In fact, there were some of the best times of my life.

But I failed to readjust my behaviour in any serious way. You can lead a horse to water, as they say; there was a whole river full of dysentery free water for me to drink from, but I chose to bask in the sun, take in the occasional drop, but slowly let my body dehydrate. My OCD was temporarily beaten, but I let it regather its strength, regroup and bide its time. It lay in the shadows, waiting to ambush me. And ambush me it did. In fact, it beat me to a pulp.

CHAPTER EIGHT: TICKING OVER

It's easy to keep OCD at bay whilst there's nothing to trigger it. Those next three years were anxious free times, for the most part. It allowed me to indulge in the occasional bit of compulsive behaviour, but not enough to break out into full-scale debilitation. The OCD hung around like a bad smell; but I was able to control it, for the most part, using it as a comfort blanket. My lapses were infrequent and went unnoticed by everyone except me. I thought I was coping and that it had been suppressed for good, or at least that it had been suppressed enough that I could stay on top of it. But OCD is a monster, waiting in the shadows, feeding off the subconscious, building up its strength, to reveal itself when the time is ready, to pounce when at full-strength and when you're least prepared to defend. Whilst my life was good, it was kept at bay, feeding off the scraps I chucked to it. I should have starved it there and then. Instead, I thought it was enough just to feel in control. However, my plunge into the depths of OCD catatonia was a good three years away and there were many wonderful times before it struck once more.

Tiana and I moved in together straight after she left university. As I was still working in London and she was aiming to, we needed to live somewhere that was cheap but on a main line to the capital. The Midlands was cheaper than anywhere south, west or east so we ran our fingers up the Thameslink, stopping as soon as we had found somewhere that we could afford. We stopped at the end of the line: Bedford. Not wanting to live in an actual town, we settled for Wootton, a little village just outside, complete with a number of old pubs, a post office and a church. We bought a tiny little cottage built in the 1860's that Tiana fell in love with as soon as we stepped inside and I fell in love with as soon as the pain had gone from whacking my head on the doorframe. The place was Alice-in-

Wonderlandesque! Picture the scene: you pull in to the driveway to see my legs through the bottom window and my head peering out the top, a hand waving from side to side in the limited distance provided. Walking inside, the old wooden front door led directly into the living room. Here, my head would touch the ceiling and I had to be careful not to wear too much hair gel or it would look like a giant slug had made its way across the room. The low ceilings were a feature throughout the original part of the cottage and within three months I had become used to its non-height-friendly ways, mastering where I should duck. In the interim, my day would start by waking at 6 o' clock in the morning, receiving my first 'whack' as I walked out of our bedroom door, another 'whack' as I reached the bottom of the staircase and a final 'whack' as I entered into the kitchen, by this time feeling fully awake. There was my haven for standing straight, jumping, dancing in a reggae style or performing any other kind of activity that required a high ceiling: the kitchen! This was the main part of an extension to the house, built in the 1930's, and it was blessed with a very high ceiling that could not be reached without jumping. I learnt early on that erratic movements could not be carried out in the front room, so I selected my dancing accordingly.

The remainder of the extension consisted of a bathroom, including the only toilet of the house and a boiler. I suppose that, when the extension was built the residents were grateful that they no longer had to walk out into the garden to relieve themselves, especially during the darker colder nights. However, my twenty-first century sensibilities did not appreciate the fact that our bedroom and the toilet were as far away as could be achieved. It was bad enough to have to go down the stairs, ducking the low ceiling and the numerous traps (see below) and coats blocking the way; however, our kitchen contained a danger that was like kryptonite to a vivid imagination: we had no curtains in there! It was a case of head down and look forward as I made my way across the kitchen, not daring to look at the potential cast of Thriller staring through the windows.

Upstairs, there was a spare room that wouldn't suffice as living conditions for a particularly short midget and a bedroom barely large enough for a double bed, a dressing table and built-in cupboards. Tiana liked to set me 'traps' in this small bedroom: plugs and brushes to tread on, wires to trip on and the like. "I don't have enough room for all of my things," she would protest.

"You don't need all of this paraphernalia," I responded in my ignorance. I consider myself quite educated for a man on the subject of a woman's vanity requirements: I can identify at least half of the items in the bedroom and the bathroom, including a general description of their purpose and tips on how to apply.

"Okay, if you want me to look like a big fat minga, I'll get rid of half of this stuff, shall I?"

"You never look fat or a minga!" I said. "You want proof of how nice you look?" – she would often be standing there naked or just in her underwear during such arguments – "is this not proof enough?" I pointed to my love appendage. "The penis does not lie!"

"You're biased," was her response.

"Biased?" I answered, incredulously. "I'm biased towards fancying you because I fancy you?"

And so on. It was all in good spirit (even when I would tread on one of those numerous bloody plug heads and get the urge to ram it up Tiana's bum!).

The garden was a reasonable size, but had not been looked after properly by the previous owners. They had let half of it grow over with trees and bushes. We (for 'we' read 'I', although Tiana would give non-requested helpful tips that

96

should be followed without question and in a precise manner or else!) spent the first year sorting that garden in a piecemeal fashion, first removing unwanted flora, then digging out flower-beds, a couple of seating areas and somewhere for a barbecue. But the garden was lively and within a month of tidying, it soon became overgrown again. I half expected to find Sleeping Beauty lying there waiting for a snog, or even a beanstalk that I could climb and pinch a giant's belongings, despite his unerring trust (oh that Jack was a 'wrongun').

Although times were tough in that house in terms of how hard we both worked, I look back at it with fondness: it was our first home and we learnt so much more about each other, falling in love with new parts of us that had been kept secret during our period of independent living arrangements. Weekdays were long and hard: we would get up early to go to work, would get back late and by the time we had eaten and tidied the kitchen it was nearly 9 o' clock. But we always made a great team and the hardness of it all never weighed us down. As long as I was doing it with Tiana, it didn't feel like work (although she would probably disagree after hearing me moan too often). But we both knew we were putting in the hard work to make it easier later down the line. And they were romantic times too: we cuddled longer and harder than we had ever done before or since; we had the freedom and the cash to go out to fancy restaurants when we had the energy; we could stay in and stay up late too, watching a movie, eating takeaways and drinking red wine.

Holidays were fantastic too. We knew that, once children came along, we would not have the money nor the freedom to go too far or to explore, so we indulged in long trips and weekends away. We travelled to Italy, visited New York, Barcelona, Bruges, South Africa and the Philippines, sometimes with other couples we knew, all over a three year period. We also toured the British Isles one year when we were a bit short of cash, the idea being to save a bit of money by not having to fly anywhere. But the plan backfired: it proved just as expensive because the cost of visiting anywhere or doing anything here is pretty hefty. Everything in this land seems to have a price on it: park your car - £5 for a few hours; sit in our café for a sandwich and a cup of tea - £10 for two people; get in to the see the museum/cave/exhibition - £12 per person; take a shit - £1! I'm going to stop whinging here: Tiana says I am like a young Victor Meldrew, but personally 'I don't believe it' (I can hear the tumble weeds…). There are some strange characters in this country though (I'm sure it's the same the world over, but when you can't speak the language, these weirdoes can often hide their ways from the tourist). I remember this couple at a B&B in York where the man was the pathetic, suppressed, quiet type and she was so fat he must have feared she might pop him in a bap and eat him one day. You know, the type where she probably threw him round the bedroom a lot and he loved every minute of it! For the three mornings that we were there, they would eat at the same time. She was one of those people that are so fat they have to wear bandages round their wrists or ankles. One morning, when offered breakfast, she turned down a couple of items claiming that she "was a very fussy eater"! I nearly choked on my egg and bacon! Tiana turned to me and said, "Yeah, she can only eat pie and chips!" We burst out laughing, attracting the attention of our fellow diners, the woman giving us an evil look and the man showing the type of courage you only show when your big brother is there to stop you getting beaten up.

Let me justify the above as I fear that it may be perceived as an attack on fat people. Now I don't have a problem with them: if they want to eat a lot, then that's up to them. I have a lot of overweight friends and relatives, a fact that's inescapable in modern day Britain. Personally, I love food, but I don't enjoy it as much if I stuff myself. What I don't like are these chubbies that don't accept that it's their own fault they're overweight. "It's my glands," they'll say, or "I've got a very low metabolism" or "I'm big-boned", etc - we've all heard the excuses. Oh, right. Well why is it, then, that when we are presented with images of famine in Africa there is never a single fat person, the camera zooming in on them, shrugging their shoulders and saying, "It's my metabolism"? Why? I'll tell you why: it's because it's bollocks! It's a silly excuse made up by lazy undisciplined people who just can't resist seeing a cake and stuffing it down. I thought of trying to market my invention for curing obesity: it's a stick that is attached to the head and has a pie dangling from the other end; the idea is, the 'chubby' will see the pie and want to eat it and chase after it and will end up losing lots of weight as a result. Not sure that I'll get the financial backing I need though.

It was during these years that we became very close to another couple that Tiana had made friends with at university. Sammy and Dennis had the same likes and dislikes as us, liked the odd tipple and generally were a real good laugh. We would take it in turns to visit each other's houses for the weekend. They are another of life's characters. Whilst we were touring our green and pleasant land, we stopped off at the Lake District where we met up with Sammy and Dennis for a few days. She was an upmarket chick from Salisbury, who rode a horse and called her Mum 'Mummy', even though she's an adult; he was from deepest, darkest, Romford. It was the kind of relationship that inspired *Uptown Girl* by Billy Joel, but I'll forgive them for that as it was written before they got together.

The first night of our stay in the Lake District, we decided to get an Indian takeaway. There were a handful of people in there at the time, but this didn't stop Dennis cocking his leg and letting out a loud, long fart! Sammy went mad! "You dirty little arsehole!" she cried in her perfect Queen's English, chasing him out of the takeaway and round a car parked outside. Tiana and I were in hysterics; Sammy didn't speak to Dennis for a good couple of hours, but he seemed to be glad of the break.

That next day we went climbing up into the mountains. I forget the names, but it was near Keswick, if that helps, and looks like a giant's foot. It was a warm day, slightly overcast if I remember, but it didn't rain and we never had to don anything sadder than hiking boots, shorts and tee-shirts. We had lunch at the top, which consisted of some sandwiches, crisps, fruit and - most importantly - a bottle of wine. Whilst we lay there resting and letting our food digest, Dennis suddenly jumped up and sprinted off down the hill, leaving the rest of us looking perplexed. There was no break in his speed as we watched him get smaller and smaller, occasionally disappearing behind a dip in the mountain to reappear a few seconds later. Close to the bottom, we could just about make out him tripping and rolling and rolling … and rolling … and rolling … until he was finally out of sight! Sammy pulled out her phone and called him. No answer! Shit – we were scared for him and started to make our way down the hill, more gingerly than Dennis, but quicker than we would otherwise have been. About a minute in, Sammy's phone rang: "I'm alright," he said in his quasi-cockney accent, "luckily a big pile of shit slowed me down." We laughed hysterically at the idea of this; however, we were muted when greeting him, realising that he was not joking. Sammy made him throw the tee-shirt away and walk home topless, showing off his pale trunk. Alongside his sunburnt face, Dennis resembled the Japanese national flag.

Soon after moving to Wootton, I changed jobs, moving to a much smaller accountancy firm in Leicester Square. There was none of the politics and back-stabbing of the bigger guys, nor the bureaucracy. My induction was more akin to a rugby club than a professional firm: at midday we hit the Indian restaurant, one meal, several drinks and two hours later we made our way to the pub; there we remained until just before five, to give me time to pack my stuff and go home! If only more accountancy firms could give that kind of induction! Of course, we worked too, and pretty hard. I enjoyed being there. The work was challenging, the clients were interesting and my colleagues were good fun (for the most part). There was only one person that nobody else liked. He was blunt, unfriendly and hated the world. He also looked remarkably similar to Jonny Rotten. One afternoon, I was telling them about this guy I knew who had been sacked for masturbating at work. Years ago, I had worked in a CD-manufacturing company. One member of staff would be allocated to look after all the old CDs that the business had made over the years, a kind of librarian. They would be kept away from the production line and it was a relatively quiet, lonely place. However, this lad was over-confident in believing that he was alone: one day, he took out a CD cover that he was particularly fond of, took something else out and proceeded to 'abuse' himself! He was caught, knob in hand, and sacked.

"Why didn't he go and do it in the loo like any normal person?" said 'Jonny' (I forget his real name). The rest of us just turned and looked at him. It soon became apparent to him that he was the only one who carried out such behaviour. For the rest of the time I was there, he became the butt of the jokes. Every time he got up to leave the room, we would hand him an appropriate picture. And there were the one-liners too: as he printed something out, someone would say, "Do you want me to pull it off for you?" And so on.

Great times at home and great times at work! It was no wonder that my OCD had little impact and no room to work in.

But then there were the blips. The first occurred around the time of the Rugby World Cup 2003. I loved my rugby and England were clearly the best team, having only lost around 4 games in as many years. Just as the tournament was starting, I had developed a cold and a bit of a cough and found myself in bed for a couple of days. It was a Friday morning and I was home alone, having taken a sicky. The New Zealand v Canada match was on, so I pulled myself out of bed and put myself in front of the box to watch. It was relatively entertaining, the Canuks actually causing the Kiwis some problems for the first half hour. I had a very chesty cough, and was producing some vile green stuff that day. During one such outburst, the line came through my head 'Tiana dies young', and right on the 'young' bit I coughed. BAD! The alarm bells went off in my head! I needed to carry out the correct ritual to get rid of this: I coughed again: 'Tiana dies OLD', the cough being carried out on the 'old'. But had I said old or young?, I thought to myself. So I coughed again, walking in to the kitchen to make sure no one walking past our front room window saw us. I did it with success this time. Phew. No, I could have done two bad ones to one good one – I would have to do it again. My neighbour was in his garden and could probably hear me, given the noise I was making and then he might see me if I stood, so I lay down on the floor and coughed again. Another good one. Or had I said 'not' in front of the old? So I did it once more to be sure; no, twice so it was evened out. And once more, so I'd done it more than I'd not done it. I lay there in this way, coughing absurdly. If anybody had seen me, they would have thought me crazy. Feeling silly, I went back into the lounge and sat back down, trying to focus on the rugby. But the first person I saw was the outside centre: the number 13 on his back! Shit - I need to see a good number to complete the ritual! So I went back into the kitchen and laid down in exactly the same place and repeated my earlier exercises. Getting up, I noticed the time: 10.13! Shit, shit, shit! I lay back down and waited until 10.16 (just in case the clock was not accurate enough). Then I coughed some more. But how many times had I done it right and how many times had I done it wrong and how many times had I done it altogether? If any one of those was a multiple of 13, I would have to do it some more until it was just right. So I did, just to make sure. Finally, getting up, I suddenly remembered: I had to look at a number that was not a multiple of 13. Staring at the ground, not letting my eyes catch sight of another number, I thought where I could look. The 2-in-1 shampoo bottle in the bathroom! I knew exactly where it was, made my way there, my hand over my eyes, feeling my way. Then I opened them, caught sight of the bottle, read the numbers 2 and 1, a couple of times just to be sure, then breathed a sigh of relief! Tiana would die an old lady!

Then I sat in a chair and cried frustrated tears. My throat was aching from the coughing, my head was aching from the anxiety. I knew deep down that what I had just done did not make any sense, but if I hadn't done it the anxiety, the nagging doubts would have played on my mind and I wouldn't have been able to enjoy anything or concentrate on anything until I had shaken off that feeling. Therefore, I had to do it. I hated myself for giving in, but knew there was no other way. I rang Tiana.

"What's the matter?" she said, "are you crying?"

"Yes," I replied. "I am."

"Why, what's happened?"

"My OCD," I answered. "It's making me cough and do stupid things?"

"What stupid things?" she asked.

"Just coughing really," I replied. "Just stupid coughing."

"Just don't do it," she said, her tone starting to change to one of being slightly annoyed. "Don't scare me like that! I thought something serious had happened! It's that stupid bloody book you bought. Ever since you bought that bloody thing you've got it into your head that you've got some strange disorder!"

"No it's not," I pleaded, pointlessly. "I've always had it. The book explained it to me."

"Look," she interrupted, "everyone gets stupid things that they do. Except most people just ignore them and get on with things. You dwell on things too much!"

"I can't help it!" I cried. "It's worse for me!"

"Yes, because you dwell on it!"

"Okay," I said, giving up trying to explain or seek some kind of understanding. "I better go."

"Are you going to be okay?" she asked.

"Yes," I said.

"You're not going to do anything stupid, are you?" she asked.

"No, of course not!" I replied. "I love you."

"I love you too."

And Tiana once again showed me that it was not worth talking to anyone about OCD unless they've got it themselves, and properly got it too. The trouble is, such people are so difficult to find because they're not prepared to disclose their problems either.

I was over this latest blip by the quarter final stages and went on to enjoy Mr Johnson and his team of legends lifting that trophy! I cried again, of course, but this time it was tears of happiness and I didn't feel that ashamed, even when Tiana's Welsh relatives smirked (they know they would have been the same!).

OCD is a self-made tragedy, a product of our natural ability to fear that which we can't control. It is put into perspective by real tragedy. My dear Nan past away around this time. She was eighty-eight years old by the time she finally let go following a year of struggling. She was a proud lady, without being unreasonable; determined, but not unrealistic. She possessed wisdom borne of experience and a heart of gold. Of course it was sad when she past away, but she got to lead a long, healthy, rich life. I was sad because I would miss her. I call it a tragedy, but only in the sense that I never wanted her to go. But maybe we need death in order to love - if we never lost anyone, maybe we would not hold them as dear to us. Maybe death is an integral part of life. Maybe without death we would not love.

Tiana had a friend called Luke. They went to school together, became close friends, hung around in the same group, went drinking together. They never became boyfriend and girlfriend; never even kissed. But they had a special place in each other's heart. He always believed that one day they would be together, a belief that was there long before the madness set in. I was aware of this when I first met him; I was also aware that his behaviour had become more and more strange in recent years. He would make inappropriate comments, take off all of his clothes in public and generally act in socially unacceptable ways, I was told. Upon first meeting him, I anticipated some form of strange activity from him, but there was none. He seemed perfectly normal to me, so much so that I questioned the diagnosis. However, soon after we met he was sent back to a mental hospital for further treatment. Tiana went to see him on her own, preferring me to stay away. She told me of his delusions that Luke and her were partners; the nurses on the ward knew her before she announced herself: "Ah, you're Luke's girlfriend," they would say. She explained the situation to them. But she did not correct Luke and I understand why.

Then one day in early 2004 Tiana had a phone call from one of her school friends. She broke down in tears.

"He's gone missing," she cried, as the call ended.

"Who?" I asked, a tone of anxiety and desperation in my voice.

"Luke," she replied. "He's in Greece somewhere, training to be a water sports teacher. His Dad went out to see him, they argued and he left! No one has seen him for days now!"

"Okay," I said, holding her tight, her head against my chest. "I'm sure he's just done a runner. He'll turn up. You'll see. He'll be alright."

He did turn up. But he was not alright. His body was washed ashore. Twenty-one years on the planet. That's all he was allowed.

Nobody is sure if it was suicide or an ill-judged misfortune. Tiana believes the latter. She likes to think that he was trying to swim from one island to another and died in the process; that he loved life too much to just give up; that his illness had fooled him into thinking he could achieve more than was possible; from what little I knew of him, she is probably right. The loneliness of his death is what she hates the most; that he was all that way out, all on his own, so loved yet so alone, so many people that would be willing to help, but nobody there to lend a hand as he was finally consumed by the unforgiving sea. He was surrounded by people and fun all his life, but died so lonely.

The funeral was the saddest thing that I have ever experienced. Unlike my Nan's funeral, where there was a feeling of naturalness about it, this had a sense of injustice. But his nature still came through that day, too strong to be suppressed by the sadness of the occasion. The music consisted of a song from the *Lord of the Rings* and dance outfit, Groove Armada; his non-religious beliefs meant that speeches concentrated on his love of life. He left a message on the answering machine just hours before he died and they played it. It was the sound of a young man full of life, ambition and love. He did not sound like a man about to die. It made the loss that much harder to understand. A good man was taken away in his prime. The saddest part of all was seeing his Mother and Father so devastated, the obvious sense of loss and bewilderment in their eyes. A parent should never have to bury their own child.

It makes my condition seem a bit pathetic. But I'm sure Luke would have empathised with me. After all, his life was dogged by mental illness, possibly brought to an end by it. We donated £100 to MIND, a charity dedicated to helping people with mental illness. Tiana wanted to and I, of course, agreed one hundred per cent.

Maybe the sense of realism that was created by these tragedies assisted in keeping my behaviour relatively stable. From the period of moving in together to being married for nearly a year, I was acting normally and loving life for the most part, only very occasionally doing something strange. Apart from the brief re-emergence of my coughing fits, there was only one significant sign of my illness that I can remember: I went through a period of having to say things in my head ('Tiana dies old', etc) at the same time as I was speaking, which caused me to talk some absolute gibberish at times and to develop a habit of mumbling. It became very difficult to hide. Every now and then, a part of the sentence going through my head would suddenly come out in my speech - "Could you turn the telly old?" or "What time are we raped dinner?" People would give me some very strange looks. Other times, I had to say something in order that I could say the good line in my head, so I would end up making some nonsensical remark just to carry out the ritual. This would particularly annoy Tiana when she was watching something or trying to read a book. But this strange episode past as I found it too difficult to carry out the rituals and soon managed to convince myself that I could not say things in my head and speak at the same time.

I will forever feel lucky and appreciative that one of the most key times in my life was not affected by my illness: 2004 was the year of my wedding and my decline was still far enough away that those memories have not been spoiled. It was a brilliant day. But first came the stag do!

CHAPTER NINE: AN EYE-OPENER

Being Tiana, planning for the wedding had begun a good two years before the big day. If I'm completely honest, it had begun long before she had met me; I wouldn't be surprised if she had clear images of what it would be like whilst I was still dreaming about going to the moon. What she would look like, the dress, her hair, the flowers, the church, the bridesmaids - they had all been well thought out long before I was ever on the scene. The two years building up to the big day were merely arranging to put the plan into action and a few finishing touches.

For some strange reason, she has often fretted about the size of her boobs and this became a particularly big issue when looking for a wedding dress. It is an interesting difference between men and women that, whilst any man would be very vocal if he is particularly well-endowed, women find it almost a handicap to be big-breasted.

"I can't wear the dresses I want to wear," Tiana would say to me. "I'm going to look stupid in my wedding dress with these stupid things sticking out!"

A man would not be upset that he could not wear a certain pair of trousers because his knob is too big.

"It's so difficult trying to find bras that fit me," she would complain.

Again, a man would not worry about pants not fitting.

"It's embarrassing going into underwear shops and asking for my bra size," poor Tiana would cry.

A man would walk up to the counter proudly and announce, "Do you have pants big enough to house this monster?", then proceed to whack his appendage down onto the counter. Not women.

But despite all her fears, she managed to find her dress in the first shop in which she looked. And it was perfect (but more of that later).

I did, however, have some say in all of these plans: at my request, she left me with the responsibility of the cake, which meant that I could taste various recipes until we had found one that was suitably sweet, chocolaty and gooey enough for me. Once I had decided on it (with her not unsubstantial input) she retook the reigns and worked out what it was going to look like! Maybe I'm being a bit harsh on her: she did always bring me along to all the wedding fairs and always asked my opinion and made sure I was happy with it before a final decision was made. Moreover, she loved organising it all and I was happy for her to get so involved. The truth is, she would get very annoyed at me if I didn't show an interest. But there was so much to think about and I often felt a little confused and overwhelmed by it all. I had no idea what a 'favour' was [they're the little gifts on the table for the guests, taking the shape of small decorated boxes or bags with ribbons round and sugared almonds inside - although we had mini eggs!] and didn't have a clue about all the traditions. But I soldiered on through the multitude of decisions, as Tiana showed no little amount of energy in perfecting the big day.

A point on Mothers-in-law, as my Dad pointed out to me: women more often than not turn into their Mothers, so make sure you look at them first. My Mother-in-law is still attractive, lots of fun and laidback I knew I'd be alright with Tiana for the next sixty or so years.

Tiana told me that she used to dream of looking like a princess, ready to marry her Prince Charming. As time went on, the image of Mr Charming changed from something out of a boyband to someone with more apelike qualities. I'm not sure where I fit on this scale, but it's probably somewhere in between. But how I looked (as handsome as I was) was merely a background detail: the wedding day is the bride's day to look their most glamorous, for everyone to be stopped in their tracks and in awe of her beauty; to be full of envy alongside their well-wishing. This day had been in her mind for all of this time, which explains the work that she put into it. And she did not disappoint. I can still put my hand on my heart and say that the most beautiful woman I've ever seen in my life is my wife on our wedding day.

But I'm jumping ahead: first came the stag do.

My best friend and best man, who goes by the name of Jim, is an absolute cretin. He is one of life's great characters. You will not meet a more laidback person. He does not really do anything, he just lets things happen around him, responding to the situation that he finds himself in. Jim has a fantastic lack of foresight, no sense of planning and is not quick to react. He is reasonably intelligent with a great sense of humour, but is mentally lazy and not overly aware of the world around him. He is a recipe for disaster! The word 'useless' can easily be defined: 'that without use' and this epitomises Jim's entire existence. By using the thesaurus on the computer, it provides me with some equally fitting descriptions: 'ineffective', 'of no use', 'a waste of time', 'futile'. But that's exactly why I like him so much: no cares, no issues, no hang-ups, never sad, always drifting between daft and ridiculous. He's the kind of best friend that everyone wants. And most of all, he's loyal, honest, trustworthy - I would go so far as to say, I love the bloke (not in a physical way, I should point out). If ever he decides to get married, I will take the opportunity to repeat all of the above, possibly making it more abusive.

Due to Jim's natural inability of organising the proverbial piss up in a brewery, I organised the stag do all myself, otherwise the two of us would probably have ended up going down the pub the night before. So I chose to go to Prague with seven of my closest friends, including Jim and Dennis. The theme was 70s gear, i.e. flares, crazy hairdos, loud shirts, etc. It will come as no great surprise that the only person not to be dressed up was Jim. He claimed that I never told him. Of course I didn't.

The fun began as soon as we stepped on the plane. Jacob, my Jewish friend, sat next to me reading a book about a Mr Coen, an Israeli spy who was eventually caught and hanged by one of the Arabic states. The front cover had a picture of his hero swinging from a rope, defiantly (!). The sub-title read: *You must not defend yourself against the Arab – you must attack*! This would not be my chosen reading on a flight, especially in these troubled times. I checked the surrounding area for anyone looking vaguely Arab/Moslem like; luckily, we were fine.

We had joked that our clothes were probably not dissimilar to Czech fashion, but upon arrival our jokes were not that far from the truth. As we made our way through passport control, we noticed that one of the locals had a thick curly head of hair and wide bottomed trousers. Of course, we pretended that he was one of us and beckoned him to come along and 'stop dawdling', etc. He gave a wry smile and muttered what I would assume to be the Czech for 'piss off, you bunch of wankers'.

Eastern Europe has (and still is in some parts), of course, gone through a great transitional period as the old Communism regimes have come to an end and it is trying to embrace capitalism. Inevitably, such countries have weaker economies, so us Western Europeans can go there and spend what to them is ridiculous amounts of money on cheap beer. And men with spending ability tend also to pay for sex. Prague was one of the first to go through this stage. Unfortunately for us, the days of 20p a pint were gone and the locals knew that drunken tourists were prepared to pay a whole lot more to taste the local specialities. Prague is still a beautiful city, but is in danger of becoming overrun with British drunkards on stag and hen dos. Such people bring in a lot of money and tend not to be as aggressive as their non-about-to-get-married-holidaymaking counterparts, so the appeal of attracting such custom is obvious. However, it is a very old city, full of culture and history and it would be a shame if this is ignored in its appeal. Maybe, as Talin and other Eastern European countries have taken over as being the destinations for cheap beer and women, its appeal as a place of historic beauty will be restored. The division into the old town and the new town, separated for the most part by a bridge, goes a long way to restoring this. The old town is full of traditional pubs and buildings and food; the new town is where you can indulge in anything from admiring naked women from afar to full-blown carnal knowledge.

Of course, we were on a stag do and a nice building does not easily grab the attention of eight beered-up lads; at least not as easily as a beautiful woman. Needless to say, we spent nearly all of our time in the new town. At around 11 o' clock on the first evening, we stumbled upon what turned out to be a strip club/brothel called *Atlas*. For the next few hours, there were very few people in there and we had the pick of the sights. I was pleasantly greeted by an attractive young lady who gave me the greatest chat-up line I have ever received: "Would you like a blowjob?" As much as that appealed to me, I was not about to wreck my marriage before it had even begun, so I declined. However, the others decided that they would club together and pay for me to have a 'dance' with the young lady. I knew deep down that I shouldn't, but in my drunken 'I love the world because I'm getting married to the greatest woman ever and she won't mind if I have one silly little dance' state, plus the fact that all of my good friends would be very grateful if I accepted their gift, I decided to go with her.

I soon found myself sitting on a bench in a 'broom cupboard' of a room with this young, dark-haired lady dancing seductively in front of me whilst slowly removing her clothes. This is when reality sinks in: even in my drunkard state, I could sense the artificiality of it all. She did not want to be there. I don't expect many of her punters looked into her eyes, but I did and it was plain to see that she did not consider herself lucky in her choice of career or having a fun time. The arrogance in me could not understand why she was not at least getting some enjoyment out of it – I am, after all, a reasonably attractive young man and, had our situations been different, we would have made a good looking and well-suited couple. And surely, when you have to put up with so many ugly or fat or incredibly drunk men trying to grab you and touch you, I must be a breath of fresh air? Who knows! I tried to ignore such feelings and just enjoy the view, but it was a bit like watching a sex scene with your parents in the room (see earlier chapter). It lasted around ten minutes, at which point she stopped abruptly and said, "That's it!" She popped her clothes back on, introduced herself, shook my hand and led me back to the main bar area. With hindsight, maybe she wanted to give herself some dignity, to say, 'yes, I may be a prostitute, but I'm still a lady with feelings'.

Very strange experience.

As the night went on, it all became even more surreal. Another woman, who looked a bit like Mariah Carey, decided she wanted me to 'shag her' and went to great lengths to let me know why it would be safe: "we use condoms, yes? Two if you want". I declined numerous times and eventually she got the point.

Then there were the sex shows that took place downstairs: a couple were 'banging away' on stage, going through all types of positions, each of them thoroughly enjoying themselves and seemingly oblivious to the audience around them, whooping and hollering, shouting advice and encouragement. The man eventually pulled out his penis and 'shot his load' all over her stomach, much to her delight! He then handed her a towel and she wiped herself down. They then both got to their feet and bowed several times to a standing ovation from the audience!

Next up was a stripper who threw each of her clothes into the crowd as she was removing them. I did not pay much attention to where her garments were going until I turned to talk to Tony, a work-mate who everyone was convinced was a homosexual until he informed us that he was going to get married – he had been the recipient of most of her garments and was now donning them himself, including a hat, frilly scarf and waistcoat! For the climax of her show, she invited a fellow stag up onto the stage and invited him to perform various acts with her. When she bent down and told him to spank her, he sat down, unscrewed his false let and began slapping her on the backside with it! The place was in uproar! To this day, I still find it hard to believe what I had seen.

The evening finished on a strange note: just before we left, I was approached by a prostitute that must have been well into her 50s. She had decided that I had offended her in some way and ran at me, shouting abuse! She had to be held back by a couple of her friends. I've no idea what I said or did, but expect it was a case of mistaken identity – this woman was frothing at the mouth trying to get hold of me! We quickly left and made our way back to the hotel.

It was around 5 in the morning when we arrived in our rooms, less Jacob, who turned up several hours later. It turned out he had been on quite a little adventure. The last anyone had seen of him, he was walking up the stairs with a tubby, small-breasted girl with lots of frizzy hair and not the greatest face in the world. He revealed that they were off to have a Jacuzzi together, or a 'jew-cuzzi' as we named it, and spent £100 for the pleasure. He could not explain why, despite so many beautiful ladies there, he decided to have a bath with the ugly one. Once in the bath, he turned down the opportunity for a shag and a blow job and decided to spend the majority of the hour sucking on her breast. He succumbed to a handjob, they dried off and he left. Outside, he climbed in a taxi but decided he didn't like the driver and ran out. He climbed into a tram, discovered it was going the wrong way, climbed into another tram, again the wrong way, and finally into a third, still wrong! So he decided to run back to the hotel. By around 10 o' clock, he turned up, found his bed occupied by another member of the group and curled up underneath the radiator.

Despite his nocturnal episode, Jacob still had enough energy to lead us round Prague later that afternoon. I forget what the destination was, but he clearly did not know where he was going and we did not have the energy to stop following him and take the lead.

That next evening, after we had woken from our naps, I had a philosophical conversation with my room-mate, Ali, who was also to be my usher. He had been happily married for a number of years, despite only being a couple of years older than me.

"You nervous?" he asked.

"Kind of, I guess," I replied. "I don't really get nervous though. More anxious. And I don't feel anxious at all. Which is a good thing." I didn't say why.

"I was cacking myself," said Ali.

"Why?" I asked. "You knew she was the right person didn't you?"

"Definitely," he answered. "I've never regretted a single moment. Best thing I've ever done. From the first time we met, we just got on so well. We just understood each other."

"Any tips for a successful marriage?"

"Talk," replied Ali. "You've always got to talk to each other about what you're thinking. Even if it's because you're annoyed - don't bottle it up. And don't take each other for granted either. Every now and then, just give her a hug, tell her what she means to you, thank her for those little things she does. Don't ever expect her to act in a certain way, or at least don't ever look like you expect it of her."

"Could you write these down for me?" I asked.

"And don't ever expect to fully understand them," he continued. "They don't understand us. Emotional creatures, women. Not like us."

"I have emotions," I said. "I even cry sometimes. Not as easily as Tiana – but she cried watching *Chitty Chitty Bang Bang*, the musical, when the car flew across the stage. I wouldn't cry at that. But I do have strong emotions."

"Yes," said Ali, "but you don't have them to the same extent. With women it's less about thinking and more about feeling."

"How do you cope with only having one partner?" I asked.

"I wank a lot," he replied.

"Not when I'm in the room?" I asked, looking across, slightly unnerved.

"I wait till you're asleep," said Ali. "Sometimes I look at you lying there…"

"Shuttup!" I interrupted, whacking him with a pillow.

"And have bloke time," he continued, "and let her have girlie time. Women and men are different, so you need to just be with your own sex every now and again."

"Sounds good advice to me," I replied.

"And never forget their birthdays or your wedding anniversary,"

"No, okay," I said, wondering whether I should have started this whole conversation.

"And don't insult her Mother," he went on.

"Never?" I asked.

"Never. And know when yes means no, when no means yes, when yes means yes and when no means no."

"Yeah, okay," I said chuckling.

"A woman is never wrong," he said, now on auto-pilot. "If she is wrong it is due to something that the man has said to mislead her. Man must apologise immediately for causing said misunderstanding."

I looked across at him. He was staring at the ceiling, looking like he was losing the will to live!

"You okay?" I asked.

"And just hold on to your balls," he continued, ignoring me. "They'll try to take them away from you," he suddenly sat up and turned to me, clenching his fist, "but don't let them!"

"And you're happily married," I said, not knowing whether to laugh or to take him seriously.

"Definitely," he replied, suddenly breaking into a big beaming smile and winking. He laid back on the bed. "Definitely."

That evening was far more relaxed. We travelled over the bridge to spend some laid back time drinking in one of the older establishment. The bridge itself is very old and beautiful. That Saturday, there were hundreds of people crossing; not just drunken hens and stags with their entourages, but lovers, families, locals, all smiling, all laughing. There were also the beggars, knelt down, their heads on their knees and their arms outstretched and holding flat caps, requesting to be filled. They were evenly distributed upon one side, gaps of ten metres between each one. It was too much to resist as I stood at the foot of the bridge looking on at the alternative race-track, complete with human hurdles: so I ran from one length to the other, leaping over each one, careful to avoid whacking them with my trailing leg! Yes, ladies and gentleman, I invented the game of 'tramp hurdling'! For the more sensitive amongst you, I did put money in their hats and most of them saw the funny side of it.

In the old town, we found a nice little pub and drank the local brew at 50p a pint. We told jokes and philosophised about the future in a steadily more drunken fashion. We went to what was reportedly the biggest club in Europe and had a little dance. Then we found ourselves back in the new town and tried to find *Goldfinger* – a famous club that we had heard so much about.

"Excuse me," I asked a taxi driver, crouching down, Dennis behind me. "Can you tell me where *Goldfinger* is please?"

"Gode-finga?" he replied in Broken English. "Who is this Gode-finga?"

"He's the man," I began to sing.

"The man with the Midas touch," sung Dennis, joining in.

"Such a cold finger!" we all sang in unison. The man drove away to the tunes of the Shirley Bassey classic, looking slightly bemused and muttering what I assume was, "Bunch of crazy English arseholes." So we found our way back to

Atlas and completed the evening much like the night before, although Jacob decided not to have the Jew-cuzzi that night.

All in all, my stag do was exactly what it should be: a chance to do bloke things with my closest mates, have a bit of laugh, but harmlessly. Some might say that we shouldn't have gone to a strip club or brothel or jumped over tramps; that people like us have taken the beauty away from Prague and made it into a sleazy, drunkard's paradise. But we never hurt anyone and gave our hard-earned cash to people more needy. All of us, with the exception of Jacob, stopped short of sexual contact for money. We never damaged anything. And Prague did pretty well out of us. And it's still a beautiful place, full of culture and colour, nice food and pleasant people. The sleaziness is on the decrease as other cheaper countries have taken up the mantle. I may go back there one day with my family, although I won't be encouraging my children to tramp hurdle.

I was so glad to see Tiana again. We hugged and kissed and swapped funny stories. Tiana had a great time in Edinburgh. Being a far more popular person than I, she had about twenty friends with her. They did typical girl things: massage, sauna, makeover, etc. And they also got very drunk, of course. But, like an OCD compulsion, the whole lap-dance thing was bugging me. I kept trying to push it to the back of my mind, telling myself that it was no big a deal, and if I felt guilty then I should suffer, not let Tiana suffer too. Especially two weeks before the wedding. But I am a compulsive being after all.

"I've got something to tell you," I said to Tiana. "You're not going to like it."

"What?!" she cried, her bottom lip quivering almost immediately. "Please don't tell me you've cheated on me!"

"No!" I began, "nothing like that! I had a lap-dance with this girl."

"You wanker!" she shouted and the tears came.

"I'm really sorry," I said. "I didn't touch her or anything. All she did was dance..."

"I specifically said not to have one!" she continued. "You even promised me – swore on your life!"

"The lads had grouped together and decided to get me one without me knowing," I pleaded, blaming my friends whilst they were not there to defend themselves. "I was drunk, we were all having fun – I didn't want to let them down!"

"I can't believe you," she said, slumping herself down on the bed. "Two weeks before the wedding and you go and do something like that! I'm not even sure if I want to marry you anymore."

"Wait!" I cried. "That's a huge over-reaction! It was rubbish, pointless. She just danced around me while I felt a bit awkward and that was it! I didn't enjoy it!"

"I can't believe you had a lap-dance with some girl," she mumbled, staring at the wall.

"It was two dances," I replied, stupidly.

"Get out!" she said.

I tried to plead my innocence, but to no avail. She made me sleep downstairs. In such a small house, I could clearly hear her cries. They continued into the early hours.

It was three days later when she spoke to me again, having successfully not said a word to me up until that point, despite my numerous attempts at an explanation.

"You know you've really hurt me," she said to me that evening.

"I know," I said, suddenly livening up and grabbing her arms fondly.

"And you've been a real selfish bastard," she continued.

"Yes!" I cried, "Very selfish! A stupid selfish bastard!" I added.

"And you didn't enjoy it?" she asked.

"No!" I replied.

"So why did you have two then?"

Shit. What do I say to that?, I thought.

"Don't worry," she went on, "you don't need to answer that."

"I'm so so so sorry!" I said. "Are you still going to marry me then?" I looked at her with eyes wide open, hoping that she'd say yes.

"Can't back out now can I?" she replied. "Everything's sorted now."

"You could sound a little more enthusiastic."

"Of course I still want to marry you, idiot!"

And that was that! Phew! I had nearly lost my future over some pointless little dance that was over before it began. I had been an idiot. But from that point on, both of us forgot about it and looked forward to our big day! The countdown had begun!

CHAPTER TEN: THE SECOND GREATEST DAY OF MY LIFE

The 1st July 2004 – my wedding day! And what a day! The sun was shining from early in the morning till late in the evening. Jim and I were staying up the road from Tiana's Mother's house with her neighbour and good friend. The night before, my Mother-in-law-to-be, Jenny, had held a big party for some of the guests that were staying in the area overnight. It had been great fun. I had got drunk but not too bad. Jim and I had been sent away before midnight – superstitions and all that! It's amazing what weird things people will believe! I woke far too early – about six o' clock. I wasn't anxious, but excited. *Really* excited. There was this buzz in the air, a kind of calm before the storm, but in the opposite sense, if you see what I mean. I tried reading a book, but nothing was going in. I tried going through my ultimate rugby team, but that didn't last very long. By seven o' clock, I could hold back no more and decided to get into my wedding suit. Realising my idiocy, I took it back off. I texted Jim to see if he was awake, but never got a response. Lazy bastard. By eight o' clock I had woken my hosts, showered, shaved and all and was downstairs, back in my wedding suit minus tie and jacket.

Jim had given me his cough whilst in Prague – it could have been disastrous! But thankfully it did not set off my OCD. In fact my disorder was nowhere in sight! My current enthusiasm for life had completely suppressed it. I won't say 'beat it into submission' – not by a long way. But it was so far away it could have been on the moon. I remember coughing a couple of times that morning and thinking how weird it was that I could have had such stupid thoughts before. I was so far away from OCD there was a smug indifference about it all.

That morning Tiana's Mum's friends were fantastic: they fed us, gave us champagne and even organised for an important rugby match to be recorded and sent to their house (they didn't have satellite). But despite their best efforts that morning dragged. I just wanted to get to the church and see everyone, especially Tiana. It was frustrating to know she was just down the road and I couldn't even talk to her. However, it was for the best: she could be a savage animal getting ready for a normal evening out; I couldn't imagine what had been let loose that morning! The tears, the anger, the frustration! Weeeeoooooh! Probably best that I was nowhere near!

Finally, it was time to get going. On the way to the church there was so much going on, it was brilliant! A huge movement of people was taking place, the streets and the roads seemingly filled with guests. I arrived at the church at around 12.30 – half an hour to spare before we got down to business. Most of the people were already there. Parents, brothers and sisters, aunties, uncles, cousins (first, second, once removed, twice removed), nieces, nephews, school friends, university friends, work colleagues and your usual selection of randoms! They were all there! Every direction I looked, there was somebody that I wanted to talk to. You could see a slight hesitation in most people, unsure of whether they should come and talk to the most important man on the planet that day. I tried my best to give them my full and undivided attention, but no doubt I seemed slightly distant, 'blown away by the love'! People told me I looked nervous, although I didn't feel it. I was still feeling incredibly excited and (as the earlier pictures were to reveal) this was represented by a gormless smile across my face.

I stood at the front of the church, looking around at all the faces smiling back at me, some of them with a wonder or curiosity; no frowns or grimacing, which was nice. I could feel the love! This is what hippies must have felt like back in the 60s and 70s. One o' clock came and right on cue she entered the church. She was beaming and looking absolutely beautiful. She has always had the most amazing dark brown eyes, slightly diagonal, sloping down towards the nose. Apparently it was the Greek blood in her. And her smile was more amazing than ever that day. She looked so happy and it was rubbing off on everyone there! Her beauty and fun attitude was contagious. You could see it in their faces as everyone began smiling and nudging each other. She had a long white dress on, not puffy (she hated puffy dresses!), with her Grandmother's long, tall veil. I remember looking across at her as she stopped beside me, smiling and telling her she looked beautiful. I can't remember if I kissed her or not at that point, but I definitely wanted to. Oh, and Tiana's cleavage, which was voluptuous and inviting at the best of times, was surpassing itself (thoughts of the wedding night briefly popped into my head). I don't mean to lower the tone on such an occasion, but they both deserved a mention! We said our vows and, though I meant every word, there was so much going on, so many lovely thoughts running through my head, I can't really remember what we said. Then came the songs, we signed lots of bits of paper then went out into the glorious sunshine. Well-wishers were everywhere, people were laughing, smiling, cracking jokes, telling us how lucky and beautiful/handsome we looked.

The day carried on in the same vein, with even the most reserved characters becoming tactile. The speeches came and Tiana's Dad was surprisingly confident for a tee-totaller. He was very complimentary and witty, although he managed to upset Jim by 'pinching' one of his jokes. Then came my own speech. I made a few jokes, including commenting on Tiana's breasts. I was meant to say, "When I first saw her, I thought 'what a lovely pair'…" then I'd turn the page of my notes and say "'we'd make'", but they laughed at the first bit and didn't hear the punchline. I even got away with managing to thank her parents for spawning her. There were some ghasps, but mostly laughter. In fact, I was getting enough laughs that some people were getting carried away and laughing at anything: Tiana's uncle chuckled when I mentioned my Nan not being able to make it because she past away recently. Once he realised he wasn't supposed to be laughing he stopped short and his face dropped. I forgave him. He's given me enough beers in the past for me not to be too harsh on him. And after the laughter, came the tears as I went into the soppy bit of the speech:

> "Tiana is my little 'pantalaimon' [read *His Dark Materials* if you don't get it – basically, it means we're inseparable; oh, and it explains the title of one of the earlier chapters]. Without her this over-crowded place seems so very lonely. I love you so much and I'm so proud that you're my wife."

And that was it! Not a dry eye in the house – well, amongst the women anyway, except for my Auntie Angie, who was always a heartless bitch. Since that day, some of Tiana's friends have told me how they had their doubts about me until that speech. Then they would act surprised when I asked them to elaborate on these doubts! Like I was going to say, "Yes, I know what you mean. I often worried that I was a bit of a bastard and likely to let her down. But now I feel comfortable that I won't turn out to be a cheating, deceitful lying git. Phew!" Someone also mentioned how Luke would have liked to have heard it. That he would finally have been convinced that I was good enough for her. I don't think anyone is good enough for her, but I try my best.

Then came the best man's speech and Jim didn't fail me. His first line went something along the lines of: "They say a best man's speech should take as long as it takes for the groom to have sex." Then he sat down to a pause then rapturous laughter! And he didn't get up! People looked from side to side. He stayed down for a good minute, which is a long time in a room full of people not saying a word. Eventually he stood and gave a belter of a speech, leaving the room in stitches.

After the speeches and the meal, we cleared the room for the disco to be sorted out and, of course, the karaoke! It was a nice opportunity to sit down with a few of our guests and just chat. Once the disco was set up, we had our first dance. When we were deciding upon our song, I had jokingly suggested *Yesterday* ('all my troubles seemed so far away', etc), but Tiana wasn't having any of it – not even a snigger. Eventually, we settled for *You're Just to Good to be True* by Andy Williams – I'd sung it to Tiana on the tube one drunken evening when we first started going out. Unfortunately, the song also reminds me of *The Deerhunter* and the wedding that takes place just before they all go off to Viet Nam and suffer horrible fates. But I tried not to think about that. Then the music changed and *Outkast*'s *Hey Ya!* blasted out of the speakers and everyone broke into spasmodic dancing, even my dear old Dad!

Then the karaoke began! Tiana and I performed *You're the one that I want* together, which went down really well. I spent much of the night running through my repertoire and generally hogging the microphone. I think I did ten songs in all! Some of them went down very well, surprisingly, although not everyone understood my David Bowie impression and just thought that I was too drunk to be singing properly. A couple of people congratulated me on the likeness, though. Everyone wanted to have a go at the karaoke! My new father-in-law performed a couple of tracks with his two brothers, my new Mother-in-law danced and sang like she was possessed to her favourite track of all time, *Loveshack*! By the end of the disco, everyone was still buzzing and smiling.

After moving the tonnes of presents to our room, we sat in the bar with a few others and drank some more. We finally went to our rooms at about 3 o' clock. What happened next is no one's business but mine and Tiana's!

Our wedding day was everything we could have asked for: everybody had a good time, everybody let their hair down, everybody saw the sunshine, oh yeah. It is definitely the second best day of our lives so far (you have to read to the end to find out what topped it!). At the time, it seemed to go on forever, much to my delight, but looking back it seemed to go so quickly! I can't recall certain parts of the day. It was brain overload.

And not an OCD symptom in sight. He was not invited and did not attempt to gate-crash our special day. But I was feeling great about life, I was happy carefree and not feeling any anxiety. I worked out from a very early age that the two are connected.

Our honeymoon was in China. We travelled all over the place as part of a touring group and saw some amazing sights: the Great Wall, the Terracotta Warriors, the Yang-tse River, beautiful temples that had escaped Madman Mao's so-called 'Cultural Revolution' and tasted some delicious food, although not as adventurous as I would have liked. I did manage to eat jellyfish, though I was not aware of it at the time. I think it was that that gave me the squirts. It seems that wherever I go I am destined to spend a good few days shitting water and China was no exception. At least I had no accidents there. Not like the Philippines. But that's another story.

Each hotel upgraded us to their honeymoon suites. Most of our companions were pleasant enough and there were one couple in particular with whom we spent most of our evenings: a middle-aged couple celebrating their 25th wedding anniversary, who were both good fun and became our foster parents for the remainder of the trip. The mainland Chinese were all very pleasant, although they stared at us a lot, especially the women, and especially Tiana's boobs. I don't think they had seen anything like them before, although no one asked for a photo with them. The shops would sell these 'chicken fillet' type accessories for bras *and knickers*! They all desperately wanted to be curvy! Compare that with our fashion designers who are so obsessed with making our women look like boys!

The mainland Chinese are much nicer than their Hong Kong counterparts, who we found to be bolshy, rude and arrogant. Maybe it is the only positive that communism has over capitalism: with the former, people have nothing, but neither do their neighbours, so they want for nothing; with the latter, everyone lusts after what they do not have. Personally, I think it's natural to strive for something better and not just settle at being content. Life thrives and progresses on change and improvement, not stability and contentment. But what do I know? I get scared of certain numbers after all. I'd fit in well with the superstitious Chinese. Four is bad there – don't they know that's the safest number? Madness!

OCD began to rear its ugly head with some silly incidents. Maybe being abroad was making me slightly anxious. But the occasions were few and far between and in no way affected my enjoyment of our honeymoon. I was still on too much of a high and loving life. His presence was there, but he had trouble keeping up with the pace of the tour and was too weak to present any real threat. I had not fed him with stupid thoughts for quite a while. To be honest, I can't even remember much about him during that time.

We came back and settled into married life with ease. The rumours I had heard about going to bed with a princess and waking up with a witch never materialised. Tiana was as wonderful as ever, and remains so to this day. We've been best friends for so long now and marriage wasn't going to get in the way of that.

CHAPTER ELEVEN: FATTENING THE BEAST

For the next few months, life was perfect. My symptoms were a rarity. We began planning for the future and a family of our own. I had always wanted children, but we had agreed to wait until after we were married, then to enjoy the early part of marriage with just the two of us. By early 2005, we had agreed that it was time to start trying for a baby. Tiana had prepared herself as meticulously as ever: she had stopped drinking and started taking folic acid, had done the research and worked out the best time to conceive, and had purchased pregnancy and ovulation tests. We had decided that we would need more money to support ourselves so I managed to get a better paid job working for a big accountancy firm in Canary Wharf. It was a long journey, but the money would justify it. And I was desperate to do well there. I needed to. I had a family to build. The pressure was on. I was entering anxious times.

Being a parent is not a decision that should be taken lightly. There's no job so important as bringing up another human being. It takes responsibility, care, understanding and massive sacrifices. A parent needs to be completely selfless. I was prepared for all of those things. People with OCD tend to be the caring sort and not overly bothered about their own existence. But that didn't stop the anxiety. Tiana would express her anxiety more passionately: would she be a good mother?, she would ask herself; what if she didn't love our child?; what if it was disabled?, and all the usual questions that any good mother should fret about.

So I began my new job – the worst job I'd ever done by a country mile. The first week, I was not given any work to do. They took me for lunch for the first day, but then I was left to fend for myself. I asked my superiors if there was anything that I could help them with ("no, not at the moment"). I read up on new areas of taxation that I thought might be useful. Half past five came and I left on time, which was of course frowned upon. Everyone else was staying for at least another hour. Then there was the dreaded journey: forty five minutes across London, followed by an hour train journey, and finally a car journey at the other end. Over two hours if there were no delays. 'If there were no delays'? Who was I kidding? This is 21st century London. As any commuter knows, delays happen nearly every day. Too many people trying to get to one place and not the infrastructure to cope.

And then there were my colleagues. The people I worked with were dull, silently ambitious and lacked character. They were the most boring bunch I'd ever met in my life. They were the people at school that sat at the front and sucked up to the teacher. There were a couple that were a good laugh, but I heard later that one of them got the sack (which was probably fair enough, if I'm honest – he had a foul mouth on him, bless him). All of us would sit around doing nothing a lot of the time and then be ridiculously busy at other times. When you were finally given work to do you were expected to stay until it was done, even if late into the evening. I couldn't stay too late – I had baby-making to do for one thing!

And I hated Canary Wharf. The big buildings, the pretentious city-goers, the big brands everywhere, the wine bars and the yar-yars! Where were the trees? Where were the mugs of bitter? Was this even England? It wasn't my England, anyway.

My days consisted of getting up around half five, getting to work by nine, sitting at my desk doing nothing or else working frantically, getting home at half seven at the very earliest, eating, washing up and sitting down with Tiana just before nine if I was lucky.

This was not an ideal situation for me: lots of sitting around doing not much, the mind begins to wander and wonder; feeling useless makes you feel worthless; I had to be doing well – this was going to be *the* job; anxiety was rife within me. The stage was set for OCD to make a comeback of mega proportions. I was weak, pathetic and vulnerable. I had the thinking time to fatten up the beast inside my brain. It was the perfect conditions for OCD to feed off. He broke my spirit, sent me into a quasi-catatonic state, fed on my fears. He pushed me into a hell of my own creation and very nearly killed me. I nearly lost everything, plummeting to the very depths of my soul.

It began with clearing my throat. The sound of it being cleared provided the 'key point' at which the 'key word' in the sentence was to be pronounced in my head. I would sit there on the train or at work by myself reading a novel or textbook respectively. I would get a frog in my throat and try to clear it. I knew that I must say some random word in my head at the same time. But sometimes this didn't work properly because either a bad word entered my head or the random word suddenly became part of a sentence which was not so random. For example, if I said the word 'train', it might be followed in my head with, 'comes crashing through our house and kills Tiana'. So I would have to clear my throat again with the emphasis in the correct place to prevent this terrible thing from happening. The line would enter my head: 'Tiana dies old' or 'Tiana is never killed by a train or anything else'. But then this might be followed by, 'except a car' or 'except by a raging elephant', or something equally weird. So I found a way to prevent this by saying 'shuttup' in my head at the end of the important sentence. This finished the possibility of the sentence being changed in a negative way. I wasted many hours thinking in such a manner.

As time went on, it got worse. It became more frequent and the rituals required to extinguish the problem became more difficult to perform, requiring greater precision. The corrective throat clearing had to be louder than the evil one. It may have to outnumber the evil one. To emphasise the key word, I began writing it down at the same time, or having it there to look at. I would sometimes carry around a piece of paper with me upon which the word was written. Or I would look for similar looking words on items around me. For example, our dishwasher had the word 'cold' on it, so I would place one finger over the 'c' whilst performing the ritual.

Throat clearing soon changed to coughing or shouting out the key word. The coughing and shouting would become louder and longer. As my behaviour became more obvious to others, I would have to find ways to cover it up or to hide somewhere. I would lock myself in the toilets on the train or at work, or find some quiet corner somewhere. I became a master at disguising my behaviour, but it was so all-consuming people would inevitably notice. As part of my attempt to hide my illness, I would have to make excuses to leave the room and sneak off to my little secret places. People at work would see me rushing around and obviously think I was busy. Maybe this deterred them from giving me work. As the rituals began taking over a greater part of my life, I became more and more exhausted.

Then came the clock-checking and looking for the right number: if I did the ritual at a time that was divisible by 13, that was no good and I had to do it again at a good time and double the number of times I did it; immediately after, I needed to look at a number that wasn't divisible by 13, otherwise I had to start all over again.

This was the way I was spending the daylight hours, but it soon affected the night time too: I began having dreams where I would be performing rituals, then would enter that space between being asleep and awake, carrying on the rituals until I had fully woken. Before I knew it, I was wide awake in a state of anxiety and in need of correcting the thought by performing a ritual. I would look at the clock and if it was on a bad number, I would stare at the clock until I could find a good time to do it. I would then look at a number in the dark that I knew was not divisible by 13, staring until I could focus in the moonlight clearly enough to see the number, just to be absolutely sure that I was looking at it and that it was 'safe'. If Tiana stirred or, worse, told me to be quiet, I would have to sneak downstairs and carry on the ritual there. Being a small house, I would go as far away as possible in order that she couldn't hear me. The knowledge that I needed to get some sleep did not leave me, especially as the sleepless nights were clocking up. If I was lucky I would get a couple of hours in before dawn. By the time morning came, I was shattered, hoping to catch up with sleep on the train, but that soon became impossible too. Without sleep, the ability to rationalise is impaired further and I did not have the strength to fight. I always feel at my most sane after a good night's sleep, but that did not happen for so long. My brain chemistry was a mess. I had no tools or hope of tidying it up.

OCD is a monster. It plays on your fears and doubts. The first few times I performed the ritual, I was reasonably convinced that I had done enough to prevent the evil event. But soon that's not enough and the doubts become stronger until they completely take over. Within a month of coughing to stop the bad event, I started to wonder whether particular sounds that I had made amounted to coughing. I soon became convinced that nearly all throaty sounds I made were a cough; with the continual repetition of lines going through my head it was inevitable that the throat sound would fall on a bad word and I would enter into a pattern of performing these coughing and number rituals. During my waking hours, I was in a complete state of doubting and fearing; it was a vicious circle. I could see no way back: I could not help making sounds in my throat – no one could, and I could never get over the connection between key words and bad words and coughing. So how could I possibly ever lead a life free of this behaviour? I had a condition and couldn't see how I could ever get out of it. My condition led me to an overwhelming feeling of hopelessness.

In the thick of my illness, my average day would be as follows. The alarm would go about five thirty. Wide awake and in a state of anxiety from my night of worrying, I would make my way downstairs to the bathroom for a shower. There the coughing would continue. Sometimes Tiana would notice as she came down to the bathroom and tell me to stop doing that stupid behaviour. I would then wait until she was back upstairs and getting dressed before I carried on the ritual. But she soon let me know she could hear me from upstairs, so I would sneak outside and sit in the car with the doors shut where I knew she wouldn't be able to hear me. I would sit there in my little hiding place where I knew nobody would hear. It was the least anxiety-ridden of my hidey holes. By the time Tiana dropped me off at the station, I was ready for a sleep on the train, feeling absolutely shattered. But there was no let up: as I moved up and down the platform I would carry on performing the rituals, people staring at me when they thought I wasn't looking. It was the same old faces so no doubt they were aware of the weird bloke. I had become one of those strange people that others would take the piss out of. In a strange twist of fate, I had become that man in the library when I was younger, sitting there with his towel over his head and a little bar of soap. On the train, I would try to sleep but eventually began questioning whether I'd coughed and would therefore need to carry out more weird behaviour. If it got out of control, I'd go into the toilet, lock the door and perform more rituals. By this time I would cough so loudly and for a long period, just to really emphasise it, that my throat was red raw. People were bound to have heard me, but I tried to look nonchalant as I walked out of there and sat back down. I was lucky if I managed to go fifteen minutes without breaking into the rituals. Crossing London, I would cough as I was walking along, trying to find signs and words that would help with the ritual. 'Old street' was a good stop for me to stare at on the underground map. 'Holborn' was okay because I could pretend the 'olb' part said 'old'. When I finally arrived at work, I tried to get stuck into something to do, which was difficult considering I was rarely given anything. There was a toilet by the lifts that I could easily sneak off into and perform the rituals as nobody else used it. There were cleaners that used to hang out in the next room and I wondered whether they picked up on my activities. One day, whilst shouting my head off in this toilet I suddenly wondered what time it was. Knowing that it could be around 4.26, I sprinted out of the toilets and jogged quickly to somebody's desk and asked him what time his computer said it was (our computers were aligned with Greenwich meantime: I checked with the speaking clock one day) – 4.25, he told me! Phew! I walked off and sat back down. Then it hit me: I didn't look – he might have been rounding to the nearest five! I walked back over to him and asked him, was it right on 25 minutes past? He confirmed this was the case. I pretended it was to do with a bet I was having with somebody and would explain it to him one day. He acted like he really couldn't give a shit, but he probably just thought I was weird and wanted to avoid me. My face would have been sweating and red with all the energy and anxiety running through me. I would visit the toilets several times a day. The way home was much like the way in. By the time Tiana picked me up, I was a hopeless wreck. I got some respite in the evenings, but not much and it would soon be time to go to bed. Despite my tiredness, I would inevitably wake around 1 o' clock in the morning and enter the vicious circle once more, getting very little sleep, sneaking downstairs several times each night, trying not to wake Tiana.

My attempts to explain my condition to Tiana fell flat. She was convinced I had developed it after reading a book and needed to learn to move on. She repeated to me that loads of people had these stupid thoughts, but didn't dwell on them. She said she even had them herself some times and would do weird things too, like tapping her hand on her thigh twice. She would get very angry at me when I continued to carry out rituals in front of her. Once Tiana told me if I loved her I would stop it – I was in the middle of a ritual at the time. I tried desperately, but couldn't stop; she shouted at me, said she was walking out because she'd had enough, but I just kept coughing, unable to stop myself. So she went. Once I finished the routine, I went looking for her, but couldn't find her anywhere. By the time I got back, she was there waiting for me. She was annoyed that I'd carried on and, moreover, hadn't bothered following her straight away. I realised she'd never understand, so I found new ways to hide it from her.

During that time, there were several nights out, lots of occasions with friends that should have been fun, but were completely ruined for me by my OCD. I'm not sure how much people noticed. A couple of people had questioned the size of my bladder, given the frequency of my trips to the toilet (my most popular haunt for carrying out rituals). I wondered whether my personality had changed noticeably. I tried to act the same, but maybe my daft comments lacked the ingenuousness and integrity they once had, like I was just acting them out. I became a ghost of my former self,

OCD having full control over my personality. He had completely taken over my life. My relationships with friends and family were completely ruined. He sat there, smiling at me defiantly. He was winning. We were alone together in that glass room. He would stare scornfully into my eyes. I wanted to jump up and smash his sodding head against the wall of the room, smash it through the glass, but if I tried he would pin me down with ease, sitting on my head while I struggled helplessly. I searched for that little door, but it was nowhere to be seen.

The philosophy and the implications of my illness did not escape me and helped make my depression worse. My studies of OCD and the brain led me to understand thoughts as a physical thing, as I have already stated. If every part of my personality was dependent on chemistry and biology, if my character could be changed by changing the make-up of my brain, where did that leave my spirit? The only conclusion I could arrive at was that I had none. When I die, that's it, my spirit goes too. No Heaven, nor Hell (except of my own making). No religion, no God watching over me. It was all Darwinian survival of the fittest. I had a defect, a spasticated brain. Under such rules, it was best that my genes did not live on. These thoughts made me feel even more lonely and worthless. I found no comfort in science. It made me a godless lump of flesh.

After nearly two months had gone by from the time I had first started the throat clearing, I was ready to collapse, to give in completely. I knew I needed to do something to break out of this behaviour before I completely broke down into a catatonic state. Each 'this is the last time', as I said to myself, was inevitably not the last time. I was losing Tiana, I would end up jobless and might enter a downward spiral from which there would be no return. I was even losing me: my whole character was changing and I became close to forgetting who I was.

It is with deep regret and shame that I confess to coming very close to suicide. How easy it would have been just to jump out in front of a train, spontaneous, sudden and final. It was my love of Tiana and my family that stopped me. The devastation it would cause her would not be fair. And there was that glimmer of hope: I had been fine before, I had lived a normal life for many years, albeit with little quirks, so why couldn't I be there again some day?

It was a rainy day when I stood at the end of the platform, as far from the edge as possible so that I could get a better run up. I rocked backwards and forwards as the no-stopping train came closer. I was sweating and panting, the lids of my eyes so far into my eye sockets that they had all but disappeared. Then I ran! Everything went into slow-motion. When you're in danger of dying, your brain is on overload, taking in every last detail, filling your mind with information and giving you more time to act. The ridges in the platform, the faded white lines and wording, a cigarette butt, all so clear. I stopped suddenly, skidding and falling to the floor, my foot slipping over the edge! The train shot by and the air pressure forced my foot back onto the platform. I rolled away, panting. People were looking over, a couple even started walking towards me.

"You okay?" asked a man. He was in his forties, I would guess, with a long raincoat, briefcase and copy of *The Times*.

"Yes," I replied, as he helped me to my feet. My heart was pounding. "Just slipped that's all."

He tried to talk to me, but I fobbed him off with monosyllabic responses. Our train came, I found a quiet corner and sat there and thought what I had done. That was serious. I could have killed myself. But I hadn't. I didn't want to die! I loved life! Especially my little Tiana! She didn't deserve this. She needed a strong husband. I was never one to give up, and I wasn't going to start now. I needed *me* back, not this wreck. All of those wasted times, I had let myself down so badly – I was smart, funny, talented! I should have achieved so much more! Could achieve so much more! There was still so much time. I had so much to live for! This was the day that I would turn things around, start living again. No, more than that: I would start living properly in this world. I needed to become a rational, objectively thinking, man.

I closed my eyes and started thinking what I could do. But I soon entered into my little fantasy world: I was inside that glass room with OCD. He was quivering in the corner, a nasty, scrawny, Gollumesque type creature, scared, spitting, snarling, panting, knowing I was on the attack, a cornered beast! There was a door on each side of the room, all of them left wide open. I threw him through one of them, out into the wilderness beyond. We were in what looked like Arizona. I beat him and kicked him for miles, over mountains, down canyons, threw him up into the air, letting him drop heavily to the ground. We entered a city with tall skyscrapers and I threw him from building to building, stopping traffic, people fleeing from my wrath! Eventually, grabbing his bloodied broken face, I looked into his eyes and saw what a spiteful, pathetic little animal he was. And I chinned him so hard he went flying into space. Exhausted from all of this, I fell into a deep sleep, missing my stop and turning up to work an hour late. But who cared – I didn't have anything to do anyway!

At lunch time I went to a bookstore and began flicking through books on OCD and other mental illnesses; but they did not have the same impact this time. None of it was new to me. So I tried looking beyond OCD theories and read up on Taoism, spiritual yoga teachings and meditations. I bought several books, took them back to my desk and started flicking through them. But my OCD was still very much there. OCD is all about thought patterns and forming positive ones. The heavily trodden paths in my brain could not be blocked off so easily. They were steadily coming back, not yet defeated by my newly discovered positive attitude. So reading was not working as much as I would have liked as I struggled to focus on books but soon ended up entering another ritual.

Inevitably, I broke down that night. I walked through the front door and balled my eyes out like a baby. Tiana couldn't shout at me this time. I wept and I wept. Through my spluttering and tears and blubbering, I told her everything, including my attempted suicide. And finally she understood. It took a fully-grown man lying in a pathetic heap on the floor to convince her, but finally she understood. And from that moment on she was brilliant, understanding and supportive. She showed me an unconditional and strong love that even an obsessive compulsive could not doubt.

"We're going to get through this," she told me.

"You don't think I'm pathetic, do you?" I whimpered, pathetically. I lay there, my head in her lap whilst she caressed my head.

"Course I don't," Tiana replied, smiling gently.

"And you won't leave me because of my weirdness?" I asked.

"Of course not!" she said, tears appearing in her eyes. "What kind of wife would I be to do that? I love you."

I was feeling a lot more positive and stronger. There was a lot of work to be done, I knew that, but we were in this together. I made a pact with myself that I would work at this every day of my life. My goal was a happy life with Tiana and whoever else might enter our family; my tools were my rationality, Tiana and a lust for life. Tiana would phone me every day and several times. She would ask me if I'd done any silly rituals and I would always tell her the truth and what exactly I'd done. My behaviour had improved, but I was still a long way from being normal. I was still deep in my OCD state but no longer threatened by catatonia. I had turned a corner. Tiana sent me details of websites and printed off factsheets for me. She also gave me a helpline to ring. One day, when things were not going so well, I phoned it and spoke to some American lady, who was very helpful. She told me to keep busy, keep my mind occupied with some activity. She said that OCD attacked you when you gave it the time of day. It was nothing I didn't know, but it felt good to hear it from another person rather than just a book. But it was difficult to take up this advice as I was stuck in a job where they never gave me anything to do. I made up my mind: I had to get out of there. And out of London too.

Inevitably, there were blips in my behaviour. One day, I had a huge panic attack. It struck me that I had completely lost count of how many days I had been doing this coughing and how many times I had coughed each day.

"I'm in the shits," I explained to her over the phone.

"What's the matter?" asked Tiana. The concern in her voice was clear.

"I don't know how many times I've been coughing each day," I replied. "And I don't know how long I've been doing this for."

"So what?" she answered. "Why does it matter?"

"I've got to rectify it," I replied. "I've got to do it a hundred times a day for the next, say, hundred days!"

"That's silly," said Tiana. "Think about what you're saying! You can't do that!"

"I have to," I cried.

"No you don't!" she exclaimed. "If you want to beat this, you have to start now! Think about what you're saying! What will it achieve?"

"I know," I said, calming down and grabbing hold of my emotions.

"You've got to do this for us," Tiana continued. She started to cry. I was hurting her – us. This wasn't what I wanted to do. "You'll look back on it in a few days and realise that you don't need to do it."

"You're right," I replied, defiantly and suddenly feeling a lot stronger again. "I'm going to do this for us! I want to be the best husband I could ever be. I need to start acting like a man! I love you so much!"

"I love you too," said Tiana. "I'm really proud of you."

"Thanks," I said smiling. My strength was renewed.

It was conversations like this, plus the look in her eyes when she was with me, that pulled me through, that helped me realise how important it was to get through this.

We arranged to see my doctor, a Mrs Cook. I sat in the waiting room, Tiana cuddling me so supportively. When they called me in, Tiana came too, holding my hand. In the doctor's room, I sat there staring at the ground, holding a booklet on OCD. Mrs Cook asked me how she could help.

"I have this," I said, my lip quivering and tears rolling down my cheek. I handed her the booklet without looking up. I didn't feel ashamed – I was well past that. I just felt shattered.

She looked at it. I didn't know what to expect. Here was a fully-grown man, in full health, reasonably handsome, well-built, in a worksuit, with his beautiful wife, yet he was crying like a baby. But she was brilliant! She really understood and gave me lots of advice. Most importantly,

Mrs Cook gave me a subscription for medication called 'faverin' (fluvoxamine, in Latin). It would help with the chemical imbalance in my brain which influenced my condition so much. It would take a fortnight before the effect would kick in. However, she emphasised that they were water wings only, i.e. they could only assist me in getting over this, and they *weren't* a cure. She also put me on a list for cognitive behavioural therapy – CBT. With my new armoury of medications and positivism, I was ready to take on OCD once more. And this time I would win. It was one thing to win a battle, but to win the war was a much bigger deal. I needed to anticipate when OCD would attack and what I would do to keep it suppressed. I needed to recognise the symptoms of when OCD was about to creep up on me, those silly little things it would tell me to do, which would only take a split second and I'd be alright after that, but in reality I would have opened the door for OCD to come streaming in. But I was not at that stage yet – first I had to get my life back.

My first step was to understand when I had coughed and when I hadn't. When Tiana was around me, I would ask, "did I just cough then?" No, she would say. This was important. She was patient and understanding with my peculiar questioning. I had to understand that any little movement of my throat was not a cough. I panicked the first few times that I moved on from the sound, but kept going over it again and again in my head, replaying the sound I had made. I knew it was not a cough. I decided what a cough should sound like and what it didn't sound like. Within a few days, I had mastered this. This had the effect of not sending me into a ritual every few minutes. And with the freed up time, I could remember what it was to think normally again. I could learn to change my thought patterns, to think more positively. Thought patterns lead to routes being trodden in your head, the more well-trodden these routes become, the more easy it becomes to carry on using them; the more they are avoided, the more overgrown they become and the more difficult it is to go down them. It becomes far easier to turn back and eventually to look for another route from the outset. The blocking off of this most dangerous of routes could not be underestimated in my battle to beat OCD. It was hard, but it took surprisingly little time: a matter of a couple of weeks.

And I worked out how to keep my mind occupied: I looked for a new job and Tiana and I looked for a new house. We were to move to Petersfield in Hampshire to be closer to our respective parents, who would hopefully be grandparents and, more importantly, babysitters! Tiana was still not pregnant, but it had only been a few months. It was still far too early to be negative, despite her fretting and the inevitable disappointment each month as she came on her period. I would spend my days phoning for jobs in the area or looking on the Internet, or updating my CV and sending it to various places! My shitty employers didn't even notice, or if they did they certainly didn't care. I also looked at houses on the Internet. Tiana would send lots of pictures over to me for me to look at. My mind was occupied with positive thoughts of a new life. This and my love for Tiana was pulling me through.

Reading one of my self-help books one evening, the first chapter instructed you to blank your mind. Then it asked you a question and you had to think of the first thing that came into your head. The question was: what do you most want to be in life? 'A husband.' That's what came into my head! That made me feel really good. Then, I was instructed to repeat the exercise for the following question: what is the second most thing that you would want to be? 'A father.' A father and a husband! For all of my desires that I thought I had, to be a husband and a father is what I most wanted to be and it made me feel so proud. My goal was there! Everything was falling into place!

It was not long before we discovered the perfect house for us. It was a townhouse in Petersfield, a small Hampshire market town. It was a new-build too, which meant the end of a chain and less stress to sell. Plus, Tiana would be living close to her parents which was great for her. I never realised just how upset living so far away from her family had made her. I had been a little selfish, no doubt partly because of being caught up in my own thoughts. But she was incredibly happy with the up and coming move and it came through in her personality. Through all of this, she needed to be feeling good too, of course.

It didn't take us long to find a buyer for our little house. It was very popular, given its charm and character. I was not sad to see it go because we had grown too big for it. And I'm glad that, despite the awful memories I have of living there, these are heavily outweighed by the good times! There were the drunken weekends when we had our friends or family round to stay, there were the quiet nights in with Tiana and I sitting watching a film together with a bottle of wine and a takeaway, there were the memories of reading to each other in bed, her cuddled up in my arms. And there was a particularly special moment, one which will always remain my favourite.

"Let me just do a test," said Tiana.

"But it's only been a couple of days," I replied, turning to her. "Wait another three days, say, and if you still haven't come on then you can do the test."

"Okay, she said. We were lying in bed at the time reading. Tiana was restless. "Let me just do it! At least it'll put my mind at rest."

"Fine," I answered. And off she went. I carried on reading, trying not to think about it. A few minutes past.

"Mark!" I heard her cry, a slightly nervous and tense vibe to her voice.

I suddenly felt anxiety run through me: this could be it! I tried to stop getting excited, just in case she told me the worst. I made my way down the stairs. She was standing in the kitchen, crying but smiling.

"I'm pregnant!" she spluttered, laughing nervously.

"Wow!" I replied. "That's ... that's brilliant!" This was the greatest news I'd ever received! But the doubts hit me: what kind of father would I make, what with this OCD of mine?

"You don't seem very excited," said Tiana, picking up on my anxiety.

"I'm ... This is ... This is amazing!" I answered. "I just want to be the best Dad I can ever be!" And, yes, I cried with happiness, smiling like the gormless freak that I am. The fear left and a wave of excitement came over me.

"Let's not get too excited," I said, trying to sound sensible and rational. "This just means we know you can fall pregnant. It's early days. Let's not build ourselves up for a fall."

Tiana nodded in agreement. But who were we trying to kid? We were both over the moon and knew we'd be devastated if we lost it now!

I swore to myself from that point onwards I would be the best father there would ever be! I knew this is what I wanted more than anything. I had a reason to live and from now on, I would do anything to ensure that everything I did for my family was positive and I would be the best father and husband I could ever be. And OCD was not going to stand in my way.

The news of Tiana's pregnancy changed everything. Finally, we had a complete goal to work for. We would be moving houses to Hampshire to be near grandparents; I had managed to find myself a new job that was only a few miles away and would take half an hour at the most to drive to; but, most importantly of all, we would have a little baby! And that's exactly what happened next! There were no hiccups, no upsets. I had gone to the depths of hell, but had clawed my way back out, and now I was virtually sprinting into heaven. We really did enter the perfect life.

CHAPTER TWELVE: MY VALENTINE

It was around 5 o' clock in the morning of 13 February 2006 when Tiana woke me, groaning.

"It's started!" she said.

"How strong?" I asked. We had attended ante-natal classes together, read all the books and watched a couple of DVDs too, so we were fully briefed as to what to do. I knew all the questions to ask, we knew all the signs and false alarms.

"Not that strong, I don't think," she replied. "Got a while to go yet."

We lay in bed for the next three hours, the contractions staying mild, with gaps of twenty-five to thirty minutes between. I held her hand and rubbed her lower back with each contraction. The time went by quickly; we went in and out of sleep, too tired to stay awake, but too excited to stay asleep. I was trying to remain calm. I needed to. I couldn't afford to get anxious on a day like this. Eventually, we got up, showered, dressed and ate breakfast. Then we sat in the front room and watched *Finding Nemo* on DVD. We had no furniture at that point (the settees had not yet bee delivered), so we both lay there on the floor, Tiana resting on a mountain of pillows. (I always hated pillows – they're a purely decorative thing that get in your way when you're trying to get comfortable; but Tiana liked them, so I have had to come to terms with them.) I continued to rub her back during the contractions, gently, whilst she groaned.

We kept track of the length of each one and the time between, writing it all down in a notepad in typical Tiana fashion. Just after midday, when the contractions were down to one every five minutes, we went to the bathroom and I ran a bath for her, lighting incense all round the room and putting some weird fancy oil in the water. I helped her in and Tiana lay there quietly, concentrating on her breathing. The contractions soon slowed down to one every eight minutes as a result of being in the bath.

"I'm hungry," said Tiana.

"Do you want me to make you a sandwich?" I asked.

"Can you get me some tinned pineapple?" she replied.

"Pineapple?" I said, slightly surprised. "You don't believe that old wives' tale do you?"

"Just get me it!" she said, slightly frustrated and in no mood to enter a discussion.

I went downstairs and emptied a tin of pineapple into a bowl, then brought it up and gave it to her – this is one old wives' tale that is absolutely true! Half way through eating it, Tiana's contractions suddenly shot to one every three minutes! It was time to make our way to the hospital!

We got her out of the bath; I dried her and helped her dress. We made our way to the car, remembering to take her pregnancy bag with her. She had, of course, put it together months before. Then we drove the half hour journey to the hospital in Chichester. Being early 21st century England and living in a small town, there was, of course, no hospital within a sensible distance, having all been closed in domino-like fashion. But we had worked out the best route a long time ago (of course!). On the way, there was a particularly large roundabout we had to cross. I was being very careful, but still nearly drove into an old man and his wife going the wrong way round the roundabout! He obviously was completely unaware of his mistake as he sat with his face almost pressed against the windscreen! Personally, I think no one over 70 should be allowed to drive.

By the time we got to the hospital it was around 3 o' clock in the afternoon. I hadn't failed to notice the date, but I really wasn't bothered: hand on heart, I really couldn't give a shit. That number had not meant anything to me for months. Secretly, I was hoping that it would fall on that day just to show that this stupid fear of a number really was a load of bollocks.

At the hospital, we managed to get the room with the birthing pool, just as Tiana had planned. The remainder of the pregnancy carried on as smoothly for a while. My poor beloved wife was really feeling the pain by now. I had continued to massage her and would try to remind her of happy times together, like nice holidays and our wedding day, to put her mind onto nice thoughts. But by around six o' clock that had ceased to work and she was taking in gas and air by the gallon! Her moans were drowning out the pan-pipe music, or whatever it was she had playing. Oh, and giving her that lovely packet of bacon flavour crisps was a waste too!

By ten o' clock, things began to take a turn for the worst: our child had managed to turn so that its spine was against Tiana's spine. The head was still facing down, luckily, but it meant that it was going to be that much more difficult for our little kiddie to pop out. The next few hours were not nice. For Tiana's dignity, I will not go into details, but suffice to say she could no longer bring up the time when I was so drunk she needed to clear up my puke. But she was so sweet all the way through. None of the swearing and calling the father everything under the sun! She would swear, then apologise, and kept asking me to help her and telling me how much it hurt and to look after her! She had lost her sense of reality a long time before and was moving about in a daze. Eventually, we had to leave the birthing pool and get her onto a bed.

Despite her state, she did tell me off once in a surreal moment: she lay there stark-whatever naked, in a hot, humid room; I could take it no more and decided to remove my tee-shirt.

"What are you doing?" she said, relatively strain free and momentarily coming back into the real world.

"I'm hot!" I replied, slightly perplexed.

"Put it back on!" she cried, laughing incredulously. She looked at the mid-wife who was looking at me as though I had just got my penis out and done 'windmills' with it. I put my shirt back on, feeling a little confused and silly. Still, this wasn't the time to go into the logic of women.

After much shouting and pleading from Tiana, the mid-wife that was assisting us eventually agreed that our little baby was stuck and that a doctor was needed. By this point, I didn't care about the baby anymore, all I cared about was that they helped my wife and relieved her from this pain. She looked so lost and scared and helpless, a look of confusion in her eyes. The mixture of chemicals and gas and air had all added to her current state. The mid-wife had mistakenly decided that Tiana was off with the fairies and that it was best to ignore her outbursts. It took a lot of straining and getting nowhere before she realised the truth. We made our way from the room containing the birthing pool (long since empty, except from some indescribable bits floating in the water) and into another room, where they put Tiana in some stirrups. Then a young female Moslem doctor in a head-scarf and called Halima pulled out the vents-touts and placed it into Tiana's long-suffering vagina. The problem was that, every time Tiana pushed, once she stopped the baby went back up again; the vents-touts held the baby still after each push so that each one was achieving something.

By the third push, we could see the top of the little head – and it was covered in hair! I was rushing between Tiana's side and looking between her legs! Despite the occasion, I was still capable of childish thoughts and couldn't help thinking it looked like my lovely wife hadn't trimmed down below for quite a while. By the fourth push, the whole of the head was out! By this time, I was smiling and crying and saying silly things about how beautiful and amazing the little thing was, et cetera! I expected it to be crying or looking around with an expression of 'where the hell am I?' on its face, but there wasn't the slightest movement! The little eyes stayed closed. On the next push the dear little thing came out and they placed it on Tiana's chest, covering her in a clean towel.

"What is it?" cried Tiana. "Girl or boy?"

"Oh," I replied, forgetting all about looking at what sex it was. "It's a boy!"

"No it's not," she answered. I had been looking at the umbilical cord and just assumed... When I tell the story now, Tiana always make a remark about, if that were true it wouldn't have been *my* son. Thank you dear! "It's a girl!" I cried! I had a beautiful baby daughter and she was so small and sweet and cute, with a little head of hair and little bits of hair on her ears and back (they soon fell out)! She reminded me of a little naked mole rate, except far more beautiful of course! And the eyes, they were amazing! Dark, dark brown, almost black, just like her Mother's! She found her little helpless way to Tiana's nipple and began sucking. I looked up at the clock: 11 minutes past 12 on February 14th – Valentine's Day! And we called her Romilly. Tiana liked the name, so I went along with it.

Tuesday 14th February 2006 is the greatest day of our lives so far.

CHAPTER THIRTEEN: TREADING WATER

Children truly are amazing. If you want to find meaning to life, watch your child being born and develop and grow, become a proper little person. The first smile, the first little giggle, the first hug and kiss that they give you, the first time they roll, then crawl, then walk and run, then dance and communicate, first through sounds, then through words … She has her Mother's dark brown, slightly diagonal eyes, but a lot bigger; she has a nose that is completely flat between the eyes, but comes out like a little button; and so much hair! She had her first haircut at 11 months! It's long, brown and very curly! She is the most beautiful thing I've ever seen, even more so than Tiana on our wedding day and that's saying something! Tiana and I fell in love with her at first sight. I live for my wife and child, which is no more than should be expected from a father and husband. After a few months, I was hassling my poor wife to produce the next one! Tiana told me I should try crapping a watermelon before being so enthusiastic.

If you really want to know what life is, hold your new born baby in your arms and look into their eyes; look at the little fingers, the tongue, the toes. Life is lying there looking back at you. Forget your churches or your temples; keep your robes and hymns; idols are no more than lifeless stone; words mere sounds. When you've created another human being and you see that little bundle of joy for the first time, nothing else matters; not your anxieties, your fears – nothing. It doesn't get any more beautiful than that.

OCD can be hereditary. I'm aware that little Romilly could develop it, so I've always watched her for signs. I can recognise them a mile off. If she does anything, I'll break her out of the behaviour, not let it develop in the way it developed in me. Having a child is not just about producing a physical creature, it's also about looking after someone that experiences and has emotions and laughs and suffers and feels pain and pleasure. She will feel anxiety and a lack of control. But if I can stop those negative patterns from forming in her brain, I will. She's not going to suffer like I have. She's going to have a fruitful life. And Tiana and I will bring her up to be more like my wife than like me. To not be so cynical or pessimistic, especially about people; to get everything she can from life, to enjoy as much as there is to experience. We're all a long time dead, after all.

For nearly eighteen months following Romilly's birth, my OCD played little part in my life. My job was going well, my family life was near to perfect, we had a lovely house and made loads of great friends in Petersfield. There were our neighbours, Steve and Karen and their two daughters, who we became very close to; then there were all the other couples we had met at ante-natal classes. And of course our families were nearby. It was support. And we would need it.

Looking back, as wonderful as those times were I was merely treading water with my OCD. I hadn't crushed it. I had learnt to manage it, but it was still a part of me, albeit no more than having a lisp is part of somebody: restrictive, but not debilitating. And given where I had come from, it was a huge improvement on my standard of living.

I felt pretty good about myself. By the time of Romilly's first birthday, I felt like I had nailed this OCD malarkey as far as I ever would. I took the fluvoxamine, or 'mental boy pills' as we affectionately called them, each evening before I went to bed. But how much good did they really do? After all, I would still get the repetitive sentences in my head and I had to avoid coughing. When I did have to cough, I made sure a neutral sentence past through my head at that time.

Around March 2007 I stopped taking my medication.

It takes around three months for fluvoxamine to leave your system.

The previous November, our office managing partner had announced that we were to move offices. The Petersfield office would be closed, as would the Fareham and Poole offices. They were to be amalgamated with the Southampton branch.

In July 2007, the move took place. There are several ways into Southampton and all of them involve a long queue. Once into the centre, you are then faced with numerous sets of traffic lights before reaching the NCP car park, where we had been designated a space. From there our office was a ten minute walk away via the rat-infested park. Some of those rodents are the size of cats. I don't mind rats, but they held a kind of symbolism for the place where my life was now heading.

If I woke at six, the journey could take just over an hour door to door, arriving at around eight o' clock; provided I could leave at four o' clock, it would take around an hour and twenty minutes to get home, otherwise it would exceed an hour and a half. Inevitably, the strict working hours I was keeping and the earlier mornings meant I was far less efficient. As much as I enjoyed working there, I knew I could not keep this up.

As for my family life, by July 2007 the harmony of our first few months in Petersfield had long since come to an end. It was around September 2006 when little Romilly fell ill. She picked up a nasty stomach bug that made her projectile vomit. I remember that first night so clearly. We heard her crying over the monitor at around ten o' clock in the evening and ran up to her room to see if she was alright – there was sick everywhere! Tiana picked her up and she projectile vomited everywhere! After every retch, she was crying inconsolably. It was heartbreaking. You could see the fear in her eyes and our inability to communicate with her made it so much harder. I took her from Tiana and ran into the bathroom with her so she could throw up into the sink. Tiana was going crazy, petrified at what was happening to our little girl. Eventually, she stopped. She was so tired, bless her. She eventually fell asleep in my arms, still crying.

We took up to our room to sleep there for the night. She woke a couple more times. We decided to call NHS Direct, who told us to ring an ambulance. The three of us were taken to Chichester hospital (the closest) by ambulance, the siren going. There we feared the worst as they carried out various tests. Meningitis was the word that we were most afraid of hearing.

Thank the Lord, it was just a stomach bug. She should drink plenty of water and whatever else could be kept down. Milk was a priority. After that, anything solid would be good. However, we were reliably informed that babies of her age could live solely on milk and water for many weeks.

By her own admission, Tiana did not cope with Romilly's illness. It was the not eating that really got to her. She went for quite a few weeks on milk, yoghurt and water. There were times when we got too confident if she held food down for any period of time and would try to give her more; inevitably, she would throw it all back up.

By November, Romilly was back to normal, eating healthily and enjoying her food. She had always been very active and by December she was walking without any assistance! Tiana was not so good. I tried to understand, but I failed miserably. I tried to be the strong husband, not showing any weakness, but Tiana said I seemed to lack emotion; so I tried talking the problems through with her, but Tiana said she didn't need to hear the voice of reason, she just wanted somebody to listen; so I listened and she told me off for not talking. And we drifted apart.

We played well together, but it seemed that we were not so compatible at the working side of things. Tiana wanted to do things a certain way and I just wasn't able to follow instructions. We carried on in this vein for the next few months, neither of us doing enough to bring us back together.

It was July 2007. I was getting up early each morning, driving the long and frustrating journey into work, arriving tired. In the evenings, I would get home, play with Romilly, bath her and put her to bed. By the time I had eaten and tidied the kitchen and carried out any other housework that needed to be done, it was getting on for nine o' clock.

It was July 2007 that I found myself a new job. But I had to give three months notice. I would not start until October. The delay was to prove a blessing.

It was July 2007 and I coughed because I needed to neutralise a bad thought. I did it the once and it felt pretty good – I got a certain sense of control and certainty from doing it. But I also felt bad for doing it and slightly anxious: was OCD on its way back into my life?, I began to wonder.

CHAPTER FOURTEEN: MY FRENCH INCARCERATION

We were due to go on holiday in August. It was our first vacation for over two years and our first with Romilly. We had really been looking forward to it. But throughout July I had been digressing rapidly, despite having started taking the fluvoxamine again. By the beginning of August, I was back to how I had been two years ago. Tiana had noticed.

"Don't worry," I reassured her, "I'm on top of it." Armed with a sense of reality and a desire to not return to those dark days, I was sure I would beat it again.

But I was wrong.

By the time our holiday had arrived, I had added a horrible new dimension to the ritual: if I had done the 'bad act' whilst touching Romilly, I could only 'neutralise' it by carrying out the ritual whilst touching Romilly. By this stage, words with 'c' or 'k' in it could amount to a cough (like 'c' in 'card'); sometimes if the release of air in my throat was to be carried out in an 'eh' sound, this could be construed as a cough too. This new development in my freaky behaviour made one huge difference: I could no longer hide it from Tiana (or at least not to the extent that I had done before). Like any good mother, she was to put the safety of her child first.

Tiana had picked out the most beautiful gites for us to stay. It was in a small village called St Giron, just south of Toulouse and lay in the shadow of the Pyrenees. As seems to be the norm, it was owned by an English couple who had taken an old run-down barn and turned it into a beautiful idyllic holiday home. By the time we arrived, my relatively upbeat mood and the beautiful surroundings suppressed my 'thought parasite' for a couple of days. Tiana would ask how I was feeling and I said I felt fine, but it was best not to discuss it so I could push it to the back of my mind.

In my typical fashion, I had to try out all the local delicacies, at the expense of Tiana's nose and despite my history of having the squirts whenever abroad (raw fish did it for me in the Philippines; it was the turn of jelly fish in China; snails did the job in Bruges). So I stuffed myself with oysters, snails and fruit des mers of various shapes, sizes and colours. Oh, then there was the cheese: "Je voudrais fromage tres faux!" I requested to the cheese-man at the local supermarche. "Tres faux?!" he exclaimed, a wry smile stretching across his face. "Oui!" I hardily confirmed. And it was gorgeous! Although Tiana made me leave it outside in the garden as the smell was that strong. When removing my trainers that I had been wearing all that hot day without socks, the stench was almost identical to that of the cheese. But far from putting me off, it just made me want to slice off a bit of my foot and have it on a bit of baguette, washed down with a fine glass of vin rouge!

Then came the trip to Biarritz to meet up with my folks: they were on holiday in San Sebastian, Spain, so we thought it would be nice to meet half way for the day. And with that came an anxious car journey. And with that came O-crapping-C-sodding-D.

It's stressful being on the wrong side of the road on the wrong side of the car. The gearstick kept disappearing for one thing, replaced by a door! Then there was the natural inclination to position myself towards the centre of the road which led to many directional expletives from Tiana! This was completely unjustified, I thought, until I scraped the side of the car going down a narrow side street. So to add to my anxiety I had Tiana feeling scared out of her wits and giving me a running commentary of what I should be doing. Romilly remained oblivious to all this as she sat in the back singing to herself or practising her speech.

To my credit, I lasted two-thirds of the journey before the thought crept in. "I don't care!" I replied to Tiana. "I'm going five miles over the speed limit!" Then it hit me: had the 'c' in 'care' come out as a cough? I started to replay the sentence back in my head, but wasn't convinced that I had remembered it properly to be sure. Tiana was shouting something at me, but I wasn't listening – all I could think of was whether I'd coughed or not. Shit, shit, shit! Right, I thought, I need to concentrate. I said the line in my head first to practice: "Romilly dies when she's over one hundred years old and God makes sure of that," with the cough coming on the hundred, and then I would need to say in my head "shut up" to bring it to an end.

In my head: "Romilly dies when she's over one hundred [cough] years old and God makes sure of that!" I did it! But then the line seemed to come into my head: "and kills her!" Shit!

"What are you doing?" cried Tiana.

"I sneezed!" I lied.

"No you didn't!" she replied. "If you're going to do that, you can't drive too!"

"I'm fine now," I lied again. I did it again and added and 'never kills her' to the end; then I did it again, quick as a flash and louder this time, again successfully, shaking my head on the 'never' bit and closing my eyes momentarily. I had done it!

"What the hell are you doing?" cried Tiana, quite rightly, a real sense of panic coming over her.

"I'm fine now," I said, quickly remembering to add a 'shuttup' in my head.

"You're not bloody fine!" she shouted, clearly shaken. "You weren't even looking at the road!" You're going to kill us all!"

"There was nothing near us," I replied. "I checked." In all my idiocy, I had checked.

"Pull over," she demanded.

I pulled over to the hard shoulder. Tiana grabbed the keys from the ignition.

"What do we do? What do we do?" she was asking herself, an anxiety and franticness in her tone.

"It's okay," I said, trying to sound calm. "I completed the ritual. I'm okay now, I promise."

"I don't believe you," she replied. And what if you feel like doing it again?"

"I promise if I feel like doing it again, I won't until we stop," I answered. "I promise. Please calm down!"

"Calm down?"she exclaimed. "How can I calm down? You almost killed us!"

"I didn't," I replied.

"I'm driving," she said suddenly.

"You can't – you're not insured on this," I replied. Listen, just let me drive. I promised I'll be fine.

"Promise me," pleaded Tiana after a while, "that you'll tell me if you feel like doing something."

"I promise," I replied. She handed the keys back to me and we went on our not so merry way.

I had two more urges for the rest of the journey, but I claimed to need the toilet both times because I had the squirts and would 'cack' myself otherwise. I blamed the perfectly good cheese. Both times, I sneaked into a service station and coughed my little heart out.

We arrived in Biarritz around half an hour late to meet my parents. Tiana was blissfully unaware and thinking all was finally hunky dory (haven't used that expression in years).

Being a supporter of Northampton Saints rugby club, Biarritz was a well known name to me, the two towns coming across each other regularly in the European Cup. So it was fascinating to see the place. It was full of colour, lots of people, interesting architecture and had a good vibe to it. My parents were in fine fiddle too, my Dad being relatively lively for him, whilst my dear old Mum was enjoying the extra attention he had been giving her. Unbelievably, they even held hands at one point.

"Look", whispered Tiana, pointing it out and giggling.

"I know," I whispered back. "If they carry on like that I might end up with a sibling!"

"That would be clever," she replied, "considering he's had the snip and your Mum's had a hysterectomy."

"Good point!" I replied. "But don't underestimate the power of my family's testicles!"

We ate at the seafront at a lovely seafood restaurant. Despite Tiana's pleading, given my delicate stomach, I still went for oysters and crab. Firstly, I knew the truth; secondly, it would give me an excuse to nip to the loo at any given opportunity; thirdly, it would provide us all with the chance to have a laugh about it later. Thankfully, all that day I only had one coughing fit. Embarrassingly, I could not find anywhere to hide, so I slipped down a side-street whilst Tiana and my Mum were shopping and my Dad was sitting outside relaxing.

"I'm going for a wander," I said. I walked down a narrow lane that adjoined the street with the seafront. It was relatively quiet, with only a handful of people using it at any one time. And I coughed and I coughed. I sat down and coughed so hard I fell backwards and landed on my back. A group of people laughed and I smiled back at them to say,

"I'm normal – I just fell!", but they averted their eyes and their faces said it all.

Eventually, I made my way back to my Dad who was by now asleep. I tried to lighten my mood.

"Why are you kissing the dog's penis?" I whispered in his ear. I had been told that you can influence somebody's dreams by whispering obscurities into their ear. "It's nice – you like the taste – like a lollipop."

"Are you two ready then?" said Tiana, suddenly appearing behind us with Romilly in the pram and my Mother smiling, but looking typically anxious. Tiana had one too many carrier bags for my liking.

"Spending our money again?" I asked.

My Dad woke at this point, looking slightly perplexed.

"Strange dreams?" I enquired.

"No," he answered quickly, looking at me with a guilty conscience. I've no idea whether it worked, but I'd like to think so. Anyway, he wouldn't admit it if I had asked.

The rest of the day went well and was pretty uneventful. We said goodbye quite late into the evening.

"Take care," I said, as we turned and left. Shit! Had the 'c' in 'care' been a cough? And had I said 'kill' in my head at the same time? And had I then said Romilly? And I was holding her at the time! And I had spoken loudly! Shit, shit, shit! I would need to do a really loud cough this time.

I spent the journey to the car trying to convince myself that I had not coughed but to no avail. By the time we got there, I carried out the ritual, stepping in front of the pram and grabbing Romilly's little hand! But she pulled away just as I was coughing!

"Get off of her!" Tiana cried. "What are you trying to do?"

"I need to touch her whilst I'm doing the ritual," I explained, trying to grab her leg this time.

"No you don't!" shouted Tiana and pushed me away from Romilly. I kept hold of her little leg and held it tight and coughed the words – but hadn't done it right! I cuddled Romilly again, but again it didn't feel right.

"Get off of her!" cried Tiana. "You're scaring her!"

I looked at Romilly's beautiful face: she looked confused, but not scared. Tiana pushed me out of the way and took Romilly out of the pushchair. I grabbed them both and did another ritual, then let go, then did it again, but still I couldn't get it right!

Tiana kicked me hard in the shin and jumped inside with Romilly, locking herself in. I banged on the door.

"Please let me do it right and I'll be okay!" I pleaded. "I won't have to do it again, I promise!"

We had caused a scene and people were gathering around. Tiana was crying her eyes out asking for help from other drivers and passers by.

"What is the matter?" one gentleman asked me.

"My wife," I replied, "she's upset with me."

Another gentleman walked over to the window and knocked on it. Tiana wound it down slightly.

"He's my husband," I can still hear her say to this day, "he's not well! Call a doctor! You *must* call a doctor!"

And all hell had broken loose. Through it all I was still scheming as to how I could get Romilly out of the car and finish the ritual. I tried all doors; I contemplated smashing a window. People were telling me to calm down in French accents; a vicar stood there bemused, possibly thinking I was possessed; Tiana was pleading through a gap in a window; I was shouting, crying, pleading, screaming; the traffic: hooting of horns, sirens, police, ambulance. Then nothing. I collapsed in the road, laying there crying like a child. I needed to complete the ritual properly, but couldn't get there. They put me in the ambulance and took me away.

I lay in the back, in a state of hopelessness, anxiety and tension running up and down my limbs, that by now all too familiar feeling of dread travelling at a rate of knots through my veins. The ambulance man in the back of the van helped to calm me, but he could only do so much. We talked about rugby and Northampton; we talked about the hairiness of Chabal and he seemed to be telling me how his name was French for 'cannibal' – I could see that! But I needed to see Romilly again, hold her tightly, love her, have her skin touching mine – and cough.

In the hospital, I spoke to a doctor, her talking in pigeon English, me in cockerel French. She asked what was wrong. Anxiety is a similar word in French. Even better, I discovered the 'o' and the 'c' are the same, but not the 'd'. She asked me to explain what exactly I did. I said I needed my daughter with me to show her. That was a convenient way for me to perform the ritual. She said they haven't arrived yet. I kept asking for them. "Je voudrais regarder ma famille, s'il vous plait?", I asked. More questions. I tried my best to answer. I explained I was not aggressive, just passionate. Questions about my medication. I explained: "faverin ou fluvoxamine; un dans le matin; un dans le soir". She wrote it down. "Je voudrais regarder ma famille, si'l vous plait?" They have not arrived. Could she find out when? She would tell me when. How long have I been like this? Now there's a question! Is it a trait, or a disorder or am I OCD itself? I believe it's the former that can lead to the second and pray it's not the latter. I'm sure it's not. The questions kept coming. I tried to answer as best as I could. "Je voudrais regarder ma famille, si'l vous plait?" "Non parce que…" "Si'l vous plait?" Through pleading tears. "Mais monsieur…", "s'il vous plait?" by now a tearful hopeless whisper.

Then eventually: "Your wife, she is arrive." At last! How I longed to hug Romilly again and finish this bloody thing.

"Oh!" I cried, jumping out of my seat. I opened the door, ran to my family crying and holding Romilly! At last! Had to do it right, and I coughed again.

"You're hurting her!"

It felt okay. I stepped back. They led me back into the room. "I'm sorry," I cried. But Tiana's face looked confused and scared, as though she didn't know me any more. I noticed my parents standing there. They looked bewildered. They had known nothing of my condition.

I sat down with the doctor once more.

"Je compris," she claimed. I did not know the French for, 'I doubt it', so I pulled a face of disbelief and shrugged.

Then it occurred to me – had I told God to make sure she was one hundred years old or had I just said it as a statement? I needed to do it again! I jumped up and went for the door, two male nurses holding me back; I shrugged them to one side and made my way through the door; I barged another man out of the way; I could see Tiana cowering against the wall the other side of the room, holding Romilly tightly, and I ran to her; my Dad tried to stop me, but I flung him to one side and finally held her. And I coughed. And this time it was right. Two doctors grabbed me either side. I thought about lifting them and tipping them upside down, but there was no longer any need. My body had gone from adrenalin-pumped muscle to a limp bag of bones. I did not want to hurt anyone anyway. They pushed me to the floor. Six of them, I think. I caught a vision of Tiana shaking and crying, my parents trying to comfort her.

"Sedate him!" she cried through blubbering and tears. I can picture her face to this day; still hear the words. "You've got to sedate him!"

They lay me on a table, still pinning me down. Six men, two women. The needle came and pierced my right bum cheek. I lay there talking to one of the nurses, a pretty blonde lady.

"It's not working," I was saying to her, feeling convinced of its impotency.

Then I was gone.

A bed in a strange room. Water – I needed water. A bottle was next to the bed. I slurped. Slept. People round me. My arm out. "We take blood." Dark again. So thirsty. More water. I woke again. Then slept. Then awake. Each time awake for a little longer. I wore a yellow suit, like most of the others. Where were my clothes, I wondered. And my wallet? Then sleep. More water. Four empty litre bottles. I needed to get out of this state. To get back to normal. What day was it? Maybe one night had past, maybe two. I ventured out of my room. 1528 was the number. I was given medicine. I was given food. Can't remember much about it. Next meal, I decided to drink the coffee and down another two glasses. Plenty of sugar. I had to wake properly. Energy stimulants. I did not know what drugs they were giving me. Maybe faverin. Maybe something to keep me sedated. I was so sleepy. I pretended to take them but threw them away. I was feeling better, beginning to think straight again. In time, I awoke properly.

"Au jourd'hui?" I asked. "Jeudi ou vendredi?"

"Vendredi, monsieur," she replied. I was right. Two days had past since I had been brought here, wherever 'here' was. Despite my condition I still had an awareness of time. Small comfort. Now I knew how those poor people had felt when

169

the calendar was changed to the Gregorian and moved forward a few days.

"Let's just let me stay here for a day and then we'll go back to the gites," I suggested to Tiana.

"No," she replied. "I've already booked my flight. I'm off tomorrow. I've got to go back. I want to see my Mum."

I pleaded but she would not listen.

"I've wasted all this money," I said, sighing.

"Don't worry about the money," she answered. "All I care about is you getting back to normal. We can go away another time."

"I'm sorry," I said.

"It's not your fault," she replied. "You can't help it. I love you so much and just want my Mark back."

"I love you so much too. You're the greatest wife any man could wish for."

I was in a hospital in Bayonne, near Biarritz, by all accounts. Tiana had made her way back to the gites and would leave as soon as possible. Arrangements would be made for my passport to be sent to the hospital and for Europe Assistance to send a doctor to meet me and travel back home with me where I would be taken by ambulance to see Tiana again and maybe to a UK hospital. The passport should arrive on Saturday.

I woke that next morning, but no passport had arrived.

"Perhaps later today," they said. "Perhaps not till Monday. We cannot be sure."

Monday? I couldn't possibly wait until then. And how long after that would it take to get a flight? I was feeling hopeless. I spoke to Tiana on the phone regularly. If I was annoying the medical staff, they did not show it. In fact, they were brilliant, very calm and very understanding.

Maybe it was the drugs, maybe the attitude of the staff, maybe the realisation that I was far better off than the other patients there (some of whom were real 'fruits de la toots', as my sister-in-law puts it). Whatever the reason, that Saturday I resigned myself to the fact that I was in a mental institute for a few days so I might as well make the most of it. First things first, I got my clothes back to help me feel more normal. Next I kept myself occupied. There were a few jigsaw puzzles there. I began with a nice easy 100 piece Asterix puzzle. Then I attempted the five hundred piece Yorkshire terrier puzzle, only to discover after a good couple of hours that there were around fifty pieces missing! I was tempted to throw a wobbly but, fearing that they might consider me to be a genuine loony and stick another needle in my arse, I resisted. Maybe it was the bloody jigsaw puzzles that sent them all mad!

Giving up with the puzzles, I began building towers out of dominoes (there were two sets and, surprise, surprise, both had pieces missing). The first tower fell down on the last piece, frustrating this old woman who told me off. She had the kind of face you'd pull if somebody farted in your cornflakes. She kept sneering at me, so I did it a couple more times to really piss her off. It was childish but made me feel better and took my mind off everything.

Then I began to draw. Just silly cartoons at first. I did a caricature of one of the patients. He laughed.

"Tres bon!" he cried through his large spectacled grey-bearded Uncle-Albertesque face. "Je m'appelle Jean-Baptiste."

"Bonjour, Jean-Baptiste," I replied. "Je m'appelle Mark.

He asked me something or other in French. I didn't have a clue what he was talking about.

"Je suis anglais," I responded. "Je ne parlez pas francais."

But that didn't stop him. He proceeded to talk to me in French, barely pausing for breath. I let him get on with it and we seemed to get on very well considering neither of us had a clue what the other was saying. At first I would try and converse, but eventually the conversations ran as follows:

"Gibber gibber d'acore gobble-di-goop avoir blah blah!"

"I can't agree more," I would rely.

"Irdy birdy hoh-hi-hoh la la," he would continue.

In the end I decided to talk to him about a giant chicken that ate a whole village down the road from my town. He showed an amazing lack of surprise at such a turn of events so either he came from a town where mass-murdering overgrown poultry were an everyday occurrence or, more likely, he hadn't understood me either.

And there were other characters there that are also worthy of a mention. There was the 'ghost lady' who would walk up and down the corridor making a 'whoo-hooh' sound like a ghost (or how they're supposed to sound, which I cannot confirm). She would occasionally break into a fit and need to be calmed down. There was a strange Moroccan looking man who would sit on the same chair all day and apparently thought he was a doctor. I would greet him with a "bonjour docteur" when I saw him, which he seemed to like, although it sometimes led to him wanting to tap the palm of my hand five times. I wondered whether he had a touch of the old OCD too – poor sod! That really would be a sign of madness.

There were others that were far more normal. Some were just very quiet; some seemed to suffer from some form of depression or paranoia, I guessed. One patient even came to my rescue, supplying me with deodorant every day after I ran out. They all seemed harmless and friendly and all spoke to me, even when I went on about the giant carnivorous chicken. Tiana told me to be careful about doing that in case the doctors decided I was insane after all, so I calmed it down a bit and made the chicken into a vegetarian.

I cannot say a bad word about the doctors, nurses, the food and the hospital as a whole. They were all very courteous and friendly and seemed to recognise that I was normal and only there for bureaucratic reasons. A couple of times they let me eat with them rather than the other patients. Whatever I asked for they would try their best to provide for me. I would often sit with them and chat about my beautiful wife and daughter or the rugby, the weather, or anything. They liked my drawings too and put my caricature of Martin Johnson up on their notice board.

That Saturday my spirits were lifted even higher when my Father came to see me. When I saw him I ran over and hugged him. I did not cry, but I felt like it and I'm sure he felt the same. There was something in his eye that day, something that I had not noticed before – a genuine affection, love even. We went and sat in my room and talked in a way in which we'd never spoken before.

"I've brought some of my clothes for you to wear," he began, and emptied a bag of tee-shirts and pants. "I know they're not quite your style, but they should do for now."

"It's okay," I replied. "Fashion is not a big thing here. And anyway I've always though you dressed like a weirdo, so the clothes should be perfect for this place." The truth is they were actually quite good clothes, but I didn't tell him that. "How long did it take to get here?"

"Three hours," he replied. "It would have been less, but they moved you to a different hospital and I had to find the way. What's it like here?"

"Everyone's really friendly," I replied.

"It seems very clean," said Dad. "And they all seem pleasant. Apparently there are more insane people in France than anywhere else in Europe, so they should be good at it!"

"It's more difficult to find the sane ones," I joked. "I'm ill Dad."

"Mmm," he replied in a questioning/understanding tone.

"I have obsessive-compulsive disorder," I confirmed. "I've always had it. It's possibly genetic, you know."

"That'll be your Mother's fault then," he joked.

"Yes," I replied. "Your side only gave me the Tourette's and the schizophrenia! It's like my brain doesn't function smoothly. If I have a problem, 'A', then I find a solution for dealing with it, 'B', but it's not always the right one. In fact, quite often it's the wrong one completely. But once that connection is formed, every time I get to 'A' my brain tells me to do 'B' and the more times I do it, the harder it is to ignore. It's like a car alarm going off and I can't stop it until I've done 'B'. I can try and ignore it and get on with something else, but that alarm is still going off and as soon as I stop doing an activity it comes back as loud as ever."

"What are you scared of?" asked Dad.

"Losing Romilly," I replied. "Something terrible happening to her."

"Why?"

"Because terrible things happen to people," I said, shrugging.

"Let me tell you something," he began. "I'm also afraid of bad things happening. Everybody is, unless they really don't care about anything. And you don't want to be like that. I worry about things happening to your Mum or you. We never had any more kids because we thought one was enough to worry about! I regret it now though: we let our fears get the better of us!"

"Yes," I interrupted, "you could have had a much better kid if only you'd tried."

"Better?" said my Dad, genuinely taken aback. "You're the best son a man could ask for! You've done well at school, got a degree, got yourself a decent job and, most of all, you have a beautiful and brilliant wife that I'm proud to call my daughter-in-law! Even if she is Welsh!" He laughed. "And as for Romilly, she's the most amazing little thing."

"Thanks Dad," I replied. "I never saw my life like that, but I guess you're right."

"Don't let your fears hold you back," he continued. "Conquer them. You're still young enough for hopes to not become regrets. The world is a beautiful place with so much to see and to offer. Whenever I get silly thoughts in my head like not walking on the cracks in the pavement or under ladders, I do it! I say to hell with this stupidity, and I do it anyway. And that way it never controls me."

"But I'm too far gone to stop doing certain things," I said. "Like saying things in my head."

"Just put other thoughts in your head," he replied. "Think about nice things. Bad thoughts will sit at the front of your mind if you keep calling on them. The more you push them back, the less likely they are to resurface."

"But they can still come back," I said. "Like if I'm in a dangerous situation."

"Well anticipate them," he answered. "And decide the best way to react. Make sure you've done everything in your power and once you're sure then that's all you can do. You can't control everything so don't bother trying."

"But I can't leave everything to chance," I persisted.

"That's why you need something beyond that," he responded. "I want to tell you the most important thing you can ever know: whatever you do, wherever you are, you must have a belief. Everybody needs a belief beyond the material world. A belief that someone is looking after you up there. For me, it's God and my Mum. I believe they're always looking after me, making sure I'll be okay. And when I wake in the night feeling scared or anxious I walk over to the window and look for that brightest star up there and know my Mum is sitting upon it, looking down on me, looking after me. And I know everything will be okay. You've got to believe in something."

"Is she looking at me too then?" I asked.

"Of course," he replied.

"I do believe in God," I said. "Even though sometimes I doubt the plausibility or how it all adds up or the things that I read in the Bible and get confused by it all, I still believe. Even when I worry that my brain has grown with the impression that there's a God because its been indoctrinated in me, even though science can prove that this is possible or that is possible, even then, I still know deep down that God exists and he loves me. Although I reckon he loves Tiana and Romilly more!"

"Who wouldn't?" We both laughed.

"Thanks Dad," I said. "You've never spoken like this to me before."

"You know me," he replied. "I bottle up my emotions because of my fears. Just like your Mum does the opposite and lets them run riot! But know this: no matter what we say or do, we love you more than anything else in the world and we're both proud to call you our son – your Mother insisted that I tell you that. I said you already know."

"I guess I knew, but it's nice to hear it!"

"Well," said Dad, standing, "I guess I'd better make a move. It's two and a half hours back and your Mother will be panicking over how you are and whether I get back safely. I can tell her everything's fine, I think."

"She should have come," I suggested.

"I told her not to," he replied. "If it wasn't very nice, I was planning on lying to her." I smiled.

And with that he was gone. A spirit had suddenly appeared in him that I had never seen before and it was lovely.

From that day on I saw my parents in a completely different light. My Dad was a proud, caring man, who wanted to be strong and dedicated to his family; my Mum was loving, temperamental, emotional and caring; and both loved me dearly and would never have me any other way (not even as a girl).

Upbeat, I spent the rest of that day drawing silly pictures and trying to make the nurses laugh. Most of them understood my humour and they all loved my cartoons.

The next couple of days were calm, tranquil and almost holiday-camp like. I resigned myself to the fact that I would be there until at least Monday and possibly more. I had access to a phone if I needed to speak to Tiana. She was back in England by Sunday morning and had decided to stay with her Mum for a bit, so I knew she was safe.

As well as drawing, I played 'babyfoot' (table football), table-tennis, 'shot some hoops' and played les boules with a few of the residents. Les boules (or petonk) is easy enough to play: the one who gets his bowl closest to the jack gets the point and if the second or third were closer than any other players' he would get two or three points respectively (each player has three bowls). But what was confusing was when each person was entitled to bowl. I gave up trying to understand and just did as I was told. One old boy thought he was the bees' knees; his favourite trick was to smack another bowl out of the way. When I did it to his, he became quite upset and had to suppress his desire to throw a wobbly. Childishly I called him names in English and put on a smile so he wouldn't know I was being rude.

There were two other main activities I carried out to pass the time. The first was a memory trick: I memorised each card in a standard deck by association: for example, Princess Diana was the Queen of Hearts because that was what she famously declared her intention to be; or the Ace of Hearts was the universe because it represented one pumping heart, spreading life through the cosmos. Having now mastered all fifty two cards, I can pull off a card trick whereby somebody shuffles the deck, I quickly flick through them making a story to connect the cards, then can ask a person to remove the card and then say which card is missing; alternatively, I can do the pure memory trick of reciting the order back to them.

The other major activity for me was to commence writing my book about two dog detectives. It is a children's tale about a cunning beagle and his haphazard sidekick as they try to solve the mystery of some stolen jewellery. It's a fun little tale featuring nine-shooters (to shoots cats with – nine lives, you see!), barkney – instead of cockney – dodgy dealers (not PC, but that's me for you!), drinking toilet water, monkeys being the dog equivalent and all kinds of weird ideas. It also meant I could do the drawings, caricaturing various breeds of dogs, cats, baboons, and goats and the world they live in. Who knows? It may get published one day.

My situation and free time and temporary independence also gave me a chance for reflection. Yes, I was in a mental institution, so there was obviously something not quite right with me. But no, I clearly was not mad (whatever that may mean). I could lead a normal life and had done (relatively speaking). I needed medicine to keep me on the straight and narrow, but so do diabetics. My illness was mental, but that only means the physical part of me that does not function properly is my brain, as opposed to a kidney or liver. I wonder whether a transplant is the answer, but that probably wouldn't be me. I understand too that we're emotional creatures and the brain is created from an emotion: the need to survive. That all the paraphernalia and tools that the core of the brain has surrounded itself with help us rationalise, but essentially we're emotional beings that can rationalise not rational beings that get emotional. The more rational the person, the better equipped she is at using these tools. It just so happens that I need a bit more help than most.

I have also come to realise that I am nothing without love and laughter in my life. I need to have people to care about and I need to be laughing and not taking life too seriously. It helps me suppress my OCD, of course, but first and foremost, it's me.

Monday morning came and so too did my passport. Doctor Lafond told me the good news. I had spoken to him before along with his friendly sidekick, but I couldn't remember when. I guessed it must have been during my couple of days with the fairies. And there were so many nurses and helpers and cleaners that there were very few I could generally place. The announcement of the arrival of my passport was a relief. If it had not arrived soon after I think I would have become a genuine patient. However, with it came the news that I would not be leaving until Wednesday – two more days! I could just about handle that, but not any more than that. I would be flying from Bilbao airport which was just over the border in Spain.

"I can't wait to see you again," said Tiana. "I really miss you."

"I miss you too," I replied. "Still, it's only two days – nothing really!"

By now, Tiana was back home with her Mother. I hated having put her through all of this. I just wanted to hug her and let her know everything would be alright.

The next two days went by reasonably quickly. I kept myself busy drawing and working on my book, *Bernard Bartholomew and The One That Got Away*. I thought of reading it to Romilly once she was old enough and could understand. I started drawing the pictures for it too, caricaturising various breeds of dogs, as well as a lion, a panther, some baboons and a goat! The other patients would come and sit with me or stand behind, looking over my shoulder, fascinated by my drawings.

It rained on the morning before my departure. I stood by the patio door looking out and reflecting on everything that happened. If I was to be a good Father and husband, I knew I needed to be rid of this illness for good. I walked out into the rain and looked up at the French sky, feeling the cool water hit my face. It felt soothing. The reality of the physical world helped to put my illness into perspective. But I was feeling upbeat too because I knew I was nearing the end of my French incarceration, my self-made nightmare. But my positive feelings hid the truth of the future for me: this was just the beginning of a long sentence.

The UK doctor arrived around 10 o' clock that morning. He was a really pleasant laidback guy with an unplaceable accent: there was a bit of West country, thrown in with some Scottish and Irish. When I brought the subject up with him, he confessed to being Northern Irish, but had spent his recent years in Scotland and now lived in Birmingham. Upon his arrival he spoke to me about my illness and the journey, assessing how 'dangerous' I would be to fly with. Given my relatively symptom-free past few days, I came across as normal and harmless and he seemed happy enough to travel with me.

Before I left, I said goodbye to all the friends I had made. The Arabic 'doctor' gave me one last diagnosis, rubbing my stomach and patting it a couple of times before passing me fit. Unfortunately, he also decided to let some spit travel from his mouth and hit my arm. With a reasonable amount of tact for me, I pretended to ignore it, but made my way to the toilet as soon as possible to thoroughly wash my arm. Once more, I got an insight into the lives of those poor hand-washers.

I left the hospital with misplaced optimism for the future.

On the journey back I talked and talked to the poor doctor – he suffered as a result of my lack of opportunities to have many conversations with somebody about more than just the weather for nearly a week. But he didn't seem to mind and was more than happy to reciprocate. I waffled on about tax saving techniques while he informed me about the ins and outs of being an anaesthetist. The journey took us through the Basque country to Bilbao Airport in Spain and then by business class to Heathrow, then finally by ambulance to meet with my beautiful wife.

As the ambulance made its way into Petersfield and to the surgery where we had arranged to meet, I went very quiet with anticipation and excitement! I could not wait to see Tiana again! And Romilly, of course, but she was still with Grandma and I would not see her until later. The ambulance turned the corner into the surgery and I spotted our car. Tiana appeared and walked over to us as we pulled up. Pulling the door open, I leapt out and ran to her. We hugged so tightly. I saw the look in her eyes, that look of love and longing and fear and the need to be hugged – I could read her eyes so well. She cried, then I cried. How I'd missed her lovely little face.

Tiana drove us back to her Mother's house where little Romilly was waiting. I was trying not to think about the rituals and how all this time I had wanted to complete it properly – to get the right feeling. I did not want that to be the first thing I did when we met up again. And I didn't do anything – not that day nor all that evening. Little Romilly was obviously pleased to see me, giving me lots of kisses and nice cuddles, but she didn't seem particularly affected or worried by the experience.

That night as I lay in bed holding Tiana tightly in my arms I felt a sense of relief that it was all over.

How wrong I was.

CHAPTER FIFTEEN: HELL

When I finally woke the next morning, Tiana was already up with Romilly and her Mother. I felt the sudden urge to complete the ritual. I lay there thinking whether I should carry it out or not. It had been over a week now and the urge had not gone away. I felt like it would never go away unless I did something about it. And it would only take a little while after all: a few seconds and it would all be over. But then again, maybe I might feel differently once I was with them all and I wouldn't need to do it, I explained to myself.

The morning past by without any incident. Being a rare hot Summer's day in 2007, we played in the garden after lunch, taking the paddling pool out. Little Romilly loved splashing about, although I had a sneaking suspicion that Mummy and Grandma were enjoying it even more! I remember desperately trying to join in with the fun and laughter, but that alarm bell kept going off in my head.

"Do you need a nappy change?" asked Tiana. I seized my opportunity.

"I'll do it," I quickly said.

"Are you going to be alright?" said Tiana, a worried look in her eye.

"I'll be fine," I lied.

"Do you want me to come with you?" she asked.

"No!" I replied in a slightly irritated tone.

I had to get this right, I remember thinking to myself. There would be no second opportunities. I bided my time. I had waiting many agonising days for this opportunity. I took off her trousers and nappy, wiped her down, put on a clean nappy, picked up from the changing mat and held her, touching the skin on her feet. Then I coughed. Bull's eye!

I made all the necessary checks to make sure I'd done it properly – I had! A sense of relief swept through me and I finally relaxed, despite the sudden appearance of Tiana and her Mother, rushing up the stairs and snatching her away from me.

"I knew it," cried Tiana, backing off and turning little Tiana away from my grasp.

"Sorry," I said, sighing. "I needed to do it. I've needed to since that day in France."

"What are we going to do?" cried Tiana, speaking mainly to herself.

"Come on, you," said Jenny. "Let's go for a walk."

Once outside, little doubts began to creep in: had I done it properly?, had I said the right thing? It was fine, I told myself. I needed to move on.

"What was that all about?" asked Tiana's Mother.

"I just needed to do it", I replied. "Ever since I was in France, I needed to do it properly."

"What do you mean, 'properly'?" Jenny asked.

"I don't really know," I answered. "Just until it felt right."

"She's been so worried," she said. "Worried about you. She's scared that you might hurt yourself or, worse, hurt Romilly."

"I'd never do that!" I insisted. "I've never even come close to hurting her!"

"Maybe you wouldn't hurt her on purpose," said Grandma. "Look, why don't the pair of you go out together for a nice meal? There's a good Indian about ten minutes from here. It'll give you both a chance to relax and spend some time on your own."

So we did.

We sat down and ordered our drinks: a white wine for Tiana and a coke for the mental boy. Then it started: had I coughed when I said 'coke'? No, I tried to convince myself. It's just the way it sounded. But the urge was too strong.

"I'm just going to the toilet," I said.

"You're not going to do your coughing in there?" asked Tiana.

"No," I lied.

"Promise?"

I smiled, went into the toilet and coughed. Then I came out and saw Tiana looking as if she was about to faint! I went to cuddle her, but before I had a chance I was pulled back inside the bathroom to cough once more! My heart desperately wanted to get back out there and hold her like she needed to be held, but my brain wouldn't let me go! Eventually I made my way out.

"That's it," I said to Tiana, hugging her and kissing her on the cheek. "No more for tonight.

So we ordered our food. But then I had another urge.

"I think I've left my phone in the car," I lied. "I'd better go and get it."

Tiana never said a word; she just sat there staring into space.

Outside, I coughed some more. Several times. Some of the fellow diners were looking at me. Eventually, I made my way back in. And sat down.

"You okay?" I asked Tiana: she was still staring into space but now she was shaking.

"I need to go," she said suddenly. She looked like she was about to throw up.

"I'm fine now," I said, smiling. But the lack of involvement of my eyes in the smile revealed it for the fraud that it was.

"Let's go!" she cried, standing up. She was panicking. "Get the bill."

Tiana stood outside whilst I paid the bill and waited for the food to take away. We could eat it at home instead, we explained to the waiter.

By the time we got to her Mother's, Tiana was visibly shaking. Grandma opened the door for us, having seen the car pull up, and Tiana fell into her arms, crying.

"You've got to stop this!" she cried. "You're turning my daughter into a nervous wreck!"

"I can't help it," I replied, a tone of despair in my voice. "It's my head." I held one finger against my right temple.

"Right," she continued, "both of you need to come in and calm down."

"I just need to go for a walk first," I replied. "I need to clear my head."

There was a little stream by their house that ran alongside a small patch of woodlands. A perfect place for me to shout my lungs out.

"Romilly dies *old*!" I cried, coughing on the 'old'. But had I said 'not' first? So I did it again, but this time said 'one hundred'! But had I said days or years? Then I did it again. And again. And soon ten minutes had gone by and I was no closer to getting the right feeling.

Tiana's Mum came out to look for me. She found me lying in the mud on the bank of the stream, my face down and coughing as loudly as I could manage.

"That's enough," she whispered to me, crouching down by my side and rubbing my back. "Let's get you inside and get you back to hospital." She helped me to my feet. "You've got to stop this now."

But I couldn't. I walked into the house, lay down and continued to cough. Then I cried like a baby and pleaded for somebody to help me stop this. "I can't take this anymore!" I said, weeping, "I can't break out of this!"

"It's alright," said Tiana, now crouched by my side. "We've phoned an ambulance. They're going to take you back to hospital where they can look after you properly."

"We all love you so much," said Grandma, kneeling the other side and stroking my hair. "We're going to make sure you're properly looked after.

Through the unceasing coughing, I remember their kind words, telling me how much they loved me. Despite my fear, I felt the warmth of their love. The ambulance drivers tried to talk to me, but I was too far gone, locked in a pattern of ritualistic behaviour.

The next few hours, everything happened around me and I was not a part of it, stuck in that little glass room that I thought I had reduced to shattered pieces two years before. I was there but I was not there: the journey to hospital, lying on the bed whilst poor Tiana whispered soothing messages in my ear, the journey to the Meadows and sitting there at two in the morning, waiting for them to get the room ready for me. Then, they lay me there to sleep and I soon dropped into Hell. I was firmly back at that place that I thought I'd never end up in again.

After just a few hours sleep, I woke that morning and coughed and coughed. Then I coughed some more. During a brief interval, they showed me round the rabbit-warren like set out: a pool room, an art room, the drinks machine, showers, toilets, bathroom, restaurant, TV rooms. It was all a blur. Every sound in my throat felt like a cough, but I resisted until the tour was over then went back to my room and coughed again.

Those next few days were very definitely the worst days of my life. I find it hard to even write about them. As I do so, I can hear the laughter of my wife and her friends downstairs, I can feel the warmth of another Christmas and thank God that I am home again. But I can still remember the darkness of those days and the fear that they could come back should I let my guard down is a very real fear. Still, it is important that I get them down on paper.

My days were filled with carrying out rituals. Each night, I would be given a concoction of tablets, including sleeping pills. I would turn out the light at 10 o' clock, hoping that the next time I woke it would be late morning. But it never was: every night I would wake in the early hours, thinking that I had coughed. So the rituals would begin, lasting several hours each time. When I did get the feeling that I had done it right, I would gingerly make my way back into bed, trying hard not to make any more throaty noises, ease myself down and pull the covers over, lying flat on my back. Inevitably, I would do something that felt like a cough and the routine would start all over again. As the hours went by, the pitch black turned to light and eventually, it would be dawn, then time for breakfast, which I would inevitably miss, being caught in the thick of a seemingly never ending ritual.

As time went on, the ritual of what I would have to say and do got longer and longer. The religious element had to be included: "Romilly dies old and God makes sure of that, Amen", then certain lines after that, such as "God is lovely", "Romilly does not die horribly", "Romilly leads a happy life"; and I had to be sure that I had not coughed when the time was divisible by 13 and would need to look at a number that was not divisible by 13 either. Then little Romilly's face would enter my head, or the visual image of certain words, so I would have to ensure that I saw her face or a good word at the point that I coughed and not whilst I was saying the bad word in my head. My whole existence had become a performance of rituals. I felt hopeless and damned.

After one ten hour bout, beginning at around 2 o' clock in the morning, I managed to crawl out of my room and into the corridor, desperate for someone to help me. I lay there on the floor, shaking, but trying to control my movements in case I set myself off again. But the staff just walked over me, ignoring my plight. One nurse even asked me to keep back against the wall out of the way of people walking past. Eventually, one lad, a fellow patient called Leo, helped me onto my feet and led me out into the garden. He spoke to me, asked what was wrong, but I could not answer – my voice had gone with all the coughing. He led me out into the garden and sat me down in a chair, then walked to the other side, pulled out a cigarette and started smoking it.

I looked around at my fellow in-mates. Most had a look of feeling lost and withdrawn. Some were so far gone, any sign of life did not seem to register on their faces. I did not want to end up like them. But in some ways I felt I already had.

Tiana came to see me on a daily basis, despite the three-quarters of an hour journey. It was difficult for her to get a baby-sitter for Romilly, but she always seemed to manage. Two things became very clear to me during this period: the first was how wonderful and generous some people can be (and can't, for that matter); the other was how strong Tiana was. She had virtually become a single Mother. She feared for me during those times, feared that she would never get her husband back, that I was a lost cause. She cried regularly. But through it all, she stayed strong, never gave up trying. If she didn't have Romilly, she may have given up; but being a Mother installs a dedication and determination that is not easily defeated.

I could see how she lost hope for me during that time. I was lost to her and Romilly, my illness taking over my waking hours and keeping my sleeping hours to a minimum. Everything I did revolved around rituals. When Tiana came to visit me, she would often find herself sitting there whilst I was on all fours coughing at the floor or at her. A part of my brain that was still in contact with the outside world could see her sitting there trying not to cry, sometimes looking at me with pleading eyes, sometimes pretending to focus on something else in the room. Each visit, she would stay as long as she could. The visits were always the highlight of my day and never pointless, even when I could not get to talk to her as I was stuck in a ritual for the duration of her stay.

After a week, I was moved to Elmleigh in Havant, which was only twenty minutes from our house in Petersfield. It was my intention to wipe the slate clean when I got there, but within five minutes of arriving I had locked myself in the toilet to carry out a ritual.

The other patients were the usual mixture of depressives, self-harmers and drug-abusers. Whoever thinks that cannabis should be legalised would be well advised to visit some of the mental institutions around and see the amount of people who suffer from mental illness as a result of smoking too much pot.

I hated being there. There was nothing to do all day except watch TV. There were cards and board games, but the other patients were too comatosed to play with. That week dragged more than I have ever experienced before or since. Going through technical information on tax helped me pass the hours – I needed to be on top of it when I started my new job. That was still a little way off and I had serious doubts as to whether I would be ready, but I used this as a goal to get better. Drawing also helped, being very therapeutic.

However, neither stopped me from counting away the minutes until 10 o' clock, when I could get my 'meds' (medication) and go to bed. But inevitably, I would get a couple of hours sleep then wake up again to carry out rituals for the rest of the night and well into the next morning.

Despite my illness, I managed to convince the doctors that I should be allowed to go. I reasoned with them that OCD breeds on boredom and thinking time: the more I had nothing to do, the more my mind would wander and the more OCD thoughts I would let in. If I were back at work during the day and going to the gym every now and again, my mind would be occupied with real things and, by the end of the day, I would be so tired I'd nod off and sleep through the night without any problem. After much pleading and enthusiasm towards my plan, the doctors eventually agreed and I was to be freed on the Friday.

Tiana was not so enamoured by my release.

"You need to be in hospital until you're better," she said.

"It's not good for me," I replied. "This is the worst place for somebody with OCD."

"Well you can't come back here," said Tiana. "Not until you've stopped this whole coughing business."

"I feel like you don't want me home sometimes," I stated.

"Don't be so stupid!" she cried. "I want you back more than anything; but *you*, not this stupid Mark with his silly coughing. I want my husband back well again."

"Well they've agreed to let me out this Friday," I said.

"They're so irresponsible!" answered Tiana. "You're not ready to come home yet. You should be given some kind of treatment first. I don't understand why they're not doing anything! How can they release you?"

"Well it's happening," I replied. "And I've got to live somewhere."

"I'll see if my Mum can put you up," Tiana said.

And she did. When I came out that Friday, I went to stay with my Mother-in-law, Jenny, and her husband, Derek. She made me very welcome, putting extra special effort into meal times and making my packed lunch each morning. Derek was an intelligent and experienced guy who was usually good fun to be with; however, there was a selfish side to him that clouded his vision when it came to me and my illness. Eventually, he let me down at a time when I needed help the most and that has been difficult to forget.

During the day, I went off to work, although there wasn't much for me to do: as I would soon be leaving, they were holding work back. This made me feel slightly worthless. Coupled with the fact that it was difficult to find work to keep myself occupied, my return had not had the desired result. I soon found myself slipping off to the toilet to make some strange coughing noises. I'm sure people noticed, but I didn't really care anymore. However, I still lied when people asked me where I'd been all this time and how I was feeling. Having used it before with reasonable success, I leant on diarrhoea, so to speak, as an alibi, throwing in food poisoning for good measure.

In the evening, I would find it relaxing to sit with Jenny and Derek and watch television. The Rugby World Cup 2007 had just started, which helped me to keep my mind off the illness. In the four years since the last World Cup, England had turned from the best team in the world into a very poor seventh at the very most. There was no chance of them repeating their previous success. So I decided I would test my cough powers out: I said to myself, "England will win the Rugby World Cup in 2007", coughing on the '2007' part. Those next few weeks would be ones of mixed emotion as England got closer and closer to the Final. We all know now what happened: after an embarrassing hammering from South Africa, England suddenly turned their fortunes round, convincingly won the rest of their pool games, beat the Aussies and the French and found themselves in the final against South Africa once more; of course, I wanted us to win, but there was a sense of dread that if they did, then just maybe I had these magical powers! To my relief, we lost. My powers had failed!

But that was a good six weeks away yet. A lot would happen in the meantime.

I was not getting better at Jenny's house. I would keep sneaking off to my bedroom, hide my head under the covers and cough away. The nights were no better. Then I would arrive at work feeling shattered. There would not be much for me to do and I would find myself nipping off to the toilets where I could carry out some rituals.

Tiana came to see me one evening with Romilly. The plan was for her to spend a couple of hours with me, then to go to her friend's house-warming party. It was all going well, until I wasn't sure if I coughed or not whilst I was in the bathroom. I did not want to spoil the evening, so I thought I would wait until they had gone and then neutralise it. Foolishly, I suggested that I came along with them to the party. Reluctantly, Tiana agreed.

We were the first there. I flicked through the CD selection, whilst Tiana and her friend, Sandra, did a tour of the flat. I remember thinking, now might be a good time to neutralise. So I did. But it didn't feel right, so I did it again. And again. And before I knew it I was stuck in a loop. I felt a tugging on my leg. I looked down and little Romilly was asking for a cuddle. I loved her beautiful little face, so sweet and totally trusting in me. Then it dawned on me: she had touched me during a ritual! Had I said the right thing?

She had only touched my trouser leg – does that count? No, I reasoned with myself, that doesn't count. It has to be skin on skin. But I still hadn't neutralised properly. Sandra's guests had begun to arrive. Soon the flat was full of people. If I was to neutralise, I would need to be smart.

"Are you okay?" Tiana asked me, a worried look on her face.

"Fine," I lied.

"No you're not," she said, not fooled by me. "I knew this was a bad idea. Why did I listen to you?"

"I'm fine!" I persisted. "I need the toilet."

"Oh no!" cried Tiana. "Don't do this in front of my friends. Why didn't I leave you at my Mum's?!"

When I had finished in the toilet, everyone had gone to the lounge to natter. Gingerly, I walked in and was greeted with lots of friendly faces. A couple of the girls tried to make conversation with me, but my answers didn't make sense and there was no proper flow to the discussions.

"I'm taking you back to my Mum's," Tiana whispered to me. "You're not going to ruin my night with my friends."

So she did, despite my pleading. Little Romilly was asleep in the travel cot, so we left her there. Tiana and I argued all the way to her Mother's. She couldn't understand why I kept acting like this; I told her she wasn't supporting me enough. There was no kiss goodbye – she dropped me off and went back to her friend's house.

I knew I needed to cough again, but touching Romilly at the same time. The nagging would not leave me until I did.

The next day, Jenny was to go to Wales for a couple of nights with her work. Derek was fretting about being on his own with me: what would he do if I turned funny? Plus, being a farm vet he was under particular stress with a

194

possible re-emergence of foot and mouth disease and 'blue tongue'. He held a senior position in the vetting world that would require him to be on call at any time and to travel up to London in the early hours. He really could do without having me to worry about. But he was prepared to do this as, after all, I was the husband of his wife's daughter and he would do anything for his wife.

The first night went okay. The second night did not. I woke in the early hours and commenced a ritual. It was a bad one. I found myself coughing and shouting as loud as I could. I kept crawling over to the window to look up at the stars, searching for an answer, for comfort, for God to look back down and tell me everything was alright, to see my Father's Mother looking back at me. But I never stared for long, before I was pulled back into a ritual. Inevitably, Derek woke and came in to try and talk to me.

"What the hell's going on?" he asked.

"Sorry, Derek," I replied. "I can't help it?"

"Have you taken your tablets?" he said.

"Yes," I answered. "It's nothing to do with that. Don't worry – I'll snap out of it in a minute."

"Okay," he replied, "but I've got to be up in a couple of hours and I really need to get some sleep."

How I would have loved to be in his position.

I made my way downstairs and kneeled in the moonlit lounge and coughed some more. Derek came downstairs with a phone in his hand and passed it to me.

"What are you playing at?" said Tiana.

"I'm stuck in a loop," I cried. "I can't get out!"

"Yes you can," she replied. "You're not even trying. I want you to phone this number." She gave me the number of the

'Crises' helpline. "Phone them and explain to them what's happening."

So I did, but they were little help. I didn't think they could be.

Eventually, I broke out of the loop, went back to my room and lay there wide awake until morning came.

I tried to go to work, but lasted about fifteen minutes before I was sent home and given sickness leave for the foreseeable future.

It was around four o' clock when Tiana phoned.

"You can't stay there any more," she said, a hard tone to her voice.

"Why not?" I asked, confused and upset by her tone.

"Because it's not fair on Derek," she replied. "Why should my family have to put up with you anyway? Your family haven't offered to help at all."

"Has he asked you to tell me to leave?" I said.

"Yes," she answered, "but I want you too. We're all fed up with you and the way your family can't be bothered to help."

"But I thought I was part of your family," I said. "And a friend. Does that not mean anything?"

"I want you to go and stay at your Mum's," Tiana continued, the hardness remaining in her voice.

"But I'll be ages away from you and Romilly," I pleaded.

"I don't want you seeing Romilly at the moment," she replied. "And I'm not in the mood for seeing you either."

So I left. I phoned my Mum and asked her if I could stay. She said I could. The journey to hers took an hour and a half longer than it should do as I stopped several times along the way to carry out some rituals. When I eventually

arrived, my Mother welcomed me with open arms, almost in tears at her poor son's plight.

Those next few days, I tried to be as helpful as possible, washing up, ironing and generally being as tidy as I could. I clearly wasn't well and would often disappear to my room to carry out rituals. Sometimes I would refuse to speak for fear that I would set myself off.

On the third night, my parents went out for a meal with friends and did not arrive back until late. In the meantime, I fell into a pattern of rituals. I managed to order myself an Indian, but only after standing outside and staring at the menu for fifteen minutes whilst I carried out my strange behaviour. Then, once I was back at my Mother's I did not get round to eating it until it had gone cold due to being stuck in another ritual.

I never slept a wink that night. My rituals varied in volume, most on the quiet side and never rising above voice level. But I couldn't seem to snap out of them; I was stuck in a permanent loop.

Morning came and I had managed to get around an hour's sleep. No matter that I had 'conquered' this particular round, though: I still needed to 'correct' the ritual involving my daughter. If only I had carried out the ritual there and then, I could be home and dry, I thought to myself. The thought kept playing on my mind. I was due to see her again on Sunday; it was only Thursday. How could I possibly wait that long?

It was around six o' clock in the morning when there was a knock on the bedroom door: my Mother.

"Are you awake?"

"Yes," I answered, climbing out of bed and answering the door. "I haven't really slept."

"Neither have I," she replied.

"What's the matter?" I asked.

"I've been having panic attacks," she said. "I'm sorry, I can't handle you at the moment. It's too much for me to deal with."

"Fine," I replied, rolling my eyes, "I'll go." I grabbed my bag and began stuffing my clothes in.

"I don't want you to go," she continued, incomprehensively.

"You just said you wanted me to go," I responded. As much as I hated that she was throwing me out, it gave me the opportunity to go and see Romilly and my mind was now set on leaving.

"I don't *want* you to go," my Mum continued, "but I can't cope with it at the moment. It's too much. I've got to think of myself for a change."

For a change?! This woman was incredible at times! She was always thinking of herself! I didn't say anything. There was no point – she wouldn't have understood and would take personal offence. She would probably even faint.

"I understand," I said, gathering the remainder of my belongings and shoving them in the bag. "I'll be off now."

I was seizing the opportunity: I would go and see Tiana and Romilly and complete the ritual at last.

"You don't have to go just yet," said Mum, slightly panicking. "Have a shower and some breakfast first."

"No," I replied, dismissively. "I'm going now. I don't want to get in your way."

"Don't be like that," she pleaded. "I just can't handle it on top of everything else that's going on."

"Oh yes," I said, momentarily stopping my packing and turning to face her. "It must be very difficult to handle the way I do the ironing, wash up, help you with the dinner and

Eventually they brought her out. She looked as beautiful as ever. I kissed her on the cheek and held her in my arms, cuddling her tightly. I held her hand in mine – I needed to get this right as I wouldn't get another chance. I braced myself.

"One hundred!" I coughed. And again, just in case I had not said her name. Then once more, as pandemonium kicked off and she was being pulled away from me by Tiana. I backed away, a sense of relief running through me, despite the panic I had caused. Karen took her and went inside. The door shut and I heard a key lock. I looked at the number of their house, 34, just to be sure that I had looked at a safe number.

"You promised!" cried Tiana, now in tears as we made our way back across the road to our house.

"Did I say 'one hundred'?" I suddenly thought aloud. "And did I say days or weeks?"

"I don't know!" cried Tiana. "I wasn't listening! You lied to me!"

"Shit!" I shouted, and turned to go back to Steve's house. But the door was closed – I couldn't get to her! No way would they open the door now! "I've got to do it one more time!" I pleaded.

"No way!" replied Tiana. "I'm not letting you anywhere near my little girl."

"But you don't understand!" I cried. "I might have done it wrong…"

"No!" she repeated, a determined look in her eye. "I can't have you going anywhere near her! You're scaring her!"

We went back in the house, Tiana pulling me by the arm and closing the door. For a few moments my desperation subsided and hopelessness pacified me. I heard the door lock and it woke me from my despair.

"No!" I suddenly shouted. "I didn't do it properly! I know I didn't!"

"It doesn't matter," said Tiana.

"It does! Something horrible could happen to her if I don't correct it!"

"No it won't," replied Tiana, grabbing me. "Please just calm down!"

"Get off!" I cried, knocking her arms away and sinking to my knees, my breath now short and fast. "I've got to correct it!" I was grabbing my head, the pain and frustration becoming unbearable.

There was a knock at the door. It was Steve. Tiana let him in. "You okay, mate?" he asked, crouching down next to me.

"Steve," I said, getting to my feet, trying to sound and appear calm and rational. "Listen: you've got to bring little Romilly here – I just need to do the ritual one more time."

"I can't do that, mate," he replied, gently but forcefully.

"Please!" I pleaded and turned to Tiana. "Please let him!"

"I'm not going to do that," said Tiana defiantly.

I grabbed the phone and threw it to the floor, smashing it to pieces.

"Calm down, Mark," said Steve.

"Aaagh!" I cried and ran to the patio doors, raising my fist to them. "I'm going to put my fist through it, I swear!"

"No you're not!" cried Tiana, running to me. "We can't afford it! Please don't hurt yourself!"

I turned round swiftly and she cowered down.

"I wouldn't hurt you," I said, relatively calmly. Noticing I still had my fist raised, I lowered it. "Please just let me finish the ritual!"

"I'm not going to do that," she repeated.

I ran into the kitchen and they both followed. I grabbed a carving knife and held it out in front of me, my hands shaking, gritting my teeth.

"Let me do the ritual!" I cried. "Or I swear I'll kill myself!"

"No!" pleaded Tiana, tears rolling down her cheeks. "I love you! I don't want to lose you! Romilly needs her Daddy too!"

"Put the knife back," said Steve, trying to sound calm.

I knew I wouldn't hurt myself. I could never do that to Tiana and little Romilly. I would be subjecting them to what I feared the most: losing a loved one. I dropped the knife on the floor and went back into the front room. The next few minutes were filled with my whining and pleading, groaning and crying. No matter how hard I tried to convince her, Tiana would not budge.

"I'll have to do it eventually," I said. "Whether it's tomorrow, a week, a month or even a year. It'll always be there, gnawing at me, nagging me to give in and correct it."

"Then you can never see her again," Tiana replied.

My words were useless. I knew that I would have to do this myself: I would smash down Steve's front door, get to Romilly and finish off the ritual.

Before I could try, the door opened and a policeman and policewoman entered the house followed by two ambulance men.

"I'm so sorry, mate!" I heard Steve say. I gave him a look that acknowledged his betrayal.

"Thanks," I said, turning to my wife. "You've both got me locked up again. Where you want me."

Through tears, Tiana explained what had happened as I sat in silence, head in hands, feeling more hopeless than ever.

Eventually, they led me out and into the ambulance van.

"Sorry!" I heard Tiana cry as the door slammed shut. I did not look up.

"We're taking you to the hospital," the ambulance man explained. "You're going to see one of the psychiatric doctors."

When we arrived at Petersfield hospital, they led me inside and upstairs to the waiting room. There they left me.

I remember the feeling of rejection most of all. I was seen as a problem, a nuisance to be palmed off to the NHS; a danger that needed to be locked away. I had never felt so alone in my life. Rejected by my wife and Mother. And the nagging feeling had not gone away: I needed to get to Romilly.

I made my way down the stairs quietly. Peering into the main foyer, I noticed the ambulance men standing there, chatting to a doctor. I made my way back up the stairs – I would need to find another way out. The fire exit! No alarm went off as I pushed open the door. I sneaked down the stairs and out into the gardens behind the hospital. Trying to look inconspicuous, I made my way round the building and through the car park. The ambulance was still there. Once I was by the entrance, I began to jog up the road – I needed to get away and get to Romilly as soon as possible. As soon as my disappearance was noticed, I knew they'd come after me.

She should be at nursery that morning as Tiana worked on a Thursday. However, would she take her in after what had happened? And she would have been sure to alert the nursery.

When I got there, Romilly was nowhere in sight. I was told that she had not been there and they had not heard from Tiana.

I made my way back home. Our street was quite; nobody was about. Walking through the door, I called their names. There was no response – where could they be? I checked every room, but there was no sign of them.

I walked back outside. Making its way down the road was a police car. They had found me. I slumped myself down on the kerb outside my house and put my head in my hands.

"Hello you," said the police woman in a gentle voice as she sat down next to me. "Well you made it back here very quickly, I must say! Did you run all the way?"

"Some," I said. "They're not here."

"I'm sure they're safe," she responded. Her radio went off. "It's okay – he's here with me. No, there's no need. He's calm. So then," she continued, turning back to me, "why did you run away?"

"They can't help me," I explained. "No one can help me now."

"They can," she replied. "And so can we. You're not well are you? Listen, because you ran away we're going to have to take you into custody." I sat up in slight surprise. "It's okay, we're not arresting you. We're just going to section you under the Mental Health Act. Unfortunately, the only way to do this is to take you to Waterlooville police station and call for a doctor to see you. Then they can make a decision as to whether you need to go back to hospital."

"No!" I cried, suddenly coming alive. "I can't go back there! I won't!" I felt like running again, but the hopelessness of it all stopped me.

I remember thinking of jumping out of the moving vehicle as we drove down the A3 to Waterlooville police station. But something inside me was telling me it would all be okay again one day. No matter how hopeless I felt, I was sure that there would be sunshine again.

The police man who rode in the back with me was asking me about my condition. He told me his sister suffered from OCD. She had to get help from a trained specialist and now she's a lot better. She still had the odd quirky behaviour, he said, but she lived a meaningful and productive life. I took comfort in his words.

At the police station I was made to sit in a small cell about one metre wide each way. They closed the metal 'gate', but assured me it was just a procedure. I no longer cared. I didn't know where Tiana was. I knew she would be safe but that wasn't the point: I needed to get to Romilly and I was about as far away from her as I could possibly get. The frustration was eating away at me.

Half an hour later, they interviewed me. They took my belongings; my shoes and my belt. My trousers nearly fell to the ground, trousers that were a tight fit only a few months before. They asked if I wanted to see a solicitor. I didn't see the point. The nice police woman who had found me informed me that my wife had been in contact and left a message: she was sorry and she loved me very much. I let out a couple of tears for her.

I was led to a cell of about ten feet by fifteen feet. But I had not been arrested. To reiterate the point, the guard left the cell door open. He sat on a chair just outside. It was at the end of a stone corridor with other cells all along one wall. There was a toilet with no seat in one corner and a sleeping area along the back wall with a wooden plank for 'comfort'. A blanket was brought into me.

"The psychiatrist will be a while," it was explained to me. He will be accompanied by Dr Loxford, your GP. They aren't free till this afternoon, so you're going to be here a while, I'm afraid. Would you like some food?"

I didn't feel like eating, but I hadn't had anything since the night before and my body was telling me I should have something. It was like something inside me was beginning to fight back – to rebel against this belief system that was doing me so much harm. And it would pass the time. I went for the lasagne. The pasta was a dark orangey brown in colour and the tomato-based sauce too vinegary. It came in a cardboard box. I had never heard of the make. A special brand just for prisoners, no doubt. Still, it was food and I ate it.

I was so tired, physically and mentally exhausted. And I was so confused. How did it come to this? A prison cell and a sectioning. I had heard the other patients talking about being sectioned and how their privileges were subsequently limited. They would have to ask for 'leave' to go out. In looniness terms, I had hit the big time! I curled up on the hard wooden bench and tried to sleep. I dozed, my brain working overtime with thoughts and images of everything that had happened, too exhausted to make sense of it all, but too excited to enter a deep sleep.

A couple of hours went by and I had heard nothing. I was content to just lie there in that state of limbo between the waking and the sleeping world. Eventually there was news: they would be another hour and a half! If I had any energy in me, I would have protested. Instead I went for the cooked breakfast, as recommended by my guard, who was, no doubt, even more bored than I was. It was passable, although the beans were almost brown, and it was a step up from the lasagne.

Eventually the doctor and the psychiatrist arrived, along with Malcolm, a 'care coordinator'. I heard Dr Loxwood's heels on the stone floor; that and the sudden buzz of something about to happen raised me out of my slumber. As they entered the cell, my heart sank as I recognised the idiot that had given me some 'PEP talks' a couple of years ago by way of therapy: Dr Taylor, the man with seemingly nothing going on behind that blank stare. He proved himself to be as useless as ever as he stood there looking gormlessly at me.

"Oh, Mark!" cried Dr Loxwood as she sat down beside me. "I'm so very sorry!"

"I just need to see my little girl," I began to plead. "What it is, you see, is that I've got to complete the ritual. I'll only need to do it once! It doesn't hurt her – Tiana thinks it does, but it doesn't. I only have to touch her."

"Listen," said Dr Loxwood in a gentle voice, "we need to work out what the best thing is to do for you."

"I know what's best," I continued. "All I have to do is be touching my little girl gently and I cough and say the right word. It can be done in a controlled environment." I turned my attention to Dr Taylor, who seemed as though he might be willing to go for it."

"Well we can consider it," he said.

My spirits suddenly lifted! But then anxiety ran through me – what if I did it wrong again? But I had no choice. "I would do it once and then that's it. And she wouldn't be in any danger and you would all be there to make sure of that anyway."

"We're going to go and have a little chat," interrupted Dr Loxwood. "We'll be a little while."

"Don't send me back there!" I pleaded and began to whimper. "I can't handle it!"

"We need to talk about it amongst ourselves," explained Dr Loxwood.

"It's no good locking me up!" I cried. "Whether I have to wait a week, a month or even a year, I'll still have to perform the ritual!"

"That's not necessarily true," said Malcolm. "If we can get you the right treatment."

"No!" I cried. "It won't help me – I *need* to do it!"

"How do you know without giving it a go?" asked Malcolm.

"It'll be wasted," I replied. "If therapy is going to be successful, I need to start with a clean slate – I need to get this one ritual out of the way."

"No you won't," said Malcolm. "I've seen it work wonders."

"We're going to go and have a chat now," Dr Loxwood repeated.

"It's not the right place for someone like me!" I explained. "I have too much thinking time on my hands. I need to be doing things. I can't just sit around! I'm going to go loopy, I know it!"

"Try and get some rest," said Dr Loxwood, standing and making her way out of the cell with the other two. "We'll be as quick as possible."

The thought of going back there scared me shitless. I couldn't bear the thought of it. I had to do the ritual. I couldn't be locked up again with just my thoughts. It was such a lonely place to be and I hated being alone, especially with me, of all people.

After thirty long minutes, they came back into the cell and announced my sentence.

"Under the circumstances," began Dr Loxwood, "we all think it's best if you go back to hospital."

"No!" I shouted. "Please!" She looked so upset, I could see it in her eyes. But she would not budge, despite my tears.

I was shaking with fear as we made the journey from the police cell back to Elmleigh. My emotions were ripped to pieces; I could think of nothing but the loneliness, of being stuck in that glass room with only OCD for company. OCD, the bully; OCD, the oppressor; OCD, the destroyer of lives; OCD.

"Control your breathing," I could hear her saying. "Try to control it or you'll hyperventilate." Her voice sounded distant, like she was talking to another person, like it was a television on in the background. I no longer cared. I felt deserted, lost, ashamed at my pathetic breakdown. The fear of that place overwhelmed me. That place. That lonely place in the early hours, when the world was at peace, at rest, and I could get neither.

Maybe I would spend the whole time trying to escape so that I could get to Romilly and finish the ritual. I would have to. What would be the alternative? Stay in the hospital until I went mad with frustration and anxiety?

I remember seeing mothers and fathers pushing prams or holding their children's hands and wishing that I could be like that, back with Tiana and Romilly, without any horrid thoughts, images and rituals ruining the magic and beauty of the family unit. But it all seemed so very far away, so impossible to reach. An unobtainable dream. Maybe one day, though, I thought to myself. Despite my desperation, I still had some hope left. Some dignity too, as I felt the embarrassment of imagined scornful looks from the people outside.

The shaking had taken over me. It became worse as I caught sight of the rectangular modern building where I had been housed once before. The police car pulled up alongside and the driver got out and knocked on a side gate. It opened and a nurse came out. I felt like the gates to Hell were opening before me; but through all my fear, I knew it was me who had allowed them to open.

My mind had made a Hell of Heaven.

CHAPTER SIXTEEN – ON THE ROAD TO RECOVERY

I walked through the doors like I was walking into the deepest, darkest, dingiest dungeon, too weak to fight anymore, submitting to my captors. The extreme fear in my expectations was in complete contrast to what confronted me: there were nurses everywhere, kind smiling faces to greet me, soft, tender words, gentle arms placed round my shaking shoulders. My trembling and mumbling continued for a little while more.

"Hey, bro!" cried a familiar voice: Leo! My good friend and fellow troubled man! I was glad to see him. "Don't worry, you'll be okay, I'll look after you. You'll be safe wiv me bruv." I could feel the genuineness in his voice and it comforted me. My shaking began to subside.

"Hello Mark," said one of the nurses. She was pretty and looked a bit like Billie Piper but with a normal set of teeth. "I remember you from before." I didn't recognise her. "I spoke to you one night when you couldn't sleep." I nodded, not wanting to offend her. But those nights were so long, I was so tired and my thoughts were focussed on rituals – I was not surprised that I did not remember her, even if she was pretty. "Let's go in the quiet room for a bit."

Kathy was her name, she told me, as she unlocked the door to a cosy looking room with a television and a couple of armchairs. The set was behind a locked glass door – apparently, some patients had a habit of throwing them across a room. We sat down in the armchairs. Another nurse came in with a jug of water, a cup and a smile. My shaking had almost stopped. I was beginning to feel what I had never thought I'd ever feel again: comfort. From nearby I could hear the sounds of the Dire Straits track, *Romeo and Juliet* – I loved that song.

"We're going to be looking after you now," said Kathy. Maybe it was the feeling that people cared again that calmed me. Those past few days, I had felt I'd been rejected by people whom I thought would love me the most. Now the kind words of strangers were feeding my hope. "It's not like over the other side, where you're left on your own. Here, there are always lots of us nurses about to talk to, to keep you company."

I nodded, trying to smile, but the look in my eyes gave away a lack of participation in the conversation.

"I hear you've got a lovely little girl," she said. Suddenly, my spirits lifted at the thought of my little Romilly.

"She's beautiful," I said with pride. I took out my phone and showed her some pictures. "Look!"

"Ah! She's a real little charmer," replied Kathy. She had a strong Portsmouth accent: like a South Londoner that's spent the last few years living on a farm.

"She's tough as nails," I continued, enthused by thoughts of my little girl. "I've knick-named her 'knuckles' and 'Titanium Girl'! The other day, she was walking along and she hit her head on the side of the table really hard, knocking herself off balance, but she straightened up and kept going! Hard as nails! Do you have any kids?"

"Yeah," she replied. "Two little boys." She pulled out a picture of them. "The eldest won a competition for cutest toddler a couple of years ago. Everyone thinks he's gorgeous."

"They're very cute," I said, wanting to add, 'but my girl's cuter!', but decided it was best not to. It would be a little childish of me.

"They're hard work, kids," Kathy said. "But they're great fun."

"I know," I replied. "Romilly needs constant attention, but I love it! I'm glad when she finally goes to bed and I can relax, but after an hour I want to get her back downstairs again to play with!"

"Listen, Mark," she began, "my shift's just finishing so I'm off now." I felt slightly disappointed. This was the first normal conversation I'd had in a long time. I was enjoying just chatting without worrying about rituals and coughing and repeating sentences in my head. "Your room should be ready by now, so one of the other nurses will show you it and help you unpack."

"Thanks," I said as we stood up and left the room.

"That's alright," she answered. I don't think she realised how strong my thanking her was meant to be: she had pulled me out of a dark place.

I was in the psychiatric intensive care unit – 'PICU' – at Elmleigh, a hospital exclusively for the mentally ill. This is where people came that were seriously ill: the paranoid, the severely depressed, the suicidal. The reason for the plethora of nurses was partly to keep the patients company and partly to stop them killing themselves – or each other! I realised this, but I still felt at peace there.

My room was just the same as the one I had occupied round the other side in the Male Ward. In fact, the whole place was a mirror image of the Male Ward, except slightly more cosy, with more cushions, armchairs and nurses. There was a pool table, lots of board games and three televisions (so there was little chance of me missing any of the Rugby World Cup just because a patient was being particularly irrational and wanting to watch something else!). There was a court yard where the patients could get fresh air or go out and smoke. No one was allowed out of the ward without being accompanied by at least one nurse.

That first day, there was an overwhelming feeling of acceptance in me: acceptance that I was very ill and that my priority was getting better, and not to be at home with my family. Tiana was strong enough to cope without me whilst I got better and she had an overwhelming amount of family and friends who were more than happy to help. Yes, my family needed me; but they needed *me*, not this OCD-consumed, out-of-control, ritualising lost soul. They were willing to wait for me. Tiana had explained this to me throughout my earlier stay in hospital, but I had refused to accept it. I was too obsessed with making sure my family was safe when there was no need for me to worry. At last, Tiana's words were accepted by me. It would be hard, I knew that, but I knew that I must get better if I am to look after them both; and I knew that I would get better, despite how low things had become. I knew that I had no choice but to remain there until I was better. And then maybe, just maybe, it would be possible to live an OCD-free life with my family.

"I'm sorry," said Tiana.

"It's okay," I replied. "You did the right thing."

"But you said…"

"I know what I said," I interrupted. "But I had lost it by then. I had lost touch with reality."

"And now?" she asked. There was a slight tone of desperation in her voice.

"I feel so much better," I replied.

"But how? How can you go from being on the edge of … of going mad to being so calm about it all?"

"I don't know how to explain it," I answered. "I just had this sudden realisation that I'm not well. A kind of enlightenment. I know that I can't neutralise anything through these rituals and that it does more harm than good."

"It doesn't do any good," said Tiana.

"I know," I replied. "But it's convincing my brain that. There's an image of Romilly that won't leave me: the fear in her eyes, the feeling that such a small thing is completely powerless against me, so vulnerable – I felt like I scared her, that her own father, the person that is supposed to protect her, scared her. I feel so sad that my own daughter could be scared of me. It's OCD that did this and it gives me so much strength to beat this thing."

"You could really hurt her," Tiana said. "You don't know your own strength."

"I know," I replied. "But I'm never going to let it happen again. I feel so much better. So positive."

"Okay," said Tiana, not sounding particularly enthusiastic.

"What's the matter?" I asked. "Don't you believe in me?"

"I don't know," she answered after a pause. "I want to. But you've tricked me so many times."

"OCD has tricked you," I corrected her.

"And how do I know this isn't your OCD trying to trick me again?" she asked.

"I don't know," I replied. "It isn't, though. I'll prove that with time."

"And maybe this feeling is just momentary," she continued. "Maybe you'll go back again after today. Back to feeling bad again."

"Maybe," I said, "but I've got to try and hold onto this feeling for as long as possible; remember how I feel at this precise moment. I really feel like I can beat this now, like I can really challenge it! And I've *never* felt like that before!

I can win this and we can all be a normal family again! It will be even better than before!"

"I hope so," Tiana replied, the slightest optimism coming through.

"I *know* so."

And I did manage to keep that feeling for a couple of days. In that time, I thought long and hard about everything that had happened. My fear was of losing my family and I had used OCD as a belief system that would stop this from happening; in reality my OCD was keeping me from my family, harming them, if not physically then at least mentally; without me, they were not as safe. OCD, my belief system, was doing the exact opposite of what it promised to do. And I was becoming withdrawn from normal society. If I carried on like this I would become like one of those OCD sufferers I had read about, unable to leave their house, only able to talk to certain people, family divided, pushed away. That was no life. I would not let that happen.

Sure enough, my OCD grew strong again, despite myself. After a couple of days, the rituals returned, attacking me in my sleep and forcing me to carry out my bizarre behaviour. But I was stronger now and was learning how to fight it. After one bad night, I decided that, in future, I would wait until the morning before I reacted. That way, I was ensuring that I got enough sleep and would be alert enough to fight. For the next few nights, I managed to delay the rituals until the morning, once I was fully awake. It was not easy and some mornings I could not break out of the rituals, still carrying them out by the early afternoon. I couldn't stop until it felt 'right'. The rituals had become particularly complex now, involving saying several phrases in my head, including requests to God; the right images would need to occur, such as Romilly smiling, and they had to appear on the 'good' word, not the 'bad' word; and I had to avoid blaspheming during the ritual otherwise it would need to begin all over again. If it was slightly wrong, or I was not one hundred per cent sure that I had said it properly, I would need to start all over again.

I realised that I would need to reduce the complexity of the rituals. So, bit by bit, I took out a particular element. First, I stopped praying straight after; then I moved on to not having to repeat the ritual if I blasphemed in my head straight after. This had the effect of reducing the difficulty of getting the ritual 'just right'. Again, this meant that I had more time to reflect on things and more energy to fight. Next, I worked on the number element, trying not to worry about the exact time that I had carried out the ritual, nor looking at a certain number straight after.

Every morning, Tiana would ask me if I had carried out any rituals and every morning I would let her know that I had. I could feel her optimism waning and the despair inside of her. She was hurting so much and could not see an end to it all. I longed for the day when I could tell her that I had not carried out a ritual. Sometimes when she rang I was stuck in a ritual and couldn't answer. I knew she knew why I wasn't answering and that this would hurt her, but there was just no stopping it. The couple of times that I did manage to pull myself away to speak to her, I would end up trying to rush her off the phone anyway so I could get back to the rituals. I longed to be with her so much, but OCD had imprisoned me. How I loved her and little Romilly and how I missed them.

When I was not performing rituals, I would spend as much time as possible with the nurses, playing pool or scrabble or cards. They were all very laid back and good fun. It was good to have them around, whether to talk to deeply or just discuss trivia. They were a connection to the outside world, a reminder that not everyone is loopy. I would spend time with the other patients too, especially Leo, but they had too many hang-ups and issues to deal with and were too far removed to be able to hold a proper conversation for long. Leo and I became very close. He had proved to me that he was a decent person by the care he had showed during my hour of need. His background was fascinating. He told me he was a vigilante of sorts, being paid to beat up drug dealers or sex offenders. Reading between the lines, drugs had been his downfall, like so many of the patients there. Leo's view of the world he inhabited was very misty: he was convinced that the nurses and doctors were conspiring against him, suppressing him with drugs and imprisonment. On a good day, Leo was happy to laugh at himself and his situation; on a bad day, he would wander around the hospital, stepping gingerly and acting cautious, suspicious of the people around him. When we were both out, we said, we'd go to a club somewhere and party and walk in there like we were a couple of 'dons'. It sounded fun, but I never realistically believed it would happen.

Eventually, I had a breakthrough! A whole morning without coughing! In fact, I managed to last out until the end of the day, when I finally gave in. Tiana sounded pleased for me, but doubtful. She kept asking me if I was telling the truth. She couldn't believe it. The next day was the same. So I made a pledge to myself: no more coughing for one whole week, otherwise something bad would happen to us all. I had effectively created a Catch 22 situation, the end result being that there was no point coughing for a whole week. So I didn't. Tiana was astounded! Of course, I didn't tell her how I had done it because I didn't want her to just think I was delaying it and would then be back to normal again. I knew by doing this that I would be able to sort my head out better and the urges would die down. A kind of a cold turkey process was going on.

After a week, it was time to cough again. But I didn't really want to bother with it. It just seemed pointless, a waste of time. But I did it anyway. I got the ritual right first time. This surprised me – it would always take several goes until it felt right. Not this time. So I vowed not to cough again for another week. I was feeling and getting a lot better.

In the back of my mind, there was always the goal of getting better in time for my new job. I knew it was crucial to start there, otherwise we could say good bye to owning a house and having any more children. It is this and the fundamental desire to look after my family that gave me the strength not to give in, to keep fighting. It was a *real* threat. Consequently, with time it became easier. I still had the occasional bad day, but I stuck to my week-long periods without coughing. There was also the fact that we had incurred enough expense in the previous two months as a result of my stay in the French hospital and my subsequent deportation: all in all, just over £5,000 was incurred. We paid it by getting an advance of Tiana's inheritance from her grandfather. It made me even shittier to know that I had disinherited my wife and made me even more determined to put things right.

I was on my own in terms of determination. The other patients seemed to have no interest in getting better. They moped around, happy to be fed at certain times, watch television for much of the day or otherwise sleep. Many of them were 'revolving door' patients: as soon as they left, they were back again. I made good friends with a lot of them and learnt a lot about mental illness in general. These were, for the most part, good, honest people, but they had been struck down by their illnesses and ended up on the fringes of society. But I did not feel overly sorry for them because of their seeming refusal to help themselves; it was as if they accepted their condition and were happy to be protected from the outside world.

By far the hardest part of all of this was not seeing Romilly for so long. It was three weeks from *that day* before I was to see her again. In the meantime, I would talk to her on the phone, which helped me get by. Tiana would call her over and tell her I was on the phone and she would rush up, grab it and call my name in a very excited tone. She seemed to understand a lot of what I was saying, although it was probably only the odd word her and there that she latched on to. She was growing so quickly, Tiana told me. And there were new words all of the time, many of which were mispronounced, giving that additional cuteness to them: 'cuggai' meant 'colouring', for example. And the conversations would always start with a 'Hiya!' and end with a 'Bubye', followed by a kiss. She was truly amazing. The sense of missing out was strong. Tiana would tell me what she was up to, such as the new words, or being able to jump, knowing her Ps & Qs, solving little puzzles, and the like. She seemed such a clever little girl for her age, if a little boisterous (she got that from her Mother!).

I feared that Romilly would forget who I was through all of this. But Tiana assured me otherwise. Every night before she put Romilly to bed, Tiana would show her pictures of me and she would say, "Daddy, Daddy, Daddy!" and kiss the photo. These were kept in a cupboard next to her room. Often, Romilly would try to open the door and ask Tiana for 'Daddy!'; then Tiana would have to get one of my photos out and Romilly would sit and look at it. It made me feel warm inside to know this, but I worried that she might start to think that Daddy was just an image that lived in the cupboard, no more real than Bob the Builder. Deep down I knew, though, she knew who I was: I was her Daddy.

"When can I see her again?" I asked.

"When you're well enough to," Tiana replied.

She was wearing her pink bra. I thought about what she looked like naked, then tried to think of something else. We had had sex once in the past three months – it was on my return from France. I longed for that carnal knowledge and would try to convince Tiana that it was fine for her to come back to my room and have sex. But she wasn't having any of it.

"It's been ages since I last ritualised though," I reminded her.

"No," answered Tiana, sternly. "You're not ready."

"But she's my little girl!" I cried. "She needs to see her Daddy and I need to see her. I promise you, I won't do anything."

"It's too soon," said Tiana. "Let's give it a little bit longer."

"What difference will that make?" I asked.

"It'll give you more time to make sure you really are better," answered Tiana. "Look, last time you saw her, you said to me that you would have to carry out the ritual again, whether it was a day, week, month or year."

"Yes, but that's not the case anymore," I said. "I was talking rubbish."

"What about when you came back from France," Tiana countered. "You were fine until you saw her again, then you had to carry out a ritual that you'd left outstanding."

"But it's different this time," I pleaded. "I know I can't do that any more."

"We'll talk to the doctors on Thursday," she replied. "If they say it's okay, you can see her at the weekend."

Although it was five days a way, I was already getting excited at the thought of seeing little Romilly again. I had waited that long, I could wait five more days. I stood up, grabbed Tiana and gave her a big smacker on the lips.

The truth was, until that point I had not pushed the issue of seeing my daughter as I was worried that I might carry out the ritual. By then, I was sure that I would not do anything again. I had accepted the uncertainty of the situation. And as the mist of OCD began to clear a little, I was sure of what I wanted more than anything else in the world: to see my little girl again, hold her in my arms and kiss her and tell her how much I loved her and how proud I was of her for being so strong.

Eventually, the nurses felt that I was good enough to move from PICU back to the Male Ward. I did not want this – it was too quiet over there, not enough nurses. But I went without too much of a fuss. I soon settled in over there. The other patients were subdued, as ever, and tended to keep themselves to themselves. There were very few nurses, possibly three or four at any one time, and they were too busy to play games with you. Overall, I found it a very calm place to be and soon settled in. I was becoming institutionalised. I would wake every morning, have a bath and then some breakfast. We would all eat together at midday and at around 5 o' clock. 'Meds' were just after breakfast and at 10 o' clock. Then I would settle down for a good night's sleep, content that I was safe inside the hospital. More importantly, I no longer worried about Tiana and Romilly's safety: they had been without me for a considerable length of time without too many problems, plus there were so many friends and family willing to help. My priority was to get better, not to worry about them, as Tiana told me many times over.

Eventually, the Saturday came when I was to see my little Romilly. I couldn't wait! I was so excited that morning when I woke and put on my best clothes to make sure that I looked nice for her. They were supposed to arrive at 10 o' clock but, Tiana being Tiana, they were of course late. I kept going out to the front desk to see where they had got to.

By 10.30 they had finally arrived. I saw the little blue Punto turn into the car park and smiled gormlessly, a buzz of excitement running through me. Tiana waved to me, then opened the back door and, for what seemed like an eternity, undid Romilly's straps and took her out. She pointed over to me, but Romilly couldn't make me out. Tiana locked the door and they came over to me. From about ten metres away, Romilly realised who I was: "Daddy!" she called and a little tear appeared in the corner of my eye. She was without doubt the most beautiful thing that I had ever seen.

We sat and played together in the 'family room'. She was as robust and boisterous as ever: there were two poufs in the room that she delighted on jumping onto and requested that I threw her on there too. We laughed and tickled each other, kissed and hugged and I let her climb all over me. All under the watchful and anxious glare of my dear wife. She was so scared that I was going to do something. I could see it in her eyes.

After about an hour, they left. Little Romilly didn't understand why I wasn't going with them – she looked confused and kept looking back and calling me as Tiana carried her away. I went back inside, so glad to have seen my little girl again and so pleased that I had not had any urges.

The visits with Romilly occurred around three times a week. Bit by bit, Tiana became less anxious and could see that my daughter and I were almost back to normal. She would often ask me if I was alright and whether I felt tempted to do a ritual around her. And I never did. Because of all of the times that I had lied to her in the past, Tiana was never wholly convinced by this. All I could do was trust in time to show her that I had changed

By the time the Monday morning arrived before my start date of Wednesday 10 October 2007, I felt that I was on top of my illness. I had not carried out any rituals for approximately a fortnight. The doctors were happy for me to begin work but to return to hospital in the evenings. I actually felt quite excited and not too anxious. I was refreshed, re-energised and ready to enter back into the real world. Ideally, I would liked to have been home too, but no one was going to let that happen just yet, especially Tiana. The role would be hard work, with a lot of expectations, but I was prepared for whatever life would throw at me by then; I'd also carried on swatting up on various technical areas during my stay at hospital.

My first day went well. A Pre-Budget Report had just been delivered by the new Chancellor, Alistair Darling, and – as the office Capital Taxes specialist – it was my role to read through the published paperwork and see what we needed to do. I got thoroughly stuck in, reading through the new legislation, making notes, drafting e-mails to other members of staff and letters to go to clients. And my new boss, Andrew Parkinson, was great to work with. He got me involved straight away with assisting him in his role as Executor of a deceased client's estate. He also dropped a little bombshell that I would be leading a Seminar on inheritance tax and estate planning in the near future – there should be around one hundred people coming along! Whilst it sounded daunting, I found myself quite excited by it. With all that was going on the first couple of weeks flew by.

Andrew knew all about what had happened. His opinion was, if you could do the job then that was all that mattered. He made it clear that I should let him know if I needed anything to make it easier for me and to avoid becoming ill again. I assured him that I would let him know.

Those first few weeks working were very strange. I would spend the day advising successful and wealthy people on tax-related issues, then return in the evening to a place filled with paranoid schizophrenics, depressives, drug abusers and other mentally ill people. One evening, whilst I was lying on my bed reading, a patient kicked my door open and started shouting abuse at me.

"What the hell are you doing?!" I shouted back, jumping up and confronting him.

"You had Sarah in here last night?!" he said. His eyes were wild. He went to head butt me, but quickly pulled back.

"Okay, let's calm down," I replied, realising that he clearly wasn't all there. "What do you think I've done?"

"I heard Sarah in here last night," he repeated. "You were shagging her."

"Look," I began in a calm tone, "I'm a married man and would never sleep with another woman behind my wife's back. I love her and my daughter too much."

"Okay," he said, suddenly cooling down. "Sorry. I suffer from schizophrenia. It's difficult for me to understand what's true and what isn't."

"It's alright," I assured him. "Don't worry about it." I left him to it and walked back to my room.

But it did not end there. He eyeballed me one day, giving me a look of real hatred. I decided that I needed to talk to the nurse. Whilst I was sure of being able to handle myself, the guy was mentally ill and capable of doing anything when your back was turned. One of the nurses, a lady called Susan, spoke to him soon after. I walked up to them both.

"I've explained to Jake that he's not got anything to worry about from you," said Susan.

"I just thought that maybe you wasn't real," Jake began. "Because you seem so normal, you go off to work and come back all smiling. You don't seem like the rest of us."

"I was very ill," I replied. "I'm a lot better, but I have to stay in here until every one is 100% sure that I am well enough to go home."

"I thought you was a reporter," Jake continued, "who'd come to write an article on me. I thought you was undercover like. I seen you on your phone, talking and that."

"Only a few weeks ago, Mark was very ill," Susan explained. "He's done brilliantly to get this well."

"Okay," said Jake. "Sorry bruv. I never meant to scare you. I was just trying to intimidate you to get you to confess or something."

"I'm too long in the tooth to be scared or intimidated," I replied, shaking his hand. He was fine from then on.

Throughout that period, my parents had been to see me several times. My Mum in particular seemed very concerned about me. Her insistence on bringing me chocolate helped appease me and eventually forgive her for throwing me out. It also helped me to look more like my normal self: since France, I had gone down from sixteen and a half stone to thirteen and a half. People said I looked like a bag of bones. Mum and I talked long and hard about everything, growing up and what we were like as a family. I learnt a lot in those visits about how difficult the early days had been.

My Dad, true to form, would sit there quietly, listening in on our deep conversations, but rarely joining in. He also proved to be good company for watching the occasional rugby match with.

It was decided: I would be going home on Monday 28th October. I couldn't wait! In order to be ready, I would spend one night at home during the week, then the Friday before at home too. I had not ritualised for about three weeks by then and was feeling very positive. Tiana couldn't believe it. She kept asking me to swear on my life or her life or even Romilly's life that I had not done anything. She was obviously very excited too, but there was also a sense of anticipation and she confessed to feeling slightly anxious. She had, after all, ran the home single handed for several weeks now and had become used to it being just the two of them.

The following Thursday would be my first cognitive behavioural therapy (CBT) session. As much as I wanted to do them, I was scared. I was scared of what they were going to ask me to do. I knew it would involve carrying out rituals and that Romilly would eventually have to be involved. They had talked of 'exposure and response therapy', which sounded pretty daunting. But I really didn't have a choice. I could not live the rest of my life like this. I read up on it: washers forced not to wash their hands, checkers to only check once … I could see where it was heading and it was making me very nervous.

The stay overs went very well. It was great to be lying in bed with my wife again, with my little daughter downstairs. I had helped bath her and played with her, although Tiana would not leave me alone with her and was still watching over me like a hawk. In bed, Tiana refused to have sex with me just yet, despite my pleading. She would not do so until I was back home for good.

On the Saturday before my date of departure from the hospital, my cousin was holding a fiftieth birthday party to which Tiana and I had been invited (I won't bore you with the reason for the age gap, but let's just say that some members of my family started young and finished late). Unfortunately, she could not get a baby-sitter, so Tiana stayed at home and I went on my own. It was to prove to be a huge mistake.

I was too cocky, too nonchalant about the effects of alcohol on my brain chemistry. It didn't help that I had left my quetiapine at the hospital too so hadn't had taken any anti-psychotics for a day. The night was going well. I was having a laugh with my cousin's son and daughter (my first cousins once removed, in case you cared about that kind of thing) and their respective other halves, dancing and doing karaoke. It was around the middle of the evening, at a time when I was sober enough to remember but too drunk to remember details that it happened: I went to the toilet and coughed. It just came out, as far as I can remember. I can recall thinking about my CBT and how I would have to do something similar and feeling confident because of the alcohol, so much so that I really didn't care about a silly cough (perhaps I should stay drunk forever!). But I don't remember what words went through my head. I could have said a bad word, as far as I know. At the time, I forgot all about it and carried on drinking and merry making. I turned up at the hospital around 2 o' clock in the morning, very drunk and singing. I had abused my privileges. This was not what the doctor ordered.

That next morning, I lay in bed awake for quite a while, not wanting to get up and discover just how bad my hangover was. The nurse came in to give me my meds and to warn me that I should not be going out and getting drunk like that as I was still in hospital and it was not fair on the other patients. A strong sense of guilt ran through me. The guilt increased as I thought of my poor wife at home on her own, struggling to get by, worrying and missing me. I felt like an arsehole. Then I remembered that I coughed; but I couldn't remember the details! It began to nag at me until I eventually gave in. The first time in weeks.

"It's just a bad day," I explained to Tiana down the phone. "I'll be alright by tomorrow, I promise."

"But I don't understand why you had to give in!" she cried.

"I've explained to you," I said.

"Why can't you just ignore it?" she asked. "I just don't understand it. What are you playing at, Mark? Why are you doing this to us?"

"I can't help it!" I explained for the millionth time. "Look, it's just a bad day, that's all."

"You're such an idiot," she replied. "This is because you missed your tablets and drank too much. I don't want you to ever drink again."

"I don't want to," I answered, biased by my current condition of being in a severe hangover. But this was not like other 'never again' statements of intent: this time there was a genuine fear in me that I had not experienced before, a fear that alcohol could release the OCD monster inside of me.

"You better be alright by tomorrow," Tiana said.

"I will be," I replied.

But I wasn't. OCD re-emerged yet again, plaguing me throughout the day. I came home straight after work for a meal with my family in preparation for the grand return. I pretended that I had been fine. Tiana questioned me; she thought something was up – I was behaving strangely, she said. I denied it and made my way upstairs.

I pulled out the little piece of paper that I had written earlier that day and placed it on the bed. I repeated in my head the sentence written down: "God makes sure that Romilly dies when she's well over one hundred years old", coughing on the one hundred. But I wasn't sure I had done it properly, so I did it again. And again.

"I knew it," came a voice from behind me. Tiana had followed me upstairs and caught me in the act.

"I'll be fine," I lied.

"Come on," she said, ignoring me, "let's get you back to hospital."

I didn't put up a fight. I knew she wouldn't agree to me staying. I would not be going home that week. I cried that night.

CHAPTER SEVENTEEN: MY GIRLS

She was not a widow – her husband was alive. She was not a divorcee, not even separated. Yet still she felt like a single Mother and to others she looked like how she felt. Every morning she would wake, shower, dress and do her hair and makeup before her daughter woke. Then she would make her way downstairs to give her little girl a bottle of milk, wash her and dress her. She gave her breakfast, lunch and dinner. Took her to the park or swimming. Took her to NCT events. Her friends and family were fantastic: they 'mucked in' as much as they could. But there was only so much others could do. She was still very much on her own.

During that time, Romilly and Tiana became the very best of friends. Each knew each other inside out, their likes and dislikes, their idiosyncrasies, their mood swings. They were closer than Tiana ever thought would be possible. Even closer than she was to her husband. If it was just going to be the two of them from now on, then she would be ready. Her heart cried out for him, hoping beyond hope that one day he would be back in their lives. But not yet. Not until he was better. If ever that happened.

Despite the emotional storm going on inside of her, Tiana stayed strong. She never broke. She couldn't afford to for Romilly's sake. Her daughter was growing by the day, it seemed. There were new words, she was more confident in her walking, even running and jumping now. And so very clever. Like most mothers, Tiana was sure that her child was the best, the most intelligent and certainly the most beautiful. But even through her blinkered vision it was clear that Romilly was a gifted child. She picked things up quickly and was far more advanced in her development than other children her age. Tiana only wished Mark was still there to see it.

By the end of each day, Tiana was shattered. She would not go to bed too late as she would need to get up with Romilly early the next morning. Not that she slept that well. She feared that he would come in the night and carry out the dreaded ritual, grabbing their daughter and holding her so tight that she would go blue and her little bones would snap under the strain. The slightest noise could wake her. So many sounds seemed like a key turning in a lock. She was scared of her very own husband. He had become the bogeyman. Her fear, lack of sleep and the energy used up in looking after a young child were taking its toll on her. There was rarely any let up. Occasionally, her Mother would baby-sit so Tiana could go out and, moreover, sleep in. Her Mother was a tower of strength for Tiana during these dark days.

Every morning, Tiana approached the phone with optimism: that this would be the day when he told her he had carried out no rituals. She hated it when he didn't pick up. She knew what it meant: that her husband would be in his room, staring at a piece of paper, repeatedly coughing. The image haunted her. And when he did pick up it was always the same: yes, he had coughed, but, he assured her, only for a little while. Sometimes he would not really be listening and would rush her off the phone. Tiana knew why: so he could go and finish another ritual.

Tiana would often look back over those last few months and the pain that Mark and his illness had put her through. The dishonesty and trickery upset her so much. She had been fooled time and time again so that he could perform his ritual. As well as the emotional strain, there was the financial burden. She had lost a large part of her inheritance. And what did the future hold? Mark was supposed to start a new job in October. She could not see how he could possibly be ready by then, despite his optimistic reassurances. She looked into what financial help could be obtained, should Mark not return to work. It was not enough to pay the mortgage. So she looked into selling the house, obtaining valuations from estate agents.

She even considered separation. If Mark did not get better, she could not live with him. Tiana did not want him to be in the same house whilst her daughter was there, fearing for her safety in case he snuck into her room one night and carried out a ritual, while she remained asleep and helpless. She talked about divorce to Mark and he tried to put it down to her anxieties. Deep down, he feared that she would leave, though, and not tell him where she'd gone. Tiana would only take so much. It was clear to anyone who knew of what had happened that Tiana's priority was her daughter, and rightly so. She would do what was best for Romilly, regardless of the consequences for Mark.

It was not like she had forgotten about her husband's plight – far from it. She was regularly chasing doctors and nurses and care-workers and psychiatrics to get him the care that he needed. She requested some kind of therapy was needed, to which everyone was in agreement but didn't seem to want to do anything about. Poor Tiana's anguish went through the roof at this complete lack of help and sense of urgency from the medical profession.

Of course, Tiana loved Mark very deeply. It broke her heart when she signed the papers in France which led to his incarceration. She hated sending him into hospital upon his return to the UK, but he had to get better. And in her eyes, the only way to get better was in hospital. He came out too early, Tiana said; she was adamant about that and did not hold back in letting the doctors know. As time went by, her sympathy towards Mark and his condition turned to anger: partly because he did not want to get rid of his illness – he seemed like he was holding onto it; but mainly because she did not understand how such a stupid thing like coughing was causing so much damage to their relationship. How could he do this to them? So when he began causing her Mother so much grief, she told him to clear off, to go and annoy his own Mother. His pathetic pleading and self-pity made her loath him even more. It came as no surprise to her that he broke down again, that he was taken back into hospital. As far as she was concerned, he should never have left.

And eventually she learned to hate him, to wish that he was dead. How much simpler it would all be with him out of the way. At least she would know where they stood, that they could get on with things and build for the future. It saddened Tiana that she had such strong emotions for a loved one and she questioned whether it made her a bad person. But it was her love for their daughter that fuelled this anger, the desire to protect her daughter from harm, to ensure the very best for her. If the world around her fell away, it would not matter as long as Romilly was safe. If that meant Mark was dead, so be it. Often when the phone rang, she hoped it was a doctor to let her know Mark had committed suicide.

She would often cry herself to sleep, looking longingly at the empty side of the bed where Mark had once lay. She even missed his snoring and smells. Often, Tiana would sleep on his side and smell his pillow and pretend he was still there, holding her in his strong arms. She knew deep down that she did not really want him dead. She just wanted him back and well again. Each time he pleaded to come home, she would tell him he was not ready, not out of spite or fear, but out of faith that one day he would be right again; just not yet. She would wait.

She loved him so very much. Always had. Always will do.

But a Mother's love for their child is unbreakable. For millennia, fathers have let their children down time and again. History is littered with bad fathers and rejected children. Man has too often been self-centred, self-preserving, more worried about getting laid, getting fed, than looking after a family. Maybe it stems from the times of living on the savannah: a man could shag dozens of women to ensure his genes survive and would not need to worry how each subsequent child was getting on – it was safety in numbers. Woman, on the other hand, needed to be choosey. If she made a wrong decision, she was stuck with it for nine months at least and nearly all women would never willingly give up or not care for their own child, so it was effectively a life-long commitment. In order to ensure their genes, they therefore had to do anything for their child. To fight and kill if necessary, if their child was threatened. Even to die for. The Mother is the ultimate selfless being, giving her all for her children. History may not be filled with great individual women thinkers, inventors, artists, musicians, leaders and politicians, but they have provided the environment for such people to survive. Without women, man would be nothing. And Tiana had all of the qualities of a Mother and a woman and demonstrated them so very clearly throughout those troublesome times. Mark would always love her and respect her for that.

Eventually the call came that she wanted to here so much: he had not coughed that morning! And when he went to bed that evening, he had still not coughed! She couldn't believe it and made him make all sorts of promises and swear various oaths to confirm that he was telling the truth. She wanted to believe him so much, but the scene had looked bleak for so long, that she found it difficult to do so. And then a week went by and another week and he still had not coughed. Every day she would ask him and every day, to her wonder and great pleasure, he responded in the way she wanted to hear.

Romilly's visits had gone well too. She was sure to watch every little move, look for every twitch or strangeness in his expression. The staring and fear that was once so evident in his countenance had nearly gone completely; there were still signs of it, so she daren't let her guard down. His conviction that he would one day have to give in, "even after a year", had impressed itself upon her such that it would take a long time before she could trust him again. The thought of leaving Romilly alone with Mark didn't even figure as a possibility.

Eventually the day was drawing nearer for Mark to come home for good. Of course, Tiana was very anxious about the whole idea. As much as she missed him and wanted him home, she had got used to being a single parent and had a routine. The idea of him coming back and getting under her feet frustrated her. But she had enjoyed it when he came to stay overnight. It felt like old times again. The night time was difficult and she would often wake up fearing that he might pop into Romilly's room and carry out the ritual. But, as far as she was aware, he never did; when asked, he swore that he had not and would not.

She was very proud of Mark for what he had achieved, especially going back to work and doing well there. It must have been difficult for him to be doing a difficult job during the day, then driving over an hour back to the hospital, passing home along the way without being allowed to go in. But he seemed to be managing.

It was understandable that she was bitterly disappointed that night before he was due to come home. She had planned a nice meal for the three of them. Nothing overboard, just a chilli con carne. She knew he liked it and so did Romilly (it was her favourite dish and did wonders for her constipation!). It had been in the slow cooker all day as it always seemed so much tastier cooked like that. But there was that look in his eyes as he walked through the door. She asked him if he was okay and he said he was fine, but she was not convinced. He was trying too hard to appear happy, but his behaviour was too erratic. And he was too keen to go upstairs and get changed. So she followed him. With each step, she became more convinced with what would be there when she opened the door. She knew exactly what he would look like: hunched up over a piece of paper, head in hands. It was too quiet, apart from the odd strange 'barking' noise. With dread, she pushed the door open and found what she had feared. Her heart sank. She knew it was too good to be true.

CHAPTER EIGHTEEN – COGNITIVE BEHAVIOURAL THERAPY

I was hugely disappointed not to be going home. I had let myself down after all of that good work. In some ways, it seemed that I was back to square one. But I wasn't. There was something lurking on the horizon that would give me more hope than I could ever have dreamed of: Cognitive Behavioural Therapy, or CBT for short.

Of course, I knew a little about CBT, its theories, and related topics. I had read up on the subject and its relationship with OCD. But it all seemed so far away from me, not something that could be achieved on your own, even using a book. It seemed to hold the key to my recovery. But the hospital, the doctors and care-workers had all played their part in fart-arsing about trying to get something arranged. My brilliant wife had been at them on a regular basis to try to get my therapy sorted out. It took them far too long already, so I dreaded to think how much longer it could have taken had she not been so persistent. Ideally, Tiana wanted the therapy sessions to take place in hospital, at least for the first few weeks anyway. She had read that a person will often regress soon after treatment before they progress and feared that happening when I was at home with them both. My set back had, by a stroke of good fortune, meant that she would get this desire.

My therapy would be with a lady called Sheila Field, whom I was introduced to during my weekly meeting with my doctors the week before the first session was due to commence. She asked me lots of questions about what I do in terms of rituals and behaviour, so I found myself repeating what I had told a hundred other doctors. She was a very short lady, of slight build and slightly Mediterranean looking. I was well aware of just how important this lady should prove to be and therefore analysed her closely, trying to get an idea of what kind of a person she was. I hoped that she would be down to Earth and would like a joke, which seemed to be the case.

As they requested, Tiana and I went to that first session together. I was so nervous. Unfortunately, there was no need to be: she had no intention of doing anything that day except talk about what I did (again!) and consider whether I wanted CBT or not! Tiana went mad!

"Look," she began, "we've waited so long for this treatment, and now you're asking him the same old questions that you've already asked! And of course he wants it – what kind of a question is that?!"

"I have to get an idea of Mark's problems in order that I can provide the best therapy," Sheila countered.

"But you did that last week!" Tiana continued, quite rightly. "Mark's been so nervous this week, he's even gone back a step. This treatment should have started straight away – weeks ago!"

"It's not as easy as that," Sheila began to explain.

"No, of course it's not," Tiana interrupted.

"Okay, we are where we are," I said, realising that the session was going in the wrong direction and fast! "Thank you, Tiana, for sticking up for me again. But let's just forget what's happened and get on with the therapy."

"Well," Sheila replied, "I need to go away and think about this all and how we're going to attack it. What I suggest is, we have a session next week at the hospital where we can actually get into the therapy properly."

I didn't look at Tiana, but I knew her eyes were rolling in her head.

"I can't believe they could prat about so much," she said to me after the meeting. "I've been trying to get this sorted for so long now. They're so bloody inefficient."

"I know," I replied, grabbing her and giving her a hug. "You've been brilliant and so strong."

"I don't feel strong," she answered.

"Well you are," I responded. "I think you've been outstanding in getting through this and you're doing such a good job with our little daughter. I'm so proud to call you my wife."

"Thanks," said Tiana. She let out a few tears and we hugged again.

"I want you to cough and have a bad thought," said Sheila. "Think of something horrible, an image or a sentence – something that will cause anxiety. But I want you to put a time limit on it. It's got to be something that will happen in the next couple of hours, for example."

"Okay," I replied. My breathing was getting faster. I was feeling very anxious already. "I can't!"

"I know it's hard," Sheila continued. "But it will get easier."

"Okay," I repeated. I thought of a sentence. "Romilly is kidnapped in the next couple of hours," I said in my head, coughing on the 'kidnapped' element.

"Right," said Sheila, "what did you think of?"

"That Romilly would be kidnapped in the next couple of hours," I answered.

"I want you to tell me out of ten how much you believe that that thing will happen because you coughed; let me know how much you believe it before and immediately after the cough took place"

"Before," I replied, "I would have believed it 9 out of 10. Now, I believe it 10 out of 10."

"I want you to live with the thought for a while," Sheila explained. "I need you to live with that uncertainty. What time frame did you put on it?"

"Two hours", I repeated.

"So," she continued, "if nothing happens in the next two hours, the cough has failed to work. Is that correct?"

"I guess so," I replied.

"I want you to really think about it – really believe that this thing will happen within the next two hours because of the power of the cough."

"Okay," I said, looking at the clock. It was quarter past three.

"Every so often, I want you to revalue your belief that this thing will happen out of ten. Don't try to neutralise the ritual, otherwise it won't work. How do you feel now? Do you think you can do this?"

"Yes, definitely," I replied, suddenly perking up a bit. The whole idea of putting a time frame on it was a good idea: it meant I could measure the ritual.

"That's really well done!" said Sheila, breaking into a smile. "You've made a huge step today by doing that. However, if we're going to really make this work, we really need to involve your little girl."

"I'm not sure Tiana would allow that," I responded.

"She's got to understand," Sheila answered, "that if we're going to nail this, we've got to work on your most feared situation."

"I'll talk to her tonight," I promised.

I left that first session feeling quite optimistic. It would have almost been good fun if it wasn't so bloody horrible. I spoke to Tiana straight after and she could sense the optimism in my voice. At last it seemed that there was light at the end of the tunnel. I told her that I had to carry out a ritual and that I would be phoning her again at five fifteen to see if it had worked.

"Has Romilly been kidnapped?" I asked once the two hours were up.

"Nope," replied Tiana. "She's sitting right beside me, playing. Do you want to talk to her?"

"Definitely," I said, smiling.

"Hiya Daddy," she began in her sweet little voice.

"Hiya Romilly," I replied. "Daddy is feeling really good about everything today!"

"Oh," she muttered (or something to that effect).

"Yes," I continued, "my therapy went really well and it looks like I'll be home soon and be a normal Daddy again."

"Yeah," she replied.

"I love you!" I cried. "Kiss kiss?"

A kissing noise down the phone.

"Ah, thank you. Can you put Mummy back on now?"

"Bubye," she said.

"Bye, beautiful," I replied.

"Thank you darling," Tiana said to Romilly. "She's cute isn't she?"

"The cutest!" I answered. "Listen, I need to ask you something."

"Go on," said Tiana. There was a nervous hesitation in her response.

"Next week, we need to involve Romilly in the ritual," I explained. "Will that be okay?"

There was a pause then a long sigh, then: "Okay. But as long as it's a controlled environment."

"Thank you," I said. I was glad that she had agreed, but a part of me was hoping she'd say no: now I had to confront my greatest fears.

"This is how it will work," Sheila explained. "We're going to bring Romilly in, you'll put her on your lap, cough whilst on a bad thought, then not neutralise it. After a minute or so, you say to me, 'I need to get a drink', then you and I leave the room. Okay?"

"Okay," I replied. I was feeling anxious, but also optimistic – I wanted to get on with this, to start fighting this illness properly and with help.

When Romilly and Tiana arrived, we all sat together in the family room and chatted and played with my little girl. After ten minutes and once the proceedings had been explained to Tiana, we got on with carrying out the ritual. I put Romilly on my knee, made sure my hand was touching her skin, and conjured up an image of her getting run over by a train. "Romilly is hit by a train today!" I said in my head, coughing on the 'train'. We then all continued, like nothing had happened. "I need a drink," I said eventually, and Sheila and I left the room.

"How are you feeling?" she asked.

"Alright!" I replied. "It's not a very comfortable feeling, but I think I can live with it."

"That's brilliant," said Sheila, genuinely impressed. "Well let's go back in and do it again."

Again?!, I thought to myself – surely once would be enough!

The next time, I thought of her being raped and coughed on the word 'rape', putting a time scale of two hours on it. "I need a drink." We left the room again.

"What about now?" asked Sheila.

"I don't like it," I said. "I don't like the feeling that I'm purposely trying to make something horrible happen to her."

"Well that's good," replied Sheila. "You need to be feeling the anxiety in order for it to work properly. Okay, third and last time."

Third?! Well, at least it would be the last for today, I thought.

This time, I imagined her being kidnapped that night, coughing on the word, 'kidnapped'. "I need a drink."

"You've done so well!" exclaimed Sheila as we got outside. "You're a right hero, you are!"

"It was tough!" I replied. Although it was not quite as tough as I thought it might be. Still, it was early days and I had to get through the rest of the day without neutralising first.

Once the therapy was over, I was allowed some time with my two girls to just have fun. I explained to Tiana what I had to do each time and she laughed at the daftness of it all, which actually made me feel better about it. If she had been shocked, it might have made me more likely to neutralise. But I didn't, and by the next day all three predicted events had not occurred. I had a real sense of pride for getting through it.

Throughout the next week, I was told to do homework: cough whilst saying a bad word, ideally holding Romilly at the same time. I would put a timeframe on each one of no more than a day. None of them came true.

I was also taught to meditate: I would close my eyes take a sweet, such as a Tic Tac or a Skittle, and concentrate on sucking it; throughout this, I should concentrate on the sweet and ignore all other thoughts; the shape, the flavour, its movement in my mouth. Such meditation allowed me to be at one with reality. It made me appreciate the amount of nonsense that went through my brain all the time. My brain was constantly trying to go off on different tangents; each time, I would need to bring it back again. I would do this twice a day: first thing in the morning and last thing at night.

The following session was more of the same. I made the images more graphic and more horrible to really boost my anxiety levels. For each one, I had to score my belief and feelings of anxiety out of ten before, immediately after and a considerable time after carrying out the behaviour. With each one, the anxiety levels and belief had decreased. For my homework, there was more of the same, but I was to record the affects from each one on a little chart.

As far as ritualising was concerned, my set back had led to just under a week of carrying them out, then I stopped once more. My therapy was working so well that there seemed to be no sign of it coming back again. So, it was decided that I would return home very soon.

All through these events, Andrew Parkinson had been the perfect boss: he understood that I had a set back and asked if there was anything the business could do to help; he agreed for me to receive therapy once a week and said I could put it down under sick pay (I did not do that, though, and made my hours up instead); I was eased into the role and given plenty of room to settle in. The excitement of everything that was going on at work helped me a lot: it kept me in the real world and didn't allow me the time to sit around and ruminate. My life was all falling back into place. The inheritance tax and estate planning seminar was still a good few weeks away and I felt I would be well on the way to recovery by then.

So it was that in early November I finally returned home. We didn't make a big fuss of it. Steve and Karen came round to welcome me back, but that was it for visitors. Romilly, Tiana and I sat down for dinner that night and it was as though I had never been away. I couldn't help smiling. I bathed little Romilly, read her a story and put her to bed, with Tiana in the background making sure I didn't do anything I shouldn't. That night we lay down together and I had the best night's sleep I had had in a long time.

CHAPTER NINETEEN – A NEW START

We had been warned that a relapse was almost inevitable. The thought of it made Tiana sick to the core. It really scared her to know that OCD was going to pounce again one day. Christmas was just around the corner – three weeks away, to be precise, when it happened.

There was a cough bug going round that December and all three of us managed to catch it. I had been coughing away merrily without having to neutralise. In fact I had not neutralised for seven or eight weeks. But then I woke one morning and coughed on a bad word, I thought. I let it go at first. Just make it through the next few hours and you'll be fine, I told myself. But I didn't make it past breakfast. I came back up to our bedroom and had to cough. Then I did it again.

"What are you doing?" cried Tiana, a tone of panic in her voice.

I ran down to the spare room, grabbed a piece of scrap paper and pen and wrote down on it: "Romilly lives until she's one hundred years old and God makes sure of that - Amen". Then I got down on my knees, read the line in my head and coughed on 'one hundred'. But it didn't feel right, so I did it again. And again. Then I suddenly remembered, I might have said that if I perform a ritual again, something bad will happen to Romilly. So I wrote down on the same piece of paper: "Nothing bad will happen to Romilly whether I cough again or not and God makes sure of that." Then I read that line, then repeated the first line, coughing on 'one hundred' again. I did it a couple more times, then got up and walked out of the spare room.

All this time, Tiana was going frantic. Romilly was still in bed asleep, luckily.

"Why are you doing this?" cried Tiana. "Why don't you just stop? I thought you were better!" At first she sounded scared, then she sounded bewildered and finally hopeless and angry.

"Wait," I said, "I didn't do it right." Back in the room I went, this time coughing on the words, 'God', 'Romilly', 'one hundred' and 'Amen'. And so it went on for another fifteen minutes or so, until I finally managed to get in the car and leave.

"Will you be alright?" asked Tiana.

"I'll be fine," I said, not knowing myself.

I drove to work feeling so disappointed with myself. I had been doing so well, yet still this had happened. When I got to work, my boss realised that I was not well. We had a chat in private and he assured me that if I needed anything he could sort it out for me. I thanked him, but there was little he could do. I went to my car three or four times that morning, pulled out that piece of paper and coughed.

By a stroke of luck, I was due to have my appointment with Sheila that afternoon. It couldn't have come any quicker!

"Your wife has told me you've had a bad day," she began. "Can you tell me what happened?"

After I had explained everything, Sheila said, "It was bound to happen eventually. You were always going to have to neutralise one day – everyone has at least one digression and this is yours. But it's not the end of the world; it doesn't mean that everything has been a complete waste of time. In fact the opposite: it's a case of having to take one step back to go two steps forward. So let's make this opportunity work in our favour."

I sat there nodding, staring at the ground. I felt like I could cry at any moment.

"Show me what you do," Sheila requested.

"Okay," I said, pulling the piece of paper out of my pocket. "This is what I read." I handed it to her, she read it and handed it back to me."

"Well let's see you do it, then," said Sheila.

So I did it. Just once.

"Now throw it away," Sheila commanded. "Before you can question whether you did it right or not. We're going to live with that uncertainty. Chuck it in the bin over there!"

At first I hesitated, then I quickly screwed the paper up and threw it in the bin. The feeling that I had not done it right quickly hit me. I wanted to do it again.

"Well done!" said Sheila. "Right now we're going to do something together: we're both going to write something bad down on a piece of paper and say it out loud and then throw the paper away."

She handed me a pen and a bit of paper. She then wrote something on another piece. I scribbled something down too.

"Right," she began. "I'll go first. 'If I don't visit my Father tonight he will die in his sleep before the morning'." Then she threw the paper in the bin. "Well I can't see him tonight because he lives in Malaga, so I can't do it even if I tried. Your turn."

I sighed, then read aloud: "Unless I cough again, Romilly will be killed today and God will make sure of that."

"Now throw it in the bin, like before," Sheila instructed.

Again, I screwed it up and threw it away. The anxiety spread through me, down my spine, making my legs and arms tingle.

"Get both pieces back out then," said Sheila, "I dare you." She was playing the role of the OCD bully that we had

250

invented together. "If you don't something bad will happen."

After a pause, I spoke: "No." I was shaking to the core. Finding that first piece of paper was so tempting – what if I had done it wrong?

"Well you've got to undo it," the bully continued. "Do you really want to take a risk over your daughter's life?"

"It doesn't make any difference," I said through quivering lips. "I can't control what will happen." I could feel Romilly slipping away from me, dying an early death because of me.

She walked across the room, picked the bin up and held it out in front of me. "Come on – take it back, while you can still save her life."

"No," I replied, turning away. I had to concentrate on not lifting my arm up and reaching inside the bin. I felt like I was sacrificing my beloved, sweet little daughter just to cure myself. Eventually, she put the bin down and returned to her normal self.

"It's this fear of uncertainty that you have," explained Sheila. "You worry about the fact that anything can happen and it is out of your control. You strive for certainty, but you can never be certain. None of us can. OCD feeds off this desire and presents you with an alternative belief system, one where certainty is possible. But the stronger you rely on this system, the more you have to do to achieve the certainty which you crave. You need to learn to live with this uncertainty."

"But I don't want anything bad to happen," I replied. Tears began to roll down my cheeks.

"None of us do," said Sheila. "But we can't control it. All we can do is ensure we've done all we can to prevent a tragedy. So we lock doors before we go to bed and only need to check them once to satisfy ourselves that we will not be burgled. But this will never give us certainty as there are numerous ways to break in. You can provide as safe an environment as possible for your daughter, but you can never be one hundred per cent sure of her safety. People with OCD often have an over inflated sense of responsibility. Tell me a situation that you fear."

"I'm scared that she might get kidnapped whilst she's at nursery," I responded.

"Apart from you, who else has responsibility in that situation," she asked. Sheila pulled out another piece of paper and drew a big circle on it.

"The ladies who work at the nursery," I replied.

"Yes, and who else?"

"Other parents coming to pick their children up. The general public. The police. Tiana. Romilly. The other children."

"There are all these other people," said Sheila. "And they all have differing responsibility. If we were to show it on a pie chart, it would look something like this."

She proceeded to draw segments in the circle, one for each person that I had named, including me.

"According to my reckoning," she explained, "you have about ten per cent of the responsibility. The other ninety per cent is a mixture of a whole load of other people. But in your eyes you have one hundred per cent responsibility. But that's not the reality of the situation. OCD blurs reality."

I nodded in agreement.

"You've got to stop putting so much pressure on yourself," Sheila continued. "It's no wonder you seek certainty when there's so much you want to be sure of."

"It was the hardest session I've ever had," I said to Tiana as I flung my arms around her. "Sheila really came into her own today."

"And how do you feel now?" asked Tiana.

"A lot better," I replied. "Like I've ran a marathon, but a lot better."

And so Christmas came and went without any more problems. It was probably the nicest Christmas we'd ever had. The pain that had gone before made the pleasure of being with each other so much greater. Romilly loved all of her presents and I loved not having a single hangover for the whole of the festive period.

With my return to family life, our sex life soon returned to normal too. In fact, it was slightly better than before for one excellent reason: we were trying for another baby! It was a huge move for Tiana to agree to it and the fact that she did reflected how far we'd come and how much she believed I had improved.

I did not have another session with Sheila until well into January due to her going off skiing for the holidays. I was still a long way off being able to fight OCD on my own, but a three week break with no CBT was bearable.

When we next met, the session became more like a trip to the psychiatrist.

"What was it like growing up in your family?" Sheila asked.

"Quiet, I suppose," I replied. "I never had a brother or sister. My Mother lost her first child, a little girl. She never quite got over it. She desperately wanted a girl, so I was a bit of a disappointment for her."

"Why didn't they have any more?"

"I'm not sure. My Dad said it's because they found the whole thing too emotionally taxing. My Mum is a very anxious person and a real worrier. She probably felt one was enough to worry about as well. But my Dad's only ever discussed it once with me. It's amazing he's even done that."

"What do you mean by that?" she asked.

"Well," I began, "he doesn't really say much. He doesn't really show any emotions. Except mockery – he likes to mock."

"How did that affect you?"

"I never felt like I was ever any good at anything," I said. "If ever I did anything well, he would never say 'well done' or congratulate me in any way. He would just say, he could have done it better, or laugh at me."

"Can you give me an example?" asked Sheila.

"I remember when he came to watch me play rugby one day," I replied. "I set up the match winning try. I looked round, all excited, wanting to see my Dad's reaction. But he'd gone. I found out later he'd left about twenty minutes in."

"How did that make you feel?"

"I always felt like I had to impress him. I was always trying really hard to try and get his approval. But it never came."

"Do you think you search for approval now from people?"

"Sometimes. A lot actually. I don't like people to not like me, especially if I like them."

"Were you popular at school, then?"

"Hardly! I didn't really have any friends. I didn't really know how to behave. I would too often mock them. And no one really liked me."

"What about your Mother?" asked Sheila. "How did she treat you?"

"She was kind and full of love for me. But she was too engrossed in her own problems. Life was never going her way, as far as she was concerned. When she was really upset, she would tell me she wanted a girl instead of me. I used to go up to my room and cry. I hated the feeling it gave me."

"Did you tell her this?"

"Of course, but she would twist it back round and say I was making her feel even worse by talking about it. I was rubbing it in, apparently."

"How did your Father get on with her?"

"He didn't really," I answered. "They have never really spoken much. He never showed her much affection. Perhaps all she needed was a good cuddle."

"Okay. Was there much order in your life?" she asked, changing the topic slightly.

"Loads! My Father was always giving out orders! He used to tell me off for making too much noise when I went for a pee! I stayed with them a little while ago, just for a few days. And it suddenly dawned on me just how many little orders he makes: don't put your feet on the settee, don't bite your spoon when you eat, don't make so much noise when you're eating... Don't cough, you're doing it on purpose."

"Sorry?" said Sheila, slightly bemused.

"He told me not to cough when I was younger. If I had a cold, I would sit there and try to hold the cough in, scared of being told off; anxious that if I did, something bad would happen."

We both looked at each other, knowingly.

"They have a lot to answer for, parents," she remarked. I nodded and sighed.

"I felt like a post script in their lives," I continued. "Whilst they carried on doing what they were doing, I was just this person in the background that occasionally got in their way. I had no guidance. Tiana got so much guidance from her parents. She knew exactly what she wanted from life and how to get it. Me – I didn't have a Scooby Doo!"

"Sorry?"

"Clue," I explained. "I didn't have a clue. I had so much talent to offer: I played rugby well, was a good drawer, I'm intelligent … But I never got the education that I should have done and didn't know what to do once I was in the big bad world. I lacked direction. Plus, I never felt like I deserved good things to happen to me."

"Why did you feel like that?"

"I don't know," I said, shrugging. "I suppose I was never encouraged in any way, never rewarded for doing something well. I guess I assumed from a young age that I didn't deserve nice things."

"That's very sad," replied Sheila. "Nearly everyone deserves nice things at least once in a while – including you! This low opinion of yourself, coupled with a lack of guidance, explains a lot: without this you needed a system you could use, something which you thought you could rely on. This and a natural inclination towards OCD probably led to your current condition."

"Don't get me wrong," I interrupted, suddenly feeling guilty over how I had spoken about my Mum and Dad. "I do love my parents very much. They rarely smacked me. I never had that unhappy a childhood. There were plenty of good times. And we get on really well now. I just think they were too bogged down in their own problems and issues."

"It's okay," answered Sheila. "There are very, very few parents who get things absolutely right. Just because we become parents, doesn't mean we're no longer vulnerable."

For days afterwards, I thought long and hard about that session. So many things now made sense: the fear of coughing, the sense of guilt when I tried to enjoy things, guilt over doing anything that might be considered immoral, always trying to please people … I didn't blame my parents. It's not like they did anything on purpose. But it made me even more determined to be a selfless parent for little Romilly, to make sure she had a happy upbringing, to ensure she grew up to be confident in her abilities and knowing how to get the most out of life, to fulfil all her dreams. I'm not delusional – I know there will still be difficult times for her, but that's all a part of life. As long as Tiana and I can do the best we can, then the rest is up to her!

The day had finally arrived: I was to stand up in front of approximately one hundred people and talk about inheritance tax and estate planning! There were three other talkers: two financial advisers and a lawyer; but I would be the main speaker, beginning and ending the proceedings. I had also added my own drawings to the slides, creating the 'Chip family', upon whom the case study would be based. It was the first time I had had to do anything like this. Was I nervous? I was absolutely 'cacking' myself!

Inevitably, the anxiety brought OCD along to the proceedings. I had anticipated this and was ready. Every time he tried to affect me, I told myself to hang on in there; if you have to neutralise, wait until the proceedings are over.

After what seemed like a lifetime of waiting around, it was finally my opportunity to speak. I made my way to the front, microphoned up, zapper in hand to work the Power Point presentation, and off I went:

"Good morning everyone and thank you for coming. This is the first time that I've done a talk to this many people, so if find yourself wanting to heckle or throw anything, please leave it until the end."

A gentle ripple of chuckles across the audience. I had them on my side. Within a couple of minutes, I was in full flow. It did not matter whether there was one hundred people listening or five people or even a thousand, all nerves and anxiety had left me. The attention of the audience seemed to remain with me, they laughed in all the right places, the occasional nodding took place, then, as I ended the talk, there was an enthusiastic applause. I sat back down. Andrew passed me a note: "Mark – that was excellent!" I beamed with pride, knowing just how far I had come in the last few months: from a broken wretch, on all fours, consumed by mental illness, to a confident young man, holding the attention of many successful and intelligent ladies and gentlemen.

As we scoffed the buffet and chatted to potential clients, I subconsciously felt my phone vibrate in my pocket. I ignored it and carried on with the socialising. A little while later, I felt the urge to see who exactly had texted me. It was Tiana – "Guess what, Marky? I'm pregnant! We're going to have another baby!"

"Yes!" I shouted, making a few people around me jump. "Sorry!"

I couldn't believe it – we were having another baby! Through all the dark times that we'd faced, we had come out the other side stronger than ever and ready to be parents once more. If it was possible, I was even more excited than I had been the first time!

Life truly is amazing.

CHAPTER TWENTY: AN ANALYSIS OF OBSESSIVE COMPULSIVE DISORDER BY AN OBSESSIVE COMPULSIVE

The mind is a terrible thing to waste. I can't remember who said it, but it's so true. I wasted mine for many years. For so long, I was in OCD's grip, letting it rule my life and affect my decisions and enjoyment. So many wonderful events that I never enjoyed fully because my mind was carrying out all these stupid pointless rituals. I won't say I don't regret it, but I don't dwell on it, as Tiana might say. Instead, I turn my weakness into my strength: I've been on a mental journey that's taught me so much about myself, my brain, the relationship between the mental and the physical. I try to avoid too much introspection and concentrate on the wonderful world around me, because there's really no point in getting bogged down in my own silly thoughts. The mind is a tool for enjoying this world, not the focal point.

Most importantly of all, I found my spirit. When I was at my lowest, when I had lost all hope, couldn't see past the material world, it was my spirit that pulled me through. My love for Tiana and for life rose up inside of me and gave me the strength to see that life is worth living, more than that, life is beautiful. I don't believe that the world is just material. There is something beyond those chemicals going through my brain, something that can't yet be explained through science. It was with me when I was stuck in the depths of my illness, my brain locked in a circle of rituals; something inside of me wanted to break out of this, more than just an instinctual desire for life, more than a Darwinian theory. I *do not* believe the world is just material. When I die, I believe my spirit will live on, if only through the people I've met and had an affect on, if only through my children and their children. I will always be a part of this world, somewhere, somehow.

Nobody really knows why people get OCD. Personally, I think it arises when the brain is being misused. I'm a big believer in everything being a product of its environment; that there's not a single part of the way we work in biological terms that isn't a reaction to the world around us. The brain has developed as a result of being in large social groups; the bigger the social groups we live in and the need to communicate to more people in more different ways, the bigger and more powerful the brain needs to be. When our brains go a bit peculiar it tends to be because we spend too much time theorising and thinking without putting it into practice. The thoughts become muddled, confused, with nowhere to go. Thoughts need an outlet, a conclusion of sorts. Otherwise, the paths in the brain could lead to unintended places. Chemicals will be released in ways in which they shouldn't be. The whole brain ends up in a bit of a pickle.

OCD sufferers have to be overly careful with their brain chemistry. In my case, I need to avoid excess alcohol and loss of sleep. OCD is far more likely to be successful in attacking me if I'm not feeling particularly good. But so what if I can't drink too much – it's actually a real eye-opener watching others getting drunk. Just like somebody with diabetes, I just have to be careful with my way of life.

I used to fear confrontation. Metaphorically speaking, I was more comfortable sitting in the corner, hiding, watching what was going on around me but not wanting to join in. Every now and again, it was inevitable that I would need to come out and confront people and issues. This would make me more anxious than most. But my CBT has taught me that, once confronted, the anxiety will lessen and eventually I will realise that there is nothing to be anxious about. Once

I have stepped out of the corner and into reality, I think realistically. CBT and meditation are my tools for coping with the world outside of my head. And they have made such a difference in my life: from picking up large hairy spiders, to giving a talk to a hundred people, I'm so much more confident in my abilities and able to stand up to confrontation. And I'm taking pride in my talents, acknowledging that I am good at a lot of things: I draw regularly and I've even started playing rugby again, having scored eight tries in my first five games! That's not mediocre by anyone's reckoning. I know I can never be certain of anything, but provided I do my best, whether it's providing safety for my family or taking on an important and difficult piece of work, I can handle that uncertainty – I can live with it.

This book is ultimately for people who suffer from OCD, especially those who have suffered, are suffering or may suffer in the future from the debilitation it causes, whether the direct victim or a family or loved one. I want you to know that there is light at the end of the tunnel. You have to remain positive, try to look objectively at things and always look to reason, to rationalise. Anticipate its onset and get yourself ready to defend. Learn sensible thought patterns. And keep yourself busy. The mind is not meant to spend most of its time cogitating and philosophising and ours are particularly vulnerable to the darker consequences of such behaviour. Use your mind as a tool to enjoy the world around you. And have something to believe in, whether it's loved ones, religion or the beauty of life itself. It doesn't really matter, as long as it makes you want to stay alive and enjoy living. Spending time with my family and friends and doing well for them is what makes me want to get out of bed every morning. You need to locate your spirit, understand it and know it, know what makes you tick.

OCD never goes away completely. It's always there. But don't let that bother you. Once you learn to suppress it, to control it, it's no more of a problem than having a peanut allergy. You stay away from peanuts and if you do cross them, make sure you know how to treat the reaction.

Obsessive compulsive disorder is the disease of our time. We've never had so much time to think about self-preservation, never been so vain. The cure, as I see it, is to look without.

My life is wonderful right now. I love my wife and child so much. Every night, before we go to bed, we go into little Romilly's room to look at her while she sleeps. She looks so beautiful lying there, so innocent and magical. Often, we will bend down and give her a little kiss; she never wakes, but I like to think she feels them and sleeps more peacefully as a result. She's the most amazing little thing ever. It seems impossible to think, as I look across at my wife's bulging stomach, that there is another one on the way that will probably be just like her. I'm a lucky man.

And then there is Tiana herself: dear, sweet, beautiful Tiana! She had proved herself to be the very best of people those past few terrible months, a tower of strength in bringing up her daughter almost single-handedly, whilst showing an unconditional love towards me, her husband. I will forever be in awe of her and in her debt.

As well as having such a loving family, I have a job that varies from bearable on a bad day to good fun on the best days, I get the evenings and weekends to do what I want, we have a good income, a nice house. All this from somebody who, not so long ago, was almost in a vegetative state. I've come so far. I've been at the very depths of a mental Hell, but I've returned and have no intention of going back. I have to be aware that it's possible I could relapse, but as long as I am aware and keep up my sensible practices it's not going to happen. Thoughts fall into a pattern and if that pattern is good, I'll be fine.

OCD really isn't worth getting worried about. There are better things to do with your life.